WASHOE COUNTY LIBRARY

3 1235 03674 6241

P9-AFK-574

THE
EVERYTHING®
TWINS, TRIPLETS, AND MORE BOOK
2ND EDITION

RECEIVED

JUL 1 2 2013

NORTHWEST RENO LIBRARY

Dear Reader,

Finding out I was having twins was certainly a big surprise. After I recovered from the shock, my feelings fluctuated from nauseating despair (or was that morning sickness?) to giddy elation. I was desperately anxious to discover how I'd actually manage to care for two babies simultaneously. At that time, there were very few books that realistically conveyed the experience of a twin pregnancy, much less prepared parents for the challenge of raising multiples once they arrived.

This is the book that I would have wanted to read prior to the birth of my twin daughters. It informs rather than alarms, preparing you to face your future with multiples. First-time parents will be relieved to know that, in some ways, managing more than one is actually easier than parenting singletons of different ages! Established parents will discover how to accommodate the unique demands of multiples while integrating the new additions into their existing lifestyle.

Every aspect of having twins has exceeded my expectations. However, the biggest surprise has been the joy I've experienced along the way. Certainly, my husband and I have seen our share of double drudgery, with hectic days followed by sleepless nights. But like many things in life, the rewards of hard work far outweigh the sacrifices. The love that you give to your multiples will be returned to you exponentially.

Pamela Fierro

Welcome to the EVERYTHING® Series!

These handy, accessible books give you all you need to tackle a difficult project, gain a new hobby, comprehend a fascinating topic, prepare for an exam, or even brush up on something you learned back in school but have since forgotten.

You can choose to read an Everything® book from cover to cover or just pick out the information you want from our four useful boxes: e-questions, e-facts, e-alerts, and e-ssentials.

We give you everything you need to know on the subject, but throw in a lot of fun stuff along the way, too.

We now have more than 400 Everything® books in print, spanning such wide-ranging categories as weddings, pregnancy, cooking, music instruction, foreign language, crafts, pets, New Age, and so much more. When you're done reading them all, you can finally say you know Everything®!

QUESTION

Answers to common questions

FACT

Important snippets of information

ALERT

Urgent warnings

ESSENTIAL

Quick handy tips

PUBLISHER Karen Cooper

DIRECTOR OF ACQUISITIONS AND INNOVATION Paula Munier

MANAGING EDITOR, EVERYTHING® SERIES Lisa Laing

COPY CHIEF Casey Ebert

ASSISTANT PRODUCTION EDITOR Melanie Cordova

ACQUISITIONS EDITOR Brett Palana-Shanahan

SENIOR DEVELOPMENT EDITOR Brett Palana-Shanahan

EDITORIAL ASSISTANT Matthew Kane

EVERYTHING® SERIES COVER DESIGNER Erin Alexander

LAYOUT DESIGNERS Erin Dawson, Michelle Roy Kelly, Elisabeth Lariviere, Denise Wallace

ILLUSTRATOR Eric Andrews

Visit the entire Everything® series at *www.everything.com*

THE
EVERYTHING®
TWINS, TRIPLETS, AND MORE BOOK
2ND EDITION

From pregnancy to delivery and beyond—
all you need to enjoy your multiples

Pamela Fierro

Guide to Parenting Twins and Multiples at About.com

Avon, Massachusetts

To Brian, my true companion, for your
continual love and support.

Copyright © 2012, 2005 by F+W Media, Inc. All rights reserved.
This book, or parts thereof, may not be reproduced
in any form without permission from the publisher; exceptions
are made for brief excerpts used in published reviews.

An Everything® Series Book.
Everything® and everything.com® are registered trademarks of F+W Media, Inc.

Published by Adams Media, a division of F+W Media, Inc.
57 Littlefield Street, Avon, MA 02322 U.S.A.
www.adamsmedia.com

Contains recipes adapted and abridged from: *The Everything® Whole-Grain, High-Fiber Cookbook* by Lynette Rohrer Shirk, copyright © 2008 by F+W Media, Inc., ISBN 10: 1-59869-507-X, ISBN 13: 978-1-59869-507-6; *The Everything® Guide to Managing and Reversing Pre-Diabetes* by Gretchen Scalpi, RD, CDN, CDE, copyright © 2011 by F+W Media, Inc., ISBN 10: 1-4405-0985-9, ISBN 13: 978-1-4405-0985-8; and *The Everything® Quick and Easy 30-Minute, 5-Ingredient Cookbook* by Linda Larsen, copyright © 2006 by F+W Media, Inc., ISBN 10: 1-59337-692-8, ISBN 13: 978-1-59337-692-5.

ISBN 10: 1-4405-3290-7
ISBN 13: 978-1-4405-3290-0
eISBN 10: 1-4405-3497-7
eISBN 13: 978-1-4405-3497-3

Printed in the United States of America.

10 9 8 7 6 5 4 3 2 1

Library of Congress Cataloging-in-Publication Data
is available from the publisher.

This book is intended as general information only, and should not be used to diagnose or treat any health condition. In light of the complex, individual, and specific nature of health problems, this book is not intended to replace professional medical advice. The ideas, procedures, and suggestions in this book are intended to supplement, not replace, the advice of a trained medical professional. Consult your physician before adopting any of the suggestions in this book, as well as about any condition that may require diagnosis or medical attention. The author and publisher disclaim any liability arising directly or indirectly from the use of this book.

Many of the designations used by manufacturers and sellers to distinguish their products are claimed as trademarks. Where those designations appear in this book and Adams Media was aware of a trademark claim, the designations have been printed with initial capital letters.

This book is available at quantity discounts for bulk purchases.
For information, please call 1-800-289-0963.

Contents

Acknowledgments

I must accord a special acknowledgement to my two extraordinary daughters, Meredith Rebecca and Lauren Marissa, whose arrival introduced me to the amazing world of twins and multiples. They continue to amaze me with their beauty and strength of character. I have been blessed.

Thanks to Barb Doyen, Kate Burgo, and Brett Shanahan for presenting me with the opportunity to write about this topic. I'd also like to thank the professionals who shared their time and expertise with me: Dr. David G. Oelberg, MD, professor of pediatrics at Eastern Virginia Medical School and director of the Division of Neonatal-Perinatal Medicine; Robin Elise Weiss, BA, LCCE, ICCE-CPE, CD (DONA), author of *The Everything® Pregnancy Fitness Book* and *The Everything® Getting Pregnant Book*; and my fellow guide writers at About.com. In addition, I am very appreciative of all the mothers of multiples who shared their personal experiences with me, especially Chris Wingard, Jen Marcus, Ann Aschenbrenner, Denise Anderson, Cindy Mayfield, Suzie Chafin, Mary Ann Magnant, and Marnie Dyer.

Finally, I am eternally grateful to the friends and family members who supported me with prayer and encouragement while I worked on this book.

Top 10 Myths and Misconceptions about Multiples

1. Multiples usually skip a generation.

2. Fraternal twins are always a boy and a girl.

3. Twins with two placentas must be fraternal twins.

4. You have to buy two (or three or more) of everything for your multiple babies.

5. All multiples must be born by cesarean section.

6. Having two kids close in age is the same as having twins.

7. Having twins is twice as hard, and triplets make it three times harder for parents.

8. Identical twins always look exactly alike.

9. It's impossible to breastfeed multiples.

10. You must have taken fertility drugs if you have twins or more.

Introduction

SO, YOU'RE HAVING MULTIPLES! As parents, you've been gifted with a treasure: a set of twins, triplets, or more—an instant family, so to speak. There's no doubt about it; this is going to have a big impact on your family. Their arrival will mean some changes for everyone.

These days, very few multiples make a surprise appearance in the delivery room. Chances are, you have some time to prepare for their entrance into this world. You'll be able to make informed choices along the way, from investing in baby equipment to selecting child care. You'll take the necessary steps to prepare your household and line up assistance so that everyone's needs are covered. You'll also be able to prepare yourself physically for the challenges of a multiple pregnancy; by taking good care of yourself, you'll optimize your chances of a healthy outcome for each baby, as well as mom.

Whether you conceived using assistance from reproductive technology or on your own, the news may come as quite a shock. Your mind is probably whirling with questions. "How could this happen?" "Why us?" The more you learn about the biology of multiples, the more you'll understand how you came to be in this position. Whether due to science, heredity, or a random coincidence, ultimately multiples are a miracle.

You're likely to experience some negative reaction to your news. "Double trouble!" "Triple terror!" "Better you than me!" However, you'll only hear that reaction from people who don't actually have multiples. Talk to the families that have been similarly blessed, and they'll respond with smiles and congratulations. They are the ones who know the true joy and amazement of raising multiples. It's important to seek them out as a source of reassurance and support.

You may have some ambivalence and anxiety about the situation as well. How will you cope? Can you afford twins or more? Will you need a bigger car or even a bigger home? Health concerns loom large. Suddenly you've been upgraded to a high-risk pregnancy, with vague threats of bed rest, pre-term labor, and complications for your babies. This book will help waylay some of your worries.

Identifying and discussing potential problems during pregnancy shouldn't alarm you. Rather, it should be informative. In the event that you encounter problems, you'll be educated about your options and prepared to deal with the consequences. With some extra monitoring and precautions, your chances are good for a healthy outcome.

Adjusting your expectations as a parent is an important component of preparing for the arrival of multiples. You'll have to switch your focus from one baby to two or more. It's easy to classify multiples as a set or a group, but as their parents, you'll quickly realize that each of your children is a unique individual. Your challenge will be to identify and meet their needs as individuals. It is a fascinating process to watch them develop as unique entities within the context of their bond as twins or multiples.

Having twins, triplets, or higher order multiples is a challenge, but one that reaps huge rewards. They bring a unique dynamic to a family, a special status that sets you apart from families with singletons. Not only are they a blessing to their parents, but they will enjoy the lifelong blessing of companionship and a special bond with each other.

CHAPTER 1

The Magic of Multiples

Welcome to the wonderful world of multiples! If you just recently made the discovery that your family is being expanded by multiples, you are probably feeling a bit overwhelmed with shock and awe at the prospect of adding a twosome, threesome, or even more. You may be curious as to how it came to pass. You may be anxious about how multiples will mesh with your family's lifestyle, and how you will meet the needs of several simultaneous siblings. Having multiples is a truly unique parenting experience, filled with fascination and occasional moments of frustration.

What's Different about Multiples?

By having twins, triplets, or other multiples, you have been granted inclusion into a special class of parents. Although they wouldn't necessarily have asked for this honor, most parents wouldn't trade it for the world. Maybe you have always had a secret fascination with multiples and suspected you would bear them. Or maybe you thought you'd be the last person on earth to have multiples. Either way, this blessing will set you apart from other families and bring a new designation to your identity as a parent.

Having multiples is extraordinary. If you gathered a group of 100 parents, only two or three would be able to claim multiples. For the rest of your life, you are guaranteed to get a reaction when you talk about your children. Gasps of "Oh!" "Wow!" "Lucky you!" and "Better you than me!" are common responses when you tell someone you have multiples.

Some might wonder why twins and multiples are a big deal. Plenty of families have lots of kids, right? What makes it so different? There are many ways that having two, three, or more babies at the same time is different than having the same number of singletons. In some ways it makes family life easier, but in others it makes things much more complicated. No matter how close in age singletons may be, the fact remains that they were born one at a time. Their parents had at least nine months to prepare for the arrival of the next child. The organizational challenges of meeting the needs of multiple newborns are simply more demanding.

ESSENTIAL

As a parent of multiples, you'll often hear people say, "Oh, my kids were only eleven months apart. It was just like having twins." There's no easy way—and no good reason—to politely explain to someone that the two situations are nothing alike. It's easiest just to smile and nod agreeably.

The Impact of Birth Order

Birth order has a tremendous impact on the structure of families. Not only does it contribute to the personality development of each individual child, but it also sets the standard for how each child is treated. Older children have more freedom, but likewise more responsibility; their advanced age makes them developmentally capable of handling it. Younger children benefit from interaction with their older siblings and learn from their experiences.

Multiples, on the other hand, lack the defined roles created by birth order. Being the same age, and generally of equal status within the family, there is no formalized structure for establishing order. The effort to create and reinvent a pecking order can generate ongoing tension for the family.

The Group Dynamic

Outsiders may look at your duo, trio, or higher order multiples and see two, three, or more kids. What they don't realize is that in addition to having these individual children, as a parent of multiples you also have to contend with a group dynamic. With multiples, parents don't simply have an extra child or two. The group dynamic adds an entirely new element. You know the old saying, "Two heads are better than one"? Working in conjunction with each other, a group of multiples is easily more daring, more creative, and more clever than any individual child on his own.

The companionship and cooperation of their same-age siblings often incites behavior that exceeds an individual child's limits. Together, multiples will invent more schemes, attempt more stunts, and create more messes. There is power in numbers, and harnessing that power is one of the biggest challenges faced by parents of multiples.

Playing Fair

Another unique challenge is maintaining equality among multiples. It's often a struggle for parents of twins or more to ensure that each child gets his or her fair share; whether it is time, attention, or material goods, it is difficult (if not impossible) to always dole out an equitable portion. Life is simply not fair. Unfortunately, you can't always convince multiples of that fact, and as a parent you can never quit striving to make it so! Soothing jealousy and stifling competition is a constant battle for parents until multiples mature to an age where they can accept and appreciate the similarities and differences among them.

The Bond They Share

The bond between a set of multiples is unique. Beginning even before birth, it is one of the longest and most enduring interpersonal relationships that a human being can have. It surpasses that of regular siblings. The intensity of this relationship often makes multiples the best of friends one moment and bitter enemies the next.

As a parent, you'll have a unique opportunity to watch your multiples' bond grow and develop from the very beginning. You'll have responsibility for nurturing each child as an individual within the context of their relationship to their co-multiples. It's never too early to start thinking how you'll accomplish that balance.

Share and Share Alike

All members of a family have to learn to share to get along. But multiples share more than most siblings. Beginning in the womb, they share space and, sometimes, a placenta. Most share a birthday. Infant multiples may share a crib, the milk from their mother's breasts, and most of their clothing.

Despite their parents' best efforts to endow them with ownership, multiples will most likely battle for custody over every toy and plaything that crosses their path. However, they'll generously share every germ and virus that comes their way. Of course, they'll share lots of fun, too, commemorating milestones and making happy memories together as they grow up. As playmates, they will have access to instant stimulation and constant companionship, often relieving parents of the burden of playing the role of entertainer.

Give and Take

Whether it is a parent's attention, the right to be first, or sole ownership of a plaything they're after, multiples can be extremely competitive with one another. Many multiples are able to channel their competitive nature into achievement when they grow older, excelling in sports or academics.

Sometimes the dynamic between a pair of multiples is one of compensating, rather than competing. Where one is lacking in a character attribute or skill, the other will step up to the plate. For example, many multiples exhibit delays in language development because the twin with stronger language skills does most of the talking for her weaker sibling, communicating for both of them.

QUESTION

Do identical twins have a closer bond than fraternal twins?
While the scientific community might argue that shared DNA makes them more compatible, the consensus among parents of multiples seems to indicate that this has no bearing on their relationship. Sometimes identical twins don't get along simply because they are too similar, while fraternal multiples craft an incredibly close bond due to their shared environment.

Myths and Mysteries about Multiples

People have long been fascinated by multiple births. Since ancient times, twins have played a role in mythology and legend. In some cultures, they are revered; in others they are considered an abomination. Twins are often used symbolically to represent the contrast between good and evil or as a symbol of true companionship.

The legendary status of twins has created some interesting misconceptions. Multiples are not identical clones of each other. They are completely unique individuals who happened to be born at the same time. They don't have ESP and can't read each other's minds, although they sometimes finish each other's sentences and often seem to be eerily in tune with each other's thoughts.

Some people mistakenly assume that twins or other multiples will be less intelligent, less talented, or otherwise deficient because they share genes. This is absolutely not the case. There is no correlation between intelligence and ability and multiple birth.

It's also not true that multiples can be characterized into opposing categories. In any given twin set, you can't label one as all good and one as all bad. There's not a "smart one" and a "dumb one," a "pretty one" and a "homely one," or a "shy one" and an "outgoing one." It just doesn't work that way. Unfortunately, sometimes people apply those labels to multiples, and if the children hear such talk often enough as they grow up, they may begin to identify and define themselves according to these views of others. Parents should be alert to these types of labels; avoid using them to describe your children and discourage others from attempting to typecast them.

What You *Need* to Know about Twins and Multiples

- **Having twins is not the same as having two children close in age.** Parents of multiples face different issues than parents of singletons. While there are some additional challenges, there are also special blessings that accompany multiples.
- **Multiples share a unique bond.** Although they can be the best of buddies, they may also contend with jealousy and animosity. Twins are not clones of each other, nor are they polar opposites. Parents of multiples must nurture their children as individuals, but also recognize the unique relationship that their children share.
- **Parents of multiples are in good company.** There are many famous twins—and parents of twins. Multiples are a popular topic in movies and literature, and also on television. Many celebrities from the realm of music, sports, and politics also have a connection to multiples.

CHAPTER 2

An Introduction to Zygosity

One of the first and most common questions that you will be asked about your multiples is "Are they identical or fraternal?" Although most people understand that these are the two basic types of twins, some members of the general public truly have no idea what these terms really describe. Twin type (this term refers to all multiples, not just twins) has very little to do with appearance, and everything to do with the originating relationship of the individuals. It's based on zygosity.

What Is Zygosity?

Most people are familiar with the terms *identical* and *fraternal*, but the categorizations don't represent twin type as accurately as the more scientific classifications of zygosity. Scientifically speaking, there are two basic types of multiples. Monozygotic, or identical, multiples are the result of a single zygote, or fertilized egg, while dizygotic (or multizygotic) multiples form from two or more zygotes. These multiples are commonly termed *fraternal*. All twins fit into one of these categories. Triplets, quadruplets, and other higher order multiples may be one or the other, or even a combination of both. For example, two children in a set of triplets may be monozygotic while the third is dizygotic. Twin typing, or determining zygosity, means figuring out which of these two types of multiples you have.

To understand zygosity, you have to start at the very beginning: conception. It starts when a woman's ovary releases an egg, or oocyte, into her fallopian tube and it travels toward the uterus. This process is called ovulation, and happens monthly. Along the way, sperm released by a male during sexual intercourse try to intercept the oocyte. If a sperm is able to penetrate, the egg becomes fertilized. The fertilized oocyte continues its journey to the uterus, dividing and combining cells to form a zygote. It implants in the uterus and begins to grow into a baby. But variations in the process can produce multiples—twins, triplets, or more. Zygosity not only defines twin type, but also can give parents valuable insight into their multiples' origin.

The zygosity of your multiples is significant on several levels. First, it's nice to have an answer when people ask whether your multiples are fraternal or identical! It's also helpful to understand how and why you became pregnant with multiples. But, more importantly, determining zygosity is important in identifying certain medical issues associated with twinning.

Dizygotic Twins

Sometimes during the ovulation process, the ovaries are prompted to release multiple eggs. There are many reasons for this occurrence. A normal female body has two ovaries, one on the left side and one on the right. Both contain thousands of eggs. Generally the ovaries take turns ovulating, but occasionally they will each release an egg in a single cycle. Some women have a genetic tendency to hyperovulate, or release numerous eggs every month. Other women might release multiple eggs on an occasional basis due to hormonal fluctuations. Sometimes hormones are influenced by medication, such as birth control pills or fertility enhancements like Clomid or Pergonal. But they can also be impacted by a woman's age (older women tend to release multiple eggs more often than younger women) or by lifestyle.

Dizygotic twins are conceived if two eggs are fertilized by sperm (*di* meaning two and *zygotic* referring to the fertilized egg, or zygote). If both zygotes implant in the uterus, you've got twins! Likewise, three zygotes produce triplets and four would equal quadruplets. Generally, even higher order multiples that are born of separate zygotes are all referred to as dizygotic, although a more accurate term would be *multizygotic*.

Dizygotic Defined

Dizygotic twins are essentially siblings that happen to be born at the same time. They are each formed from a separate egg and a separate sperm. Just as related children within a family have a variety of appearances and characteristics based on the combination of genetic traits they inherit from their parents, dizygotic twins can also be very alike or very different. They can be boys, girls, or one of each.

When people talk about twins being hereditary or skipping a generation, they are referring to dizygotic twins. Women with a gene for hyperovulation are more likely to conceive twins since they routinely release multiple eggs. Their daughters have an increased chance of having twins as well, if they inherit the gene. However, if a woman gives birth to a son, his impact on the twinning process is irrelevant, as men do not have ovaries or ovulate. However, his daughter may inherit the hyperovulation tendency and produce twin grandchildren, thus causing the gene to "skip" a generation.

Causes of Dizygotic Twinning

Many other interesting characteristics influence dizygotic twinning. A woman's chances of conceiving dizygotic twins increase when:

- She's had a previous multiple pregnancy
- She's over age forty-five

- She's already had several other children
- She is a dizygotic twin herself, or her mother or maternal grandmother was a twin
- She has irregular sexual intercourse
- She consumes a lot of dairy products (not including those from organic sources)
- She has a BMI (body mass index) higher than 30
- She conceives shortly after discontinuing birth control pills. (This is not recommended due to the risk of birth defects.)

FIGURE 2-1
Egg-Splitting
Chart

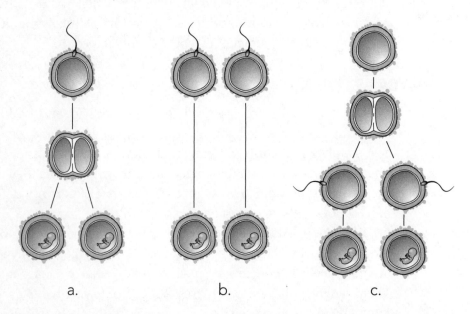

a.   b.   c.

▲ (a.) Monozygotic (identical) twins form from a single egg that splits after fertilization. (b.) Dizygotic (fraternal) multiples result when more than one egg is fertilized. (c.) Polar body twins are the result of single ova that splits prior to fertilization.

Monozygotic Twins

As opposed to dizygotic twins, monozygotics form from a single zygote. (*Mono* means one.) For reasons yet to be exactly determined by science, a single fertilized egg sometimes splits and divides the contained cell matter between two individual zygotes; both begin the process of dividing and combining cells to form embryos, resulting in two babies.

No one knows exactly what causes an egg to divide. Several theories have been formulated, but none are accepted as fact. Some scientists believe that it is related to the age of the egg, while others suggest that an enzyme in certain sperm is the cause. But no one knows for sure, and monozygotic twinning remains one of the great magical mysteries of life. A zygote can split more than once. Some triplets, quadruplets, and one documented case of quintuplets, the Dionne sisters, are monozygotic.

FACT

Dizygotic twins generally outnumber monozygotics by about two to one. Interestingly, monozygotic twinning rates remain steady despite an overall increase in multiple births. Further, monozygotic rates are the same across populations; you're equally likely to have identical twins whether you're Japanese or African.

Because they have formed from a single zygote, monozygotic twins share the same genetic makeup. Since many human physical characteristics are determined by genetics, monozygotic twins may share a remarkable resemblance. This is why the term *identical* is a common way to describe them. However, environmental influences also affect appearance, so no two twins are ever exactly alike.

ESSENTIAL

Monozygotic twins are always of the same sex. The only exception is an extremely rare condition where a chromosomal abnormality in male (XY) monozygotic multiples results in the loss of a Y chromosome in one twin, producing a female (XO).

Other Zygosity Variations

Although monozygotic and dizygotic are the two accepted categories of twinship, there are some subtypes that deserve mention. You may or may not be able to determine whether your multiples fit into one of these categories, but they are interesting to consider.

Half-Identical or Semi-Identical Twins

You may have heard of a third type of twinning. The theory of polar body, or "half-identical," twins provides a tidy explanation for dizygotic twins with a strong resemblance. A polar body is a small cell within the egg that divides off and usually degenerates and dies after fertilization. If, for some reason, the polar body divides off prematurely from the egg, it may also become fertilized by a sperm and develop as an embryo. No one is sure why or how it happens, and it appears to be very rare.

Developing from a single egg, but separate sperm, the twins share about 75 percent of their genotypes: 50 percent from their mother but only 25 percent from their father. They would be more "identical" or similar in appearance than dizygotic twins, but less so than monozygotics.

Researchers reported another rare classification of twinning in a report in the *Journal of Human Genetics* after analyzing the DNA of a set of twins that were identical on their mother's side but shared only half of their father's genes. It was determined that two separate sperm had fertilized a single egg, and then the egg split into two. Sesquizygotic twins—also called "semi-identical" twins—are distinct from polar body twins because the egg split after—rather than before—fertilization. At this time, these rare hybrid types of twinning are very difficult to identify and confirm without access to sophisticated genetic testing technology; the services that test zygosity for consumers do not provide this level of analysis. Parents may suspect their twins fit into these categories, but they probably won't ever know for sure.

Dizygotic Variances

While not an alternate twin type, other categories of twins are subsets or special types of either monozygotic or dizygotic twinning. Among dizygotic twins, two unique divergences have been identified.

Superfetation occurs when a second egg is inadvertently released in a subsequent reproductive cycle despite the fertilization of the first. The result is multiples that are conceived at different times, up to twenty-four days apart. Superfetation may account for discrepancies in fetal size and development in dizygotic multiples. If confirmed during the pregnancy, the "older" baby may be delivered days or even weeks before his twin to promote optimal gestational well-being.

Superfecundation, on the other hand, describes a situation where dizygotic twins have different fathers. It happens when an ovulating woman has intercourse with multiple partners within a short span of time. Two eggs are fertilized by sperm from different men. Several cases of superfecundation have been identified and confirmed, including a case in Europe in the 1970s where the babies were of different races.

Mirror Image Twins

Mirror image twins are an example of a special type of monozygotic twins. About 23 percent of monozygotic twins are classified as "mirror image," in that they exhibit reversed asymmetry in certain physical characteristics. For example, hair whorls rotate in opposite directions, moles or birthmarks are featured on opposite sides of the body, or the two have opposite hand preferences. In very rare cases, vital organs may develop on opposite sides of their bodies.

There's no way to diagnostically confirm mirror image twins, except by observation of their features. It's believed that mirror image twinning occurs due to a delayed split, about a week after fertilization, when the developing embryo has a clearly established right and left side. Mirror image twins generally share a placenta and other characteristics specific to monozygotic twins.

Conjoined Twins

Conjoined twins are a type of monozygotic multiples, originating from a single zygote that splits into two. However, they take their time splitting apart, with the consequence that they do not entirely separate, and begin to develop with connected tissue or organs.

With an increase in media attention focused on conjoined twins, it may seem that they are becoming more common. However, conjoined twins are an extremely rare type of monozygotic twins, representing only 1 in 500,000 pregnancies. The majority of conjoined twins are female, although no one is exactly sure why that is.

Generally, conjoined twins result if the split is delayed more than twelve days post-fertilization; the later the split, the more tissue and organ function is shared. Every set of conjoined twins has a unique connection, but about three-quarters of conjoined twins are connected at the torso. The degree of conjoinedness determines the outlook for the babies; few sets are able to survive without surgical separation. Many do not even survive in the womb—more than half are stillborn, and about 35 percent survive only one day.

Surgical separation of conjoined twins attracts much media attention, but unfortunately, many conjoined twins are not candidates for surgery. Babies who share major organ function cannot survive separately, putting parents in the unthinkable position of having to sacrifice one child for the survival of the other. Advances in medical technology are giving parents more hope, however, as doctors gain more expertise in the treatment of this unique kind of twinning.

FACT

> Conjoined twins are sometimes known as Siamese twins, a reference to Chang and Eng Bunker, the first set of conjoined twins to gain world renown. Born in Siam in the early 1800s, they traveled the world as circus performers before settling down and marrying sisters in North Carolina.

Although some conjoined twins live into old age, most are afflicted by health complications due to strain on their shared organs. It is estimated that about 50 percent of conjoined twins are stillborn, and many more do not survive more than a few days after birth. Even with a minimal connection, it is difficult for conjoined twins to lead a normal life. Modern medical technology makes surgical separation of conjoined twins an increasingly viable option, even when vital organs are shared. Success stories like Egyptian brothers Ahmed and Mohammed Ibrahim and American sisters Kendra and Maliyah Herrin provide hope for a healthy future.

Twin Typing In Utero

So how will you know what kind of multiples you have? In the past, some multiples never knew the truth about their origin. But as modern technology provides new ways to reveal the clues, conclusive information is more accessible. In some cases, doctors can even identify zygosity before the babies ever arrive.

Using Ultrasound

The babies' arrangement in the womb may provide some clues about their zygosity, although the signs aren't always conclusive. First, an ultrasound examination can provide a tip-off: the sex of the babies. If they are of opposite sex, they are obviously dizygotic. However, if their gender cannot be determined, or if all babies are of the same gender, they could be either monozygotic or dizygotic.

Placenta Analysis

Doctors can also use ultrasound to examine the placenta. Studying the placenta can be helpful in determining zygosity because the placental structure of monozygotic and dizygotic twins sometimes varies.

In any pregnancy, single or multiple, the fertilized egg travels to the uterus and implants in the uterine wall; from this point it is referred to as an embryo. The process may take several days. About a week after fertilization, the placenta begins to form along the inner wall of the uterus. Dizygotic multiples will implant individually in the uterus and develop individual placentas. Monozygotic twins, on the other hand, may follow one of several courses depending on when the zygote splits. If the split occurs early, within four days post-conception, monozygotics will act much as dizygotics; they'll implant separately and, at least initially, have two distinct placentas. Early forming monozygotics can be indistinguishable from dizygotics.

ALERT

Determining zygosity before birth is tricky since the evidence is often inconclusive. Unless doctors can definitively identify two fetuses of the same gender with a shared placenta and a shared sac, they can't be sure whether the multiples are dizygotic or monozygotic. To complicate matters, two placentas may fuse together over time, appearing as a single entity.

The majority of monozygotics, about two-thirds, experience the split between four and eight days post-fertilization. They will share a placenta and be enclosed within a shared chorion (the outer layer of the sac that contains a fetus), but will develop individually within separate and distinct amnions (the inner membrane surrounding the sac of amniotic fluid). These twins are referred to as monochorionic monozygotics. A small percentage of monozygotic twins, less than 2 percent, split after the amnion forms on or about day eight, and develop jointly within a shared amnion. Monoamniotic multiples will also share a single placenta and chorion. Doctors can often use ultrasound technology to determine the number of placentas and the structure of the chorion and amnion by identifying the membrane separating them. The absence of a distinguishing membrane may indicate monozygotic twins.

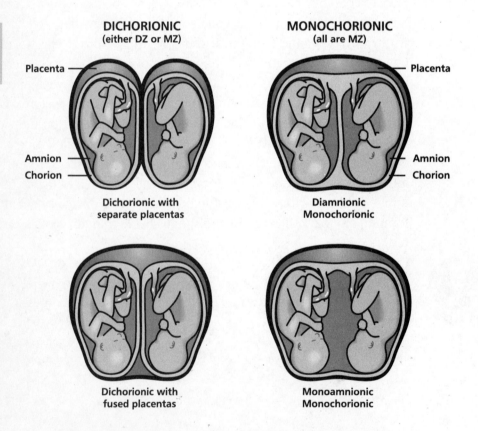

FIGURE 2-2
Chart of Membranes

DICHORIONIC
(either DZ or MZ)

Placenta

Amnion

Chorion

Dichorionic with separate placentas

Dichorionic with fused placentas

MONOCHORIONIC
(all are MZ)

Placenta

Amnion

Chorion

Diamnionic Monochorionic

Monoamnionic Monochorionic

▲ Depending on when the egg splits, monozygotic twins will have two separate placentas (dichorionic) that may or may not fuse together. Or they may share a single placenta (monochorionic) but have individual amniotic sacs. Monoamniotic twins are encased in a single sac.

After Birth

Sometimes you can't determine the zygosity of multiples until after they are born. After your babies are delivered, your physician may examine the placenta(s) visually or send them to a laboratory for pathological testing. Most monochorionic multiples are identified by laboratory analysis of the placenta after birth.

In the meantime, your babies may confirm or confound your suspicions by their similarities or dissimilarities. Even monozygotics may appear radically different due to their birth experience (perhaps one was a breech delivery) or factors in the uterine environment. On the other hand, some dizygotics have a strong resemblance as infants that fades as they grow older.

What if you still don't know for sure? If you have same-sex babies that look alike but had two separate placentas, they could be either dizygotic or monozygotic. If you want to know the truth, further testing is required. Sometimes a simple blood test will reveal the secret; if the babies have different blood types, they are dizygotic. But if they share the same blood type, you'll have to take the next step and pursue a DNA test.

In most cases, doctors won't routinely order DNA testing to determine zygosity, and insurance won't cover the costs. Fortunately, several private companies now offer twin-type testing services. The process is fairly simple, the results are usually conclusive, and the cost is minimal; several companies offer the test for less than $300.

ESSENTIAL

Because twins and other multiples provide scientists with such a rich resource for research, there is great interest in studying them. Many research studies will cover the cost of zygosity testing for participating multiples. It's one way to unlock the secret of your multiples' origin, while helping scientists unravel the secrets of the universe!

DNA testing determines zygosity by comparing cell samples from each child. Monozygotic twins, evolving from a single gene set, will have comparable samples. Dizygotic multiples, on the other hand, will exhibit differences in their DNA, since each child inherited a unique genetic package from their parents.

Zygosity Fast Facts

- **Twins and multiples are classified by zygosity.** Zygosity is a way to describe twins based on how they form.
- **Dizygotic—or fraternal—twins are the result of two separate sperm/egg combinations.** They are essentially two siblings who are conceived at about the same time and share a womb. Dizygotic twinning can be hereditary or influenced by environmental factors such as maternal age, diet, or body type.
- **Monozygotic twins are commonly known as identical.** Only about one-third of twins are monozygotic, forming from a single egg/sperm combination that splits and develops into two individual embryos. Because they share the same combination of DNA, they can be remarkably similar and may look alike. Monozygotic twins that separate late form conjoined twins.
- **Twin type can be difficult to determine.** Sometimes zygosity can be confirmed before birth by using ultrasound to assess placental structure. However, DNA sampling will more conclusively confirm whether multiples are monozygotic or dizygotic.

CHAPTER 3

Supertwins: Triplets and More

While twins have become fairly commonplace in our society, triplets and higher order multiples remain relatively rare. Nearly everyone knows a twin or a family with a set of twins in their genealogy. But many people live their entire lives without ever crossing paths with a quadruplet or sextuplet, except the ones they see on television. Discovering that you're about to be responsible for so many babies can be quite daunting! Each additional baby that you welcome into this world represents an increase: in risk, in challenge, but also in blessings.

What Are Supertwins?

The term *supertwins* is used to refer to multiples of three, four, or more. Another term that is commonly used is *higher order multiples*. More descriptive names are assigned to specially designate the number of babies.

- **Three babies:** Triplets
- **Four babies:** Quadruplets (quads)
- **Five babies:** Quintuplets (quints)
- **Six babies:** Sextuplets
- **Seven babies:** Septuplets
- **Eight babies:** Octuplets
- **Nine babies:** Nonuplets
- **Ten babies:** Decaplets

Higher order multiples are conceived like anyone else, when a sperm meets an egg. Most supertwins are multizygotic, meaning that each individual embryo starts as a single egg-and-sperm combination. Sometimes a pair of individuals within the multiple set will be monozygotic and the rest will be dizygotic. In rare situations, the entire multiple set is monozygotic, the result of a fertilized egg splitting multiple times.

FIGURE 3-1
Supertwins
Zygosity
Permutations

Triplets

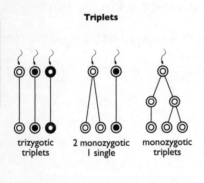

Quadruplets

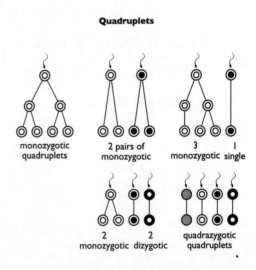

▲ Higher order multiples may be multizygotic, monozygotic, or a combination.

There's no doubt about it. If you're expecting triplets, quadruplets, or more, you've joined a rather elite club of parents. The birth rate for higher order multiples (triplets and more) jumped 400 percent between 1980 and 1998. However, despite this increase, they remain a relatively rare event. Take a look at the statistics.

- Naturally occurring triplet births occur in approximately 1 per 8,500 births.
- Naturally occurring quadruplet births happen only 1 per 600,000 births.
- The odds of having quintuplets in nonassisted conceptions are 1 in approximately 50,000,000.
- In 2008, about 1,950 sets of triplets and 85 sets of quadruplets were born in the United States.
- Triplets and above represented less than two-tenths (.147) of 1 percent of all live births in 2008.

How did you get so lucky? If you played the lottery with the same odds, you'd likely be a big winner!

Reproductive Technology and Supertwins

Much of the rise in supertwin birth rates over the last thirty years is attributed to advances in reproductive technology. New techniques and procedures increase the ability to produce viable pregnancies. The MOST (Mothers of Supertwins) organization estimates that 82 percent of higher order multiples (triplets and higher) are the result of fertility treatments.

Fertility Drugs

Treatment for infertility takes many forms, depending on a couple's specific needs and issues. Fertility-enhancing drugs are often the first step for couples. Prescription drugs such as Clomid (clomiphene citrate) or Repronex (human menopausal gonadotropin) manipulate a woman's hormones to induce and regulate ovulation. Sometimes the drugs cause hyperovulation, or the release of multiple eggs. This increases the odds of more than one egg becoming fertilized, and a resulting multizygotic multiple pregnancy.

Although the chances of conceiving twins while taking Clomid are estimated at about 7 percent, the drug is not generally associated with an increased risk of higher order multiples. However, other more powerful drugs are employed when Clomid fails to produce a pregnancy. These can have an extreme impact on ovulation, generating the release of numerous eggs, which, if fertilized, lead to the development of many fetuses.

The ART of Reproduction

Assisted reproductive technology (or ART) is the collective term used to describe procedures that involve manipulation of both a female egg and male sperm outside of the female body. There are several approaches that are used, depending on the cause of the infertility issue.

- **In vitro fertilization (IVF):** Eggs are harvested from the mother's ovaries and combined with sperm in a laboratory. (*In vitro* is Latin for "in glass.") The fertilized eggs—or embryos—are then placed into the mother's uterus.
- **Gamete intrafallopian transfer (GIFT):** GIFT is similar to IVF, but the eggs are fertilized inside the woman's body rather than outside. The mother's eggs are removed from her ovaries and placed in her fallopian tube along with sperm from the father.
- **Zygote intrafallopian transfer (ZIFT):** ZIFT is a combination of GIFT and IVF. It is also known as tubal embryo transfer. Eggs are fertilized in the lab, then placed in the mother's fallopian tube (rather than the uterus, as in IVF).

In the past, reproductive specialists would often transfer multiple eggs or zygotes with the assumption that not all of the eggs would implant in the uterus and produce a viable pregnancy. In order to enhance the chances of conception—up the odds, so to speak—they would transfer five, six, or seven embryos. The practice become a source of controversy because of the increased number of risky multiple births that resulted.

What about Monozygotics?

Limiting the number of embryos reduces the chances of dizygotic multiples, but it doesn't rule out multiples completely. An interesting relationship has been observed between monozygotic twins and ART. Reports indicate the monozygotic twinning rate following ART procedures is up to ten times higher than the natural occurrence of this type of twin. One theory proposes that the delay in the zygote's growth and implantation gives it more time to split, but the cause remains as much a mystery as spontaneous incidence of monozygotic twinning.

FACT

The American Society of Reproductive Medicine refined its guidelines in 2009 to limit the number of embryos transferred in in vitro fertilization cycles in an effort to reduce the number of higher order multiples as an outcome of assisted reproduction. The rate of supertwins has actually declined since the late 1990s, and is expected to continue to decrease as the guidelines are put into practice.

Whether by uncontrolled ovulation stimulation or overzealous embryo transfers, clearly reproductive technology has resulted in an increase in higher order multiples. Multiple birth is actually considered a complication of reproductive treatment, not the primary goal. Nevertheless, as a result, many previously infertile couples now find themselves the parents of triplets, quadruplets, or more.

Extreme Supertwins

While many animals give birth to litters, the human body is designed to bear only one baby at a time. Generally, two are easily sustained, but every additional baby pushes the situation to an extreme as competition for space and resources increases.

In recent years mothers have given birth to extreme supertwins like sextuplets, septuplets, and even octuplets. Higher order multiples such as these are not a new phenomenon, but their ability to survive has only been established in recent years as medical technology has grown to accommodate the extreme stresses of pregnancy and prematurity.

The first recorded set of surviving quintuplets was born in Canada in 1934. The identical Dionne quintuplets—Annette, Yvonne, Cecile, Marie

Reine, and Emilie—became wards of the province of Ontario and were unfortunately turned into a public spectacle. Supertwins remain the subject of public curiosity as media outlets and reality television programs insist on keeping these extreme families in the spotlight.

ESSENTIAL

The Suleman octuplets, born in January 2009, are the first surviving set of octuplets. The six boys and two girls were born to an unemployed, single mother in California who already had six other children. Although the octuplets continue to be remarkably healthy, the situation generated a great deal of criticism and controversy.

Special Medical Considerations

For many supertwins, merely being born seems a miraculous event. The struggle for survival in the womb puts a strain on both the mother's and babies' health. Each additional baby increases the demands on the mother's physical ability to provide sufficient space and nutrients for everyone. A supertwin pregnancy requires careful monitoring and often, more intense medical intervention.

Multiple Challenges for the Mother

Many conditions of pregnancy are intensified in mothers of higher order multiples. Each additional baby contributes to the hormonal fluctuations raging within her body. These hormones that control pregnancy cause many of the typical symptoms such as mood swings, cravings, fatigue, and nausea; the increased levels of these hormones in a mother carrying three, four, or more babies are likely to intensify her experience of the symptoms.

Perhaps the biggest concern in higher order multiple birth is preterm labor. Because of the risk, many mothers of higher order multiples experience more medical intervention. While a twin mother may be able to avoid bed rest or hospitalization during her pregnancy, it is more common for mothers of triplets or quadruplets to require treatment to prevent preterm labor. It is virtually assured that mothers of quintuplets and higher will spend time in the hospital prior to delivery.

Why are higher order multiples more likely to be born early?
The average uterus is designed to accommodate about ten pounds of baby. Supertwins usually weigh only half of the average birth weight of their singleton counterparts, but their combined weight easily overwhelms the capacity of the uterus. The risk increases exponentially with each additional baby.

Every pregnancy experience is different, and not every mother of supertwins will have a complicated pregnancy. However, increased tendencies for many complications exist. For example:

- Morning sickness and nausea in early pregnancy may be intensified, leading to improper nutrition and dehydration.
- Iron-deficiency anemia is more common and severe.
- Complications from the placenta, such as placenta previa or abruptio placentae, are more likely to occur.
- One in three mothers of multiples will contract preeclampsia or pregnancy induced hypertension, which can raise her blood pressure to dangerously unhealthy levels.
- Virtually all mothers of multiples higher than triplets will have to deliver by cesarean section, which carries an increased risk of infection, blood loss, and complications, and generally requires a longer recuperation period.

If you're expecting higher order multiples, it is vital that you receive prenatal care from a physician experienced with your situation. Simply having delivered twins is not sufficient experience for treating a woman expecting three, four, or more babies. Obstetricians and perinatologists that specialize in higher order multiples are most accessible in large cities or teaching hospitals, but they are becoming more common as the demand increases for specialized care for multiple births.

In addition, you should plan to receive care from a hospital with a Level III maternity division. This designation provides assurance that the facility is prepared to meet the needs of high-risk obstetrical patients and can treat the full range of newborn afflictions once your babies are born. Some mothers choose to receive care in another city or even another state in order to ensure the best possible treatment in the event of complications.

Risks to the Babies

The biggest single risk for higher order multiples is premature birth. Without sufficient opportunity to develop in utero, premature babies are at risk for numerous complications and disabilities. Some are apparent at birth, as severely premature infants struggle to maintain the basic operation of life. Other consequences don't manifest themselves until later in life, as the children develop cognitive and motor skills.

Because prematurity is so common for the majority of higher order multiples, it's important to recognize the potential consequences and be prepared for any eventuality. It's estimated that in 40 percent of supertwin births, at least one of the babies will suffer permanent physical or neurological damage due to complications. The risk can't be underestimated. The chapters in this book pertaining to preterm labor and premature babies will provide you with further information on the topic, as well as guidelines for improving the odds of a favorable outcome.

ALERT

A normal singleton gestation is forty weeks. According to Mothers of Supertwins (MOST), the average gestational age for triplets is 34 weeks. For quadruplets it is 32 weeks. And for quintuplets, it is only 30 weeks.

Amid all the risks and complications, parents of higher order multiples should have optimistic hope. Advances in medical technology improve the odds for at-risk babies with every passing day. New drugs and treatments allow mothers to sustain their pregnancies longer, and neonatal care gives even extremely premature infants the opportunity to thrive.

Multifetal Reduction

One of the most controversial issues faced by parents of higher order multiples is the option of selective reduction. Many parents are horrified by the mere suggestion, while others firmly believe that it is the only way to ensure a healthy outcome.

Multifetal selective reduction is the practice of reducing a higher order multiple pregnancy (usually to a twin pregnancy) in order to minimize risk and maximize the potential viability of the remaining fetuses. During an outpatient procedure, a needle is inserted into the mother's uterus, either through the vagina or abdomen. Ultrasound guides the needle as it injects potassium chloride into one or more of the embryos. The chemical halts the embryo's development and the embryo is eventually reabsorbed by the body.

When Reduction Is Warranted

Medically, selective reduction is an accepted method of improving the odds. Despite the successful delivery of babies such as the Suleman octuplets and McCaughey septuplets, many situations of extreme multiple pregnancy result in the loss of some or all of the babies.

The procedure is usually recommended only in incidences of quadruplets or higher and is generally performed toward the end of the first trimester. That doesn't give parents a great deal of time to consider their options. They may feel pressured by the dire predictions of their doctors or conversely by their own religious or moral convictions. It is a tremendously agonizing decision, with no clear answer.

Making a Difficult Decision

If you are faced with making a decision regarding multifetal reduction, it's imperative that you receive qualified advice from a variety of sources. In many cases, parents are put into this position after undergoing extensive fertility enhancements to get pregnant in the first place, so most likely you will already have a good relationship with at least one professional in this area. Ask your reproductive specialist for objective statistical information regarding the potential outcomes for your pregnancy. In addition, consult a qualified perinatologist or other specialist in higher order multiple pregnancy. They may offer a different assessment of your pregnancy's potential.

Once you have compiled a balanced view of your options and the medical risks and benefits involved with each, you'll have to confront the emotional aspects of your situation. Because it is such a controversial issue, you may find it difficult to discuss with friends or family members, especially if they have strong opinions on the subject. Choose your confidantes carefully. It may be helpful to seek guidance from a trusted religious adviser who can help you reconcile your beliefs with your choices. Perhaps your most valuable resource at this difficult time is the support of families who have faced a similar predicament. Networking with other parents will provide an opportunity for you to discuss the outcome of their choice, whether they decided for or against reduction.

ESSENTIAL

There are several organizations that can provide support for parents facing this situation, including national groups like MOST (Mothers of Supertwins) or The Triplet Connection, as well as local chapters of multiples clubs. You'll find contact information for these and other organizations in Appendix A.

Preparing for Supertwins

It's not uncommon for families to have three, four, or five children. However, having them all at once is a completely different scenario! As you read through this book to prepare yourself for the birth of multiples, there are several things you should keep in mind as a parent (or parent-to-be) of supertwins.

First of all, once the babies arrive, you'll be immediately outnumbered. Where parents of twins can divide their time equally between two babies, you'll always have someone waiting in the wings for your attention. In this type of situation, it is essential that you establish routines to ensure that everyone's needs are met.

Secondly, every additional baby represents an increase. Everything is "more." You'll need more help, have to buy more supplies, and require more medical monitoring. At the same time, your babies will likely have less time in your womb, so it's vital that you make the most of your pregnancy. You'll have to eat more—and gain more weight—than a mom of a singleton or even twins. You'll need to get more rest and spend more time off your feet.

Finally, even though there are more demands, the rewards also increase exponentially. Your children will enjoy the spotlight of their special status as supertwins. They will share a unique bond with their same-age siblings. Your family will include a ready-made playgroup and they will never be without companionship. And as parents, you can look forward to three times the smiles, four times the giggles, or five times as many hugs!

Spotlight on Supertwins

- **Sometimes multiples come in sets of three, four, five, or more.** The term *supertwins* describes triplets (3), quadruplets (4), quintuplets (5), sextuplets (6), septuplets (7), or octuplets (8). They are also known as higher order multiples.
- **Reproductive technology is responsible for the birth of many supertwins.** Although they are still a relatively small proportion of all births, reproductive technology, such as fertility drugs or in vitro fertilization, produces hundreds of sets of supertwins each year.
- **Supertwins can be monozygotic, dizygotic, or a combination of both.** While most supertwins are dizygotic (resulting for separate egg/sperm combinations), in vitro fertilization does produce some incidence of monozygotic multiples where a zygote splits two or more times.
- **A higher order multiple pregnancy presents numerous risks for the mother and babies.** Supertwins are at increased risk for premature birth and the resulting health complications. In addition, moms of supertwins may encounter medical complications during pregnancy or delivery. In some cases, parents may have to consider a selective reduction of the pregnancy in order to promote an optimal outcome.

CHAPTER 4

The First Trimester

So you're pregnant! You may or may not even know that you're having multiples during the first twelve weeks of your pregnancy, but it is definitely a time of discovery, surprising physical changes, and emotional upheaval. If you've been pregnant before, you may think you know what to expect, but there are some unexpected differences when you are pregnant with more than one.

Signs and Symptoms of Multiples

Some mothers are fully aware that they are pregnant with two or more babies from the very beginning of their pregnancy. They may have strong and accurate powers of intuition or, more likely, they are under the supervision of a reproductive specialist who is monitoring every step of the conception process. However, most women who spontaneously conceive twins, triplets, or more won't begin to suspect anything out of the ordinary until their pregnancy progresses.

Suspicious Signs

Multiples manifest their presence in several ways, but no one symptom distinguishes itself as a clear indicator. Some mothers of multiples report a strong suspicion based on one factor or a combination of signals, while others experience absolutely nothing out of the ordinary. Any of the following indicators may come up in the first trimester. If you experience them to an unusually extreme degree, it may be a sign that you are carrying multiples.

- **Weight gain:** A singleton mother gains, on average, five to seven pounds in the first trimester. Anything more could indicate multiples . . . or excessive junk food consumption.
- **Abdomen size:** With multiple babies in her womb, a pregnant woman tends to outgrow her regular clothing and require maternity gear sooner. Although it is difficult to estimate fundal size (the size of the uterus) in early pregnancy, sometimes an increase is evident, indicating multiple babies.
- **Fatigue:** Excessive fatigue is one of the most commonly reported complaints for mothers of multiples in the early stages of pregnancy. With their bodies busy taking care of the babies, there is little energy left over for carrying out their daily routines.
- **Fetal movement:** It's very unusual for a mother to experience fetal movement in the first trimester, yet there is some evidence to suggest that the sensation is more acute when there is more than one baby moving around.
- **Nausea:** Extra babies can intensify the symptoms of morning sickness.

You may be aware of some or all of these indications, or none at all. Perhaps your doctor or midwife brought the symptoms to your attention during a routine exam. However, they are also all normal consequences of pregnancy, which makes it quite difficult to tell whether they are truly a sign of multiples.

A Certain Something

In addition to physical symptoms, many mothers of multiples report an unexplainable hunch or vague suspicion early in pregnancy. Often it's triggered by unusual circumstances that bring multiples to the forefront of their attention. Perhaps they dream about having twins or find themselves running across several sets of multiples in a public place. Or they may encounter mysterious phenomena that occur in sets of twos or threes. One expectant mother of twins discovered that the eggs she'd bought for holiday baking all contained double yolks; two days later an ultrasound revealed that she was having twins!

Hearing Heartbeats

You might assume that multiple babies would be easily identified by listening for multiple heartbeats. Unfortunately, that is not an effective practice in early pregnancy. Distinct heartbeat sounds are usually only detected toward the end of the first trimester, about week twelve. Even then, what sounds like an additional baby might actually be an echo of the mother's own beating heart. In other situations, multiple babies that are positioned fairly close together may have indistinguishable rhythms that are misinterpreted as a single heartbeat.

ALERT

The phenomenon of one audible heartbeat is particularly common with monochorionic monozygotics (see Chapter 2). Not only do they have similar heart rhythms, but also they tend to settle close to each other because they are contained in the same sac.

hCG Screening and Multiples

One of the earliest ways to detect the possibility of multiples is by monitoring the level of human chorionic gonadotropin (or hCG) in the mother's body. hCG is a hormone secreted by the fertilized egg(s). It regulates the production of other hormones, such as progesterone and estrogen, until the placenta develops and assumes that role.

hCG is the substance detected by common over-the-counter pregnancy tests to ascertain if a woman is pregnant or not. These tests measure the amount of hCG in a urine sample to determine whether there is enough of the hormone to indicate pregnancy.

But hCG monitoring of a blood sample provides a more comprehensive picture of the woman's status. It not only indicates whether an egg is fertilized, but can be used to determine whether the fertilized egg, implanted in the uterus, is developing into an embryo. An hCG blood test can also suggest the presence of more than one embryo. A single hCG measurement doesn't tell the story. Rather, samples are taken every few days during the early weeks of pregnancy, and compared. With each passing day, increasing amounts of the hormone are detectable in the pregnant mother's system. hCG production peaks toward the end of the first trimester, so it is generally monitored only in the first few weeks of pregnancy.

▼ hCG LEVELS IN SINGLE AND TWIN PREGNANCY

Days from LMP*	hCG Range** for Singleton Pregnancy	hCG Range for Multiple Pregnancy
28	9.4—120	9.5 - 120
33	300—600	200—1,800
36	1,200—1,800	2,400—36,000
40	2,400—4,800	8,700—108,000
45	12,000—60,000	72,000—180,000
70	96,000—144,000	348,000—480,000

*LMP is the date of the start of the last menstrual period.
**hCG is measured in mIU/mL

As the chart illustrates, hCG measurements are quite inflated when a multiple pregnancy is present. However, they are not considered a completely reliable indicator of twins or more. In most cases, a high hCG reading will only prompt further investigation.

Confirming That There Is More Than One

The only way to authenticate a multiple pregnancy in the first trimester is with visual confirmation via ultrasound. Other indications and testing may arouse suspicion or contribute evidence, but you won't know anything for sure until you and your doctor peek inside through the magic of ultrasound technology.

Your caregiver may suspect multiples for several reasons. In addition to the symptoms and hCG indicators mentioned earlier, predisposition factors such as your age, a previous multiple pregnancy, history of twinning on your mother's side, or fertility treatment should always be considered valid reasons to screen for multiples early in the pregnancy.

Using Ultrasound

If multiples are suspected, a brief ultrasound scan can help determine the proper course of action to ensure the healthiest possible outcome for mother and babies. Early detection of multiples is the best option for families, giving them more time to prepare physically and psychologically. Ultrasound technology can be successfully used to diagnose a multiple pregnancy as early as four weeks, but it is generally used about halfway through the first trimester when individual heartbeats are distinguishable.

ESSENTIAL

Advances in ultrasound technology mean that very few multiples make a surprise appearance during delivery. As recently as 1970, nearly half of twins, triplets, and other multiples went undetected, but in recent times, less than 10 percent remain undiagnosed.

Types of Ultrasound

Two types of ultrasound are used routinely in pregnancy: vaginal and abdominal. Generally, abdominal ultrasound is utilized later in pregnancy, while vaginal scans (also called transvaginal sonography, or TVS) provide the most reliable information in the first trimester. A probe inserted into the vagina sends out high-frequency sound waves. As the waves bounce off the inner contours of the body, they are transmitted as electrical signals to a computer, which processes the results and displays a view of the womb on the screen.

Your doctor or radiologist will interpret the images to identify the cervix, uterus, and any embryonic or placental development. To parents, the images may appear as blobs or shadows, but the trained eye can clearly identify the number of embryos and their developing circulatory system, and can even pinpoint gestational age.

Just keep in mind that early ultrasound detection is not 100 percent accurate. Sometimes one embryo is shadowed behind another, and not visible using a two-dimensional scan. Ultrasound can also produce false evidence of multiple embryos if an empty sac is misinterpreted as a viable embryo.

Physical Changes

The first twelve weeks of a pregnancy are a very busy time, physically, for a mother of multiples. While your mind may be slow to adjust to the concept of having twins, triplets, or more, your body wastes no time in preparing to accommodate their needs in the womb. There are many different ways that you will experience the effects of the marvelous miracles growing inside you. In many aspects, the early pregnancy experience for mothers of multiples is very similar to a singleton situation. Some of the symptoms may be exaggerated, but they are generally of the same nature.

Changes in Your Digestive System

The impact on your digestive system is one of the most acute—and uncomfortable—side effects of pregnancy. Fluctuating hormones decrease the muscle tone of your stomach and intestines and slow down your ability to move food through the digestive tract. At the same time, your expanding uterus is crowding your digestive organs. The result? Heartburn, indigestion, nausea, vomiting, constipation, or a combination of all of the above!

Although it's called "morning sickness," this unpleasant stomach distress can occur at any hour of the day or night. Just as your appetite increases, your ability to process the food decreases. Everything may smell and taste different. You may crave foods that you didn't care for previously, while your stomach turns at the mere thought of old favorites. Believe it or not, morning sickness may actually be your body's way of protecting your unborn babies. Some researchers believe that the nausea and vomiting are a way of ridding your body of potentially toxic chemicals and protecting the fetuses from harmful foodborne bacteria.

FACT

Morning sickness can be harmful if the vomiting becomes severe or excessive enough to result in dehydration. This condition, called *hyperemesis gravidarum*, occurs in about 5 percent of multiple pregnancies and requires medical treatment. Let your doctor know if you are unable to keep down any food or fluids over a twenty-four-hour period.

Every woman copes with morning sickness differently. What works as a solution for one pregnant woman may make symptoms worse in another. Trial and error will help you find the best remedy for your situation. Take heart; it's a temporary condition of pregnancy, and your symptoms will likely be alleviated by the second trimester.

Here are some common recommendations for relieving morning sickness:

- **Graze.** Small, frequent meals and regular snacks keep your stomach happy.
- **Avoid greasy or fatty foods.** They take longer to digest and stay in your stomach longer.
- **Stay away from spicy fare.** It can aggravate symptoms by irritating your stomach tissue.
- **Have someone else prepare the food.** Cooking odors may trigger nausea.
- **Try bland foods.** Nibble on bland snacks that are high in carbohydrates and protein, such as whole-grain crackers, low-fat yogurt, or nuts.
- **Try motion sickness bands.** Wear a nausea-controlling acupressure band, such as those sold to combat seasickness.
- **Look at alternative treatments.** Talk to your doctor about homeopathic remedies such as ginger or vitamin B_6 supplements.

- **Don't rush out of bed in the morning.** Give yourself time to relax and your stomach will, too.

Changes in Your Circulatory System

Your circulatory system will also experience major changes during pregnancy. Blood flows to and from the placenta(s) to deliver oxygenated blood and extract unoxygenated blood from the babies. There is a drastic increase in the amount of blood (blood volume) that your body has to circulate. Each additional baby increases the volume by about 10 percent.

Your breasts may become swollen and sensitive. The nipples and areolae may darken, and you might notice prominent blue veins, especially if your skin is particularly fair. Many women find that their bras are one of the first things they outgrow during pregnancy. Some mothers of multiples gain two or three cup sizes by the end of their pregnancy.

The pressure of the extra blood flow causes your veins to dilate. This phenomenon is the cause of varicose veins, one of the unfortunate effects of pregnancy that doesn't disappear after delivery. Another particularly unpleasant consequence is the development of hemorrhoids, which occurs when the veins around the rectum become enlarged and protruding. The majority of mothers of multiples have to contend with the resulting itching and discomfort throughout their pregnancy.

ESSENTIAL

That extra radiance known as "pregnancy glow" isn't simply a symptom of happiness at having multiples. It's caused by an increase in blood flowing close to the skin's surface. Enjoy the glow, but also be careful. Your skin may react more sensitively to the sun or skin-care products.

Drinking lots and lots of fluids, particularly water, helps your body accommodate the production of all that extra blood. You'll also benefit by upping your iron intake. You might notice that you're craving iron-rich foods such as red meat or leafy green vegetables. It's a good idea to discuss your iron intake requirements with your doctor, who might recommend supplements.

Weight Changes

In a normal singleton pregnancy, weight gain is minimal in the first trimester, usually less than five pounds. However, some would say that when you're carrying multiples, an earlier weight gain produces healthier babies, based on the assumption that twins and especially higher order multiples have a shorter gestational period. Unlike a singleton pregnancy, where most weight is accumulated in the later months, weight gain may be accelerated in the earlier months with multiples.

At the same time, excessive weight gain can produce its own set of problems, during pregnancy and beyond. Gestational diabetes, high blood pressure, and even postmenopausal breast cancer have been linked to unhealthy weight accumulation during pregnancy. In order to strike the right balance and achieve a healthy weight gain for both yourself and your babies, you need to be more aware of your weight fluctuations, beginning with the first trimester.

FACT

Weight gained in the first trimester is the hardest to get rid of postpartum, since it is composed mainly of fat stores. It is not until the second trimester that the combined weight of the babies and placentas are reflected in your weight total.

By the end of the first trimester, you will likely see the scale inch upward, especially after the tenth week. Some of the increase, about two pounds, can be attributed to the extra blood volume and retained fluid. The rest is primarily accumulated body fat. Some women, depending on the severity of their morning sickness or the shape they were in prepregnancy, actually lose weight. Your initial prenatal visit with your doctor or midwife is an excellent opportunity to discuss the issue. At that time, your caregiver should assess your weight goals based on your individual situation.

Other Early Effects

Some of the early effects of pregnancy are difficult to distinguish from your body's normal functions. But when there's more than one baby in the womb, these manifestations of impending maternity may be experienced more intensely. They are often a clue that there's something different about this pregnancy.

Fatigue

The one symptom most commonly experienced by expectant mothers of multiples appears to be fatigue. From occasional drowsiness to overwhelming exhaustion, nearly every pregnant woman feels her body's call to slow down and rest. It's not hard to imagine why. Before pregnancy, your body kept itself pretty busy taking care of your own needs. Now it has to attend to the demands of two, three, or even more additional beings. With the busy baby-building boom going on, there's not much energy left over for mom!

It's important to listen to your body's cues and give it the rest it requires. Take naps, go to bed earlier in the evening, and sleep late when possible. Fatigue is generally temporary, and most overwhelming during the first trimester. There really is no remedy for it, except to give in and rest.

Spotting or Bleeding

It's normal to have some spotting or bleeding during the first trimester, but that doesn't mean that it's not frightening. The appearance of blood can make an already emotional pregnant woman frantic with worry. The most common type of bleeding during the first trimester of pregnancy is sometimes called implantation bleeding. It coincides with the timing of the first missed period and is often misinterpreted as the onset of menstruation. Instead, it is merely a result of the fertilized eggs burrowing into the soft lining of the uterus. It is usually lighter than a menstrual period and should only last a day or so.

Bleeding or spotting can also occur for a variety of other reasons in the first trimester and does not necessarily indicate an impending miscarriage. The majority of women who experience bleeding go on to have a healthy pregnancy. You should, however, notify your doctor or midwife, especially if the blood is bright red or accompanied by cramping, pain, or fever.

Your Emotional State

There is nothing quite as shocking as the surprising revelation that you are carrying multiples. Whether you find out immediately after an assisted conception or late into your pregnancy, the discovery that you are carrying two, three, or more babies pushes your pregnancy into a new dynamic. Suddenly you are labeled a "high-risk pregnancy." Immediately there are more worries. Along with a new level of excitement, the questions loom. What will go wrong? How will we cope? Can we afford this?

Your fluctuating hormones only serve to heighten the emotion of the moment. You may find yourself hysterically laughing at your unbelievable fortune one minute, then sobbing with distress the next. Mood swings are a normal consequence of pregnancy. The surging hormones affect the neurotransmitters in your brain that control your feelings; the sensation often peaks in the last half of the first trimester.

Don't fret if you feel overwhelmed or out of control. You still have several months to prepare for your new arrivals, and you'll be able to put that time to good use. Educating yourself about multiple birth—by reading this book, for example—is an excellent way to get a handle on your situation. As you learn more, you'll feel better equipped to handle the adventures ahead.

ESSENTIAL

Talking to other families with multiples is extremely reassuring during your pregnancy. Appendix A of this book contains several resources for finding support, locally or online. As you come in contact with parents in similar situations, you'll see that life with twins, triplets, or more is truly a joyful experience, despite the challenges.

The Babies' Development in the First Trimester

Your babies have been very busy since their conception. They've evolved from a sperm and an egg into a zygote, traveled down the fallopian tubes, implanted in the uterus to become an embryo, and established a placenta. At the end of the first trimester, they officially graduate from embryos to fetuses, as they will be known for the duration of the pregnancy.

Setting up shop in your womb, they've developed within a cushioning fluid-filled sac called the amnion, where they lie protected by a second membrane called the chorion. Depending on their zygosity and exactly how the development of the zygotes began, two co-multiples may be sharing the space.

As early as four weeks post-conception, the embryos have established the foundation for many of their major organs. In each embryo a tiny heart beats. A brain and a primitive central nervous system have formed. By eight weeks, the skeletal system forms a network of bones and many organ systems begin to function. At the end of the first trimester, the babies will be about the size of a travel tube of toothpaste and weight about an ounce apiece.

First Trimester Highlights

- **Some pregnancy symptoms are amplified with multiples.** Mothers who are expecting more than one may experience more fatigue, nausea, weight gain, or mood swings than in a normal pregnancy. Or they may not feel anything out of the ordinary.
- **Most multiples are discovered during the first trimester.** Symptoms and intuition may hint at multiples, and hCG screening or Doppler scans may arouse suspicion, but ultimately ultrasound will reveal whether there's more than one. Regardless of the signs, ultrasound is the most reliable way to confirm twins or multiples. Routine use of ultrasound in the first trimester means few multiples make a surprise appearance later in pregnancy.
- **Mom's body is busy building babies.** Physically, mom will undergo a roller coaster ride in the first trimester as her body prepares a place to nurture her babies. Morning sickness may make an appearance, bringing uncomfortable sensations of nausea and loss of appetite. No part of her body is immune to the effects of pregnancy, as her digestive and circulatory systems adjust to accommodate the pregnancy process.
- **Meanwhile, the babies are busy growing.** So much happens during the first trimester! Out of microscopic collections of cells, skeletal structures and functioning organs are organized, ready to grow and develop in the months ahead.

CHAPTER 5

The Middle Trimester

Welcome to the second trimester. After getting acquainted with pregnancy in the first trimester, you'll have a chance to settle in during the next few months. As you grow accustomed to the idea of having multiples—and grow physically—you are likely to experience a period of relief and rejuvenation. The nausea and exhaustion of the first trimester often give way to a period of enhanced energy and vitality.

Your Body's Changes

Your body is busy during the second trimester! By this time it is generally very difficult to conceal your pregnancy. The height of your fundus, the name for the top of your uterus, exceeds that of a singleton pregnancy by several inches. In fact, by the end of the second trimester, you may have the appearance of a full-term singleton pregnancy, causing you to attract concern for your "imminent" delivery.

What You're Feeling

The second trimester brings good news and bad news. Some of the problems that plagued you during the early weeks of pregnancy will start to dissipate, such as the nausea and queasiness of morning sickness and the extreme exhaustion. However, in their place, some new symptoms may make an appearance.

Your appetite may increase to ravenous proportions. Take advantage of your hunger to fill up on healthy foods, such as lean proteins, fresh fruits and vegetables, and whole grains. As your constant urge to urinate eases, you may find it easier to sleep through the night. However, you may be visited by frequent, vivid dreams.

One physical phenomenon that pregnant mothers of multiples are particularly prone to is round ligament pain, a sharp pinching discomfort in the abdominal area. It occurs as the ligaments that support your uterus stretch to accommodate its rapid expansion. Sometimes it will happen when you move or stretch suddenly, or it can come out of the blue, even while you're at rest. Aside from the discomfort, it can be an alarming experience if you confuse the sensation with the onset of contractions. Round ligament pain usually eases after a moment, but if it recurs, be sure to discuss your symptoms with your doctor.

As you grow, your skin stretches to cover your expanding abdomen. Stretch marks may make an appearance on your breasts, belly, or hips. They indicate a separation of collagen, a substance that lends elasticity to skin. They may be pink or purplish, but will probably fade to a light silvery shadow after pregnancy.

Some other common symptoms that you may experience during these middle months are:

- Constipation
- Swelling (edema)
- Nasal stuffiness
- Bleeding gums
- Headaches

There is some good news. Many women attain a radiant appearance during this period of pregnancy. The extra circulation drives more blood to the hair follicles, skin surface, and nail beds. The result? Thick, lustrous hair; clear, luminous skin; and strong nails that grow faster than you can say "manicure." Enjoy the beauty benefits of this special time!

Changes in Sexual Desire

After a few months of wanting sleep rather than sex, you may experience an awakening in the second trimester. Many moms, and appreciative dads, report an increase in sexual desire during this time. Sometimes extreme concern about preterm labor may prompt your caregiver to recommend abstinence, but unless you've been advised to restrict sexual activity, you can take advantage of your increased appetite. Most couples will enjoy a second honeymoon period before the advancing pregnancy literally gets in the way of sexual relations.

The Babies' Development

Your babies are having a busy season as well. Having developed into recognizable human form, they enter the second trimester with the appearance of newborns, only smaller. In the second trimester, they grow rapidly, from about twenty grams to nearly a pound in weight. By the end of the second trimester, they are each about 8 inches in length.

At that size, they still have plenty of room to move around in the womb environment, and you are likely to experience their gymnastic routines with increasing frequency and intensity. Most mothers of multiples detect the sensation of fetal movement, called *quickening*, earlier than moms of singletons; however, if you've never been pregnant before, it's easy to mistake the feeling for gastrointestinal bubbles.

FACT

Most expectant mothers experience quickening by the twentieth week of pregnancy, but it's not uncommon for moms of multiples to discern the feeling as early as twelve weeks.

As the second trimester passes, the babies will become more and more active. They'll establish rhythms of activity and rest according to your routines, although often in contradiction to your schedule. For example, during the times of day when you're most active, your body movements lull them into tranquillity, yet you'll find them wide awake and most active when you're still.

Weight Gain

Most women are particularly concerned with how their pregnancy will impact their body. Gaining weight is a given during pregnancy, and as you might expect, the amount of weight increases in a multiple pregnancy. In a singleton pregnancy, the average woman gains between twenty-five and thirty pounds during her pregnancy. Only a third of that is fat and maternal tissue; the rest is a combination of the baby, placenta, amniotic fluid, and increased blood volume. When you double or triple the number of babies, you can expect the amount to increase proportionately.

What to Gain

The amount of weight that you gain during your multiple pregnancy is dependent on a number of factors. Your prepregnancy size is one determinant. If you were overweight before becoming pregnant, you'll need to gain less than if you were underweight. However, if you carried a few extra pounds before becoming pregnant, don't view this time as an opportunity to shed them. You will still need to gain weight during pregnancy, but just less than someone who was underweight at the outset. Likewise, if you were underweight before pregnancy, you will have to gain more weight faster in order to provide an optimum environment for your babies to grow.

Your doctor can advise you as to the optimal amount for your individual situation, but a general guideline is thirty-seven to fifty-four pounds for twins, fifty to seventy pounds for triplets, and ten additional pounds per baby for higher order multiples. It may be beneficial to gain more if:

- You were underweight before becoming pregnant.
- It's your first pregnancy.
- Your pregnancy was the result of infertility treatment.
- Severe morning sickness decreased your appetite in the first trimester.
- You are expecting higher order multiples.
- You are or were a smoker.

▼ RECOMMENDED WEIGHT GAIN IN MULTIPLE PREGNANCY (IN POUNDS)

Type of Pregnancy	Underweight (BMI <18.5)	Normal Weight (BMI between 18.5–24.9)	Overweight/ Obese (BMI >25)
Singleton	28–40	25–35	11–25
Twins	40–59	37–54	25–50
Triplets +	60–80	55–75	45–65

When to Gain

The timetable of your weight gain is every bit as important as the amount. In a multiple pregnancy, it is particularly important to gain weight early, prior to the third trimester. In a singleton pregnancy, the mother may record little gain in the first trimester, with the pace accelerated later in the pregnancy. If you've had a baby before, your pregnancy may have followed that pattern. But that's not the case when you're having multiples.

Because multiple pregnancies are often cut short due to preterm delivery, more weight has to be gained in a shorter amount of time. Gaining steadily throughout the first and second trimesters helps you establish extra stores of fat and nutrients. The babies will rely on those stockpiled deposits in later pregnancy when their nutritional demands are greater. The amount of weight you gain in the first half of your pregnancy has a significant impact on your babies' development in the second half. The pounds you accumulate now will sustain them later, resulting in a longer gestation and bigger, healthier birth weights for the babies.

ALERT

Some caregivers use the rule "24 in 24," advising that mothers of twins try to gain twenty-four pounds by the twenty-fourth week of pregnancy, or the end of the second trimester. But some experts in multiple births feel even that is too conservative and encourage gaining up to twenty-five pounds by week twenty.

The pace of your weight gain should be accelerated throughout this second trimester. For one thing, it is easier earlier on. Later as your uterus expands and crowds your stomach, it will be more difficult to fill it up. Also, your hormones are finally cooperating with your efforts. The appetite-killing effects of morning sickness dissipate, and you'll often feel ravenous. Your body is encouraging you to build a nutritional reserve.

In the second trimester, you should aim to gain one to two pounds per week, depending on your situation and the number of babies that you're carrying. Your doctor or caregiver can make recommendations based on your specific situation, taking into consideration your prepregnancy weight and condition of your multiples.

Why Gain?

Recent research has established the benefits of early and adequate maternal weight gain, particularly for multiples who are already at a higher risk for problems. What mom eats during pregnancy directly impacts the nutritional environment for her babies. Providing optimal nourishment results in babies that have higher birth weights, even if they are born prematurely. At the same time, evidence suggests that increased intrauterine growth rate may reduce the likelihood of premature birth. After birth, well-nourished babies are healthier and hardier, able to recover more quickly from illness or trauma. And the benefits last beyond pregnancy; healthy babies become healthier adults.

Many elements of your pregnancy with multiples are beyond your control. You cannot determine when your babies will be born or whether they will face consequences from prematurity or medical conditions. At times you may feel out of control of your body, unable to command the forces at work inside your womb. But you can take control of your diet and weight gain during this important period of your—and your children's—life. The importance of eating the right foods in the right amounts cannot be underestimated, and following recommended guidelines to gain weight is critical.

Think Positive

For many women, weight gain carries complex psychological and emotional baggage. The idea of gaining nearly fifty pounds or more can be frightening and staggering. Try to keep it in perspective. Gaining the weight is a good thing; it's a sign of healthy development for your babies. Remember, too, that a good percentage of your weight gain will be lost at delivery. Finally, keep in mind that you're not just adding pounds; you're adding two or more new members to your family. In comparison, you'd likely accumulate more weight if you had serial singleton pregnancies.

Maternity Clothes

It's time to go shopping! By the second trimester, you'll have outgrown your prepregnancy outfits and will require maternity clothing. Before you spend a bundle on new attire, you'll want to consider the big picture, which is growing bigger every week! While you should have no problem fitting into standard maternity styles during the middle trimester, you may need to update your wardrobe every few weeks to accommodate your escalating girth.

The most important factor in choosing clothing is comfort. Choose soft, flexible fabrics with a bit of stretch, garments that give and move when you do. Recent fashion trends have produced new styles of maternity clothing that sit below the belly, instead of stretching across it, and many women find this a more comfortable option. It's also more practical for moms of multiples, whose bellies exceed the measurements of the average pregnancy.

Consider your lifestyle and activities when selecting clothes. Many of your prepregnancy routines will be altered in the months ahead; you may have a reduced work or social schedule and won't require as many special occasion outfits as you did previously. A few pairs of comfortable pants in basic colors are a good foundation. Mix and match with a variety of tops and blouses to extend your options. Remember that your bust line may expand as your pregnancy progresses, so consider tops with roomy armholes and a generous fit across the bust. When buying skirts or dresses, choose hemlines that fall below the knee. As your belly grows, it will pull up the fabric of your skirts, risking an overexposure of your thighs!

FACT

Generally manufacturers advise women to buy maternity clothes according to their prepregnancy size. However, mothers of twins or multiples may wish to size up. Buy one or two sizes bigger in anticipation of your expansion in the months ahead.

Keep in mind the season as you choose maternity clothing. Lightweight fabrics and layers are preferable; even in the dead of winter, your "buns in the oven" will provide an internal radiator that keeps you warmer than normal. Your bulky sweaters and heavy overcoats won't get as much use while you're pregnant. Likewise, if your pregnancy spans into the next season, you won't have to invest in another wardrobe as the weather changes.

Smart marketers are considering moms of multiples as they develop their maternity wear products. Blouse and dress styles that are fitted on top and flowy around the middle work well; the extra fabric will cover the larger size of a belly with multiples without fitting poorly in other areas. Browse the Internet for companies that cater to moms of multiples, but check sizing options and return policies carefully.

Maternity clothing can be a big expense in pregnancy. If you have any opportunity to borrow outfits, take advantage of that! Some local clubs for parents of twins organize maternity clothing swaps or sales. Consignment shops are another good option for bargains. And don't be afraid to look outside the box for clothing options. Your husband's closet may proffer a comfy T-shirt or crisp button-down shirt. Check the plus-size department at a discount store for extended sizes of basics like pants, shorts, and tops; pair them with more expensive pieces to stretch your options and give your wardrobe more variety.

Special Considerations for Higher Order Multiples

If you are expecting triplets or more, the second trimester is a special time. The likelihood of restricted activity, bed rest, hospitalization, or early delivery looms large in the third trimester, so it's especially important for you to utilize your time in these middle months wisely.

While you're feeling up to it, plan to do your shopping to stock up on supplies and get your home ready for the new arrivals. Schedule time together with your spouse or with your older children. The changes facing your family in the months ahead will prevent you from enjoying quiet time for quite a while. But don't overdo it. You don't want to raise your risk or complications by pushing yourself too hard.

Making It Through the Middle Trimester

- **Mom's body stays busy.** There's good news and bad news for mom during the trimester. Some of the more unpleasant symptoms subside, such as morning sickness, but aches and pains may intensify.
- **Gain and growth are hallmarks of the second trimester.** These middle months are a time of increased appetite and escalating girth. Weight gain is particularly important during this time; the extra stores of fat and nutrients are going to sustain mom and babies in the months ahead.
- **It's time for a wardrobe makeover.** The extra gifts associated with a multiple pregnancy put mom into maternity wear sooner than if she was expecting one baby. Maternity wear is a good fit during the second trimester, but mom may also be comfortable in larger sizes of loose clothing.

CHAPTER 6

The Final Trimester

You're getting close! The final trimester with multiples may be a few weeks shorter than a singleton pregnancy, but it can feel like an eternity to a pregnant mother who is growing increasingly uncomfortable. But it's also a time of great joy and anticipation, and of finalizing some important decisions and preparations.

Staying Comfortable

There's no doubt about it, the last few months of a multiple pregnancy can get uncomfortable. For one thing, you've expanded to accommodate two or more growing babies! You may feel gigantic, and realize that you're only growing larger. Despite your overall lack of energy and a stern admonition from your doctor to rest as much as possible, your increased girth may make it impossible to relax comfortably. Meanwhile, as they grow, the babies are putting increasing pressure on your muscles, ribs, lungs, stomach, and bladder. As the time to deliver draws near, your emotional discomfort may increase as well. Fears about your babies' safe entry into this world and your future as a family may seem more relevant as the time of their arrival gets closer.

Life in the third trimester doesn't have to be miserable, however. Keep your situation in perspective; it's temporary, after all. Despite the physical discomfort they cause inside of you, your babies are much better off in your womb than born prematurely. This is a time for frequent positive reinforcement and support; remind yourself that things could be much worse and adopt an attitude of gratitude for each extra day of nurturing that you can give your babies.

Dressing for Success

You may find that you've outgrown your maternity wardrobe. Even the largest sizes of maternity wear may not cover your expanded midsection. Many mothers find that the best option for late pregnancy is to skip the maternity store and invest in a couple of plus-size outfits. Designed to accommodate larger women, they should fit comfortably over your belly. You don't need much to carry you through these last few months; a few T-shirts and elastic-waist pants will do. You may have to sacrifice fashion for a while, but you can look forward to returning to style once the babies are born.

It's not just clothing that doesn't seem to fit right in the last few months. You may have problems getting your shoes on your feet, and not just because your belly is in the way. Pregnancy hormones soften up the ligaments in your body, and your feet actually expand. You may find that yours have increased a size or two, and your shoes don't fit anymore. Since you may spend some portion of the third trimester off your feet, you don't need to invest a lot of money in new shoes. Comfort is the utmost priority, and so is convenience. Unless you want to get help with lacing and tying, slip-on shoes are the best option for the latter stage of pregnancy.

ALERT

Even if you lose weight after you deliver, your feet may not ever return to their old shoe size. A pregnancy hormone called relaxin softens up joints and ligaments, including those in feet. Sometimes this causes feet to spread out and widen, and they don't always return to their prepregnancy shape.

If you are plagued by backache and muscle discomfort, you may want to invest in an undergarment that supports the weight of your expanding belly. It helps take the pressure off your back and can provide a great deal of relief. You'll find such products available at maternity and baby stores, and the cost may be covered by your insurance plan. Buy a product intended for late pregnancy, even if you plan to start wearing it before the third trimester. As a mother of multiples, you'll need the extra support earlier in your pregnancy.

A good bra will also provide comfort. As your breasts prepare for nursing, they are likely changing shape and size, and your prepregnancy bras won't fit the bill, so to speak. If you haven't already, invest in several good-quality maternity bras. If you're planning to breastfeed, you can even consider starting to wear nursing bras. They'll do double duty, providing extra support for the last few months of your pregnancy, and easy access to your breasts once the babies arrive.

Working It Out

If she hasn't already, your doctor may advise you to stop working during the last portion of your pregnancy. Any job that requires a lot of standing, strenuous physical activity, or long hours is probably not the best way to spend your last weeks before the babies are born. However, some mothers are able to continue at their jobs until shortly before they deliver. Discuss the risks and benefits with your medical provider if you are having twins and your job allows you to be relatively sedate and comfortable while you work. Mothers of higher order multiples will likely have fewer opportunities to stay on the job.

If you do continue to work, take it easy. Stay off your feet as much as possible. Take frequent breaks and drink plenty of water throughout your workday. If your job involves repetitive hand motion, such as typing or filing nails, carpal tunnel syndrome may make the activity uncomfortable. It's made worse during pregnancy when increased blood volume through arteries and veins compresses the nerves in the hand and wrist, resulting in tingling, numbness, and pain.

ESSENTIAL

The symptoms of carpal tunnel syndrome can be alleviated by wearing a splint or restricting activity, but ultimately the only thing that will make it go away is delivery of the babies.

On the Go

As it gets closer to the time when your babies will arrive, your list of "to-dos" gets longer and longer. Unfortunately, you may find that you're less productive in the last trimester. You may experience difficulty getting in and out of a car; you may even need to restrict your driving if your shape prevents you from sitting safely behind the wheel. This is a great time to take advantage of Internet services and do your shopping from the comfort of home.

As relaxing as it may sound, this is not the time to plan a vacation getaway. While mothers of singletons are considered safe for air travel up to week thirty-six, that's not the case with mothers of multiples, who are at increased risk for preterm labor. Many airlines have policies denying travel to women in the last month of their pregnancy; with twins or more, you'll look like you're near your due date even if you're months away. If your doctor does give you permission to travel by air (which is unlikely in the third trimester), you will need a letter indicating that you can safely fly in order to board the aircraft.

At Home

You may feel inclined to "nest" as your due date gets closer, making your home clean and ready for the babies. Leave the heavy-duty work to someone else, however. Activities that require heavy lifting, pushing, or climbing are simply too risky. Slaving over a hot stove isn't recommended either, although short bouts of standing in the kitchen may be acceptable. If your doctor approves, use that nesting energy to make and freeze casseroles to eat later; you'll likely have less time to prepare meals when you're busy feeding the babies.

When Will You Deliver?

As you reach the third trimester, the birth of your babies may seem imminent. With so much attention focused on the risks of preterm labor, you may be anticipating an early arrival. (Chapter 13 deals with the risks and signs of preterm labor in detail.) Even though you've made it past the critical point for survival, your babies will benefit by spending the majority of the third trimester in your womb, rather than in the hospital.

For many mothers of multiples, the last trimester is cut short. About half of twins, and the majority of higher order multiples, are born at least a month early. It's important to remain aware of the signs of preterm labor. You'll be scheduled for more frequent visits with your health care provider so that he can assess any signs of impending labor, as well as the condition of your babies.

Overdue and Over It

Despite the focus on preventing preterm labor, not all multiples are born early. Half of twin pregnancies last longer than thirty-six weeks. You may find yourself in the final weeks of the third trimester feeling like there is no end in sight. It can be an uncomfortable time, full of relief that your babies are close to term, but with anxiety looming about labor and delivery.

There is medical evidence to suggest that post-mature pregnancy poses risks for both the babies and their mother. The discomfort of late-term pregnancy and the strain on the mother's organs may prompt doctors to intervene if labor is not imminent. Some argue that thirty-eight weeks should be considered full term for twins (thirty-five weeks for triplets), and recommend delivery when a mother reaches that point. Other experts maintain that forty weeks is the standard milestone, whether there is one baby or more.

Whether early or late, it's difficult to predict the exact date of your babies' arrival. Throughout the final trimester, your medical care providers will review the babies' status and your own health. Your body may go into labor on its own—ideally, close to term, but possibly earlier. Or your doctor may recommend an intervention to deliver the babies in an effort to optimize their health or your own well-being. You will have to work as a team with your medical advisor to determine the best possible course of action to ensure a healthy outcome.

ESSENTIAL

Because the risk of preterm birth is heightened for multiples, much attention is focused on delivering early, rather than late. However, a review of the National Organization of Mothers of Twins Clubs' database indicates that 13 percent of its membership didn't deliver before their due date.

Making a Birth Plan

A birth plan has become a standard practice for expectant mothers who want to maintain some level of control over their birth experience. It is a document that communicates your wishes and expectations to the medical professionals who will be participating in your care. It is not intended to be antagonistic or confrontational, and should respect both your concerns and your caregivers' expertise.

What's the Point of a Birth Plan?

Moms of multiples who prefer to retain some control over their birth experience may be frustrated by the increased level of medical intervention required when there are twins or more. A written birth plan is a good way to express your desires regarding the birth in a way that optimizes the medical staff's ability to accommodate you.

It's important to develop your birth plan in plenty of time before you actually give birth. Given the risk of preterm labor, that can be earlier rather than later in a multiple pregnancy. The first part of the third trimester is an excellent time to start developing it. You'll want to provide ample time to review your plan with the appropriate caregivers, including your obstetrician, peri-natologist, midwife, doula, pediatrician, and neonatologist. Be willing to discuss any concerns they might have, and once you've finalized the plan, ask them to sign the document to indicate their approval of your requests. Ask that a copy be placed in your medical chart. In addition, bring several copies of the signed plan to the hospital with you so that you can share them with any other staff members who are assigned to care for you or the babies.

Things to Include in Your Plan

Your plan should encompass any aspects of the birth process that you have strong feelings about. Include references to any options for labor, delivery, recovery, postpartum care, breastfeeding, circumcision, and newborn care. State the names of any people whom you want involved in your care, including your spouse/partner, coach, or doula. Be sure to specify your preferences for each baby by clear references to Baby A, Baby B, and so on.

ALERT

While your birth plan should be comprehensive, keep it concise. Significant information will be overlooked if it is too wordy. Keep it short and simple, and you're more likely to have it implemented to your satisfaction.

Some important items to address in your birth plan are below.

DURING LABOR:
- ☐ Mobility (being able to walk around)
- ☐ Access to food and liquids
- ☐ Placement of IVs
- ☐ Atmosphere of the labor environment (control of lights, noise)
- ☐ Administration of pain medication
- ☐ Anesthesia preferences
- ☐ Nonmedical pain relief options
- ☐ Performance of vaginal exams
- ☐ Presence of support persons
- ☐ Limits on visitors, including observation by medical students

DURING DELIVERY:

☐ Episiotomy options

☐ Ability to record the birth

☐ Pushing position

☐ Avoidance of unnecessary intervention

☐ Cutting of the umbilical cord, including a request for partner to cut it

☐ Collection of cord blood for banking, if desired

IN THE EVENT OF A C-SECTION:

☐ Anesthesia preferences

☐ Catheterization preferences

☐ Presence of partner during procedure

☐ Ability to remain alert

POSTPARTUM:

☐ Rooming-in preferences

☐ Feeding instructions

☐ Privacy requests, including private room preference

ISSUES SPECIFIC TO MULTIPLES:

☐ Attempts to turn second baby before delivery (external cephalic version)

☐ Ability to see and hold babies between deliveries

☐ Interactions with neonatology staff in the event your babies are admitted

☐ Requests for co-bedding

Ultimately, make your birth plan flexible and accommodating of emergencies and contingencies. Recognize that you and the medical professionals who treat you have the same goal: a safe delivery and healthy babies.

FACT

You can find more assistance with developing a birth plan in pregnancy books and online. A particularly good resource for multiple birth labor and delivery has been developed by Karen Kerkhoff Gromada and is available on her website *www.karengromada.com*.

Preparing for Delivery

In most cases, giving birth to multiples will require a hospital visit. Although some mothers of multiples opt to deliver at home or at a birth center, it is generally not recommended for the safety of all involved. Instead, a hospital equipped with a Level III NICU (neonatal intensive care unit) can provide optimal care for multiples in the event that they require extra care. The third trimester is a good time to begin preparing for your hospital visit.

What to Pack

Often the onset of labor comes unexpectedly. If you put off packing your bag and making arrangements, you may be caught unprepared. It's a good idea to start assembling the things that you need so that you're ready when the time comes.

If you're being hospitalized for preterm labor, you'll need additional comfort items and entertainment to help you pass the time. If you're headed to the hospital planning to deliver, you'll need to consider the babies' needs in addition to your own.

FOR LABOR YOU'LL NEED:
- ❑ Comfortable nightgowns (not pajamas)
- ❑ Underwear (comfortable old pairs are best; they may get messy)
- ❑ Socks
- ❑ Watch or stopwatch
- ❑ Pain management tools (focal point picture, massage balls, music)
- ❑ Camera
- ❑ Journal and pen

FOR RECOVERY YOU'LL WANT TO HAVE:
- ❑ Sanitary pads (they'll also be provided by the hospital)
- ❑ Address book or a list of people to contact with the good news
- ❑ Bathrobe
- ❑ Slippers or socks
- ❑ Essential toiletries

FOR GOING HOME:

❏ Car seats

❏ Clothing for each baby (don't forget coverings for heads and feet)

❏ Baby blankets

❏ An outfit for you to wear home (not prepregnancy size)

IF YOU PLAN TO NURSE, CONSIDER PACKING:

❏ Nursing bra

❏ Nursing pads or breast shields

Coverage at Home

Depending on how you deliver, you can expect to be away from home for at least a night or two. If you have a C-section, it can be four nights or more. You'll need to arrange coverage of your responsibilities at home while you're away.

If you have other children, arrange to have someone come and stay with them in your home. It will be less disruptive for them to remain in familiar surroundings. Have a backup plan in case you have to make a hasty departure for the hospital and your original arrangements fall through.

Pets also need care while you're away! Have a neighbor or pet sitter stop by to feed and walk your animals as needed. Your pets need the extra attention during this time of transition for your family.

You'll want to share the good news about your babies with everyone you know, but you may be unable to spend a lot of time spreading the word while you recover. Instead, rely on online social media, like a blog, Facebook, or Twitter. Record a greeting on your voicemail that friends and family can call to get updates or designate a contact person to provide information. You'll only have to make one phone call, and your helper can do the rest.

Choosing Names for Your Multiples

Selecting names for your children is one of the most important decisions you will make on their behalf. It can be a difficult decision, especially considering that you have yet to meet the little ones you're assigning this lifelong label to. With multiples, you not only have to consider the individual nomenclature, but you'll also want to think about how their names interact as a group.

In the past, "twinny" name sets were popular, such as, Sharon and Karen, Michael and Michelle, or Jim and Tim. The trend has shifted in recent years to more subtle combinations, often with the same initial letter. Jacob and Joshua is a perennial favorite for boys. Both names start with the same letter, and both have Biblical roots, yet they sound distinctly different when pronounced. For girls, Olivia and Sophia or Isabella and Gabriella are among the most popular combinations. This time, they have the same last letter and a similar cadence when spoken, but don't have the same initial, a helpful distinction if you plan to monogram any of your twins' items! Clever combinations based on meaning or themes are also a trend among multiple names. Consider triplets named Faith, Hope, and Charity or twins named London and Paris.

QUESTION

How do we decide which baby receives which name?
That can be a tricky determination. In utero, most multiples are identified by the labels "Baby A," "Baby B," "Baby C," and so on. You might select names that start with those letters or use that to determine an alphabetical order. Other families assign names based on birth order, womb position, or personality estimates.

Naming style is a source of controversy among the multiples community. Some families try to avoid names that rhyme, start with the same letter, or otherwise appear matched. They feel that it compromises their multiples' sense of individuality. Others enjoy choosing a corresponding combination that clearly indicates their children's status as multiples. Ultimately, it's a matter of personal preference. Sometimes there is an expectation that twins' and multiples' names should be coordinated, and you may be met with a reaction of disappointment if you announce unrelated names.

To start the process, brainstorm a list of names that you and your partner like. You can turn to baby-naming books and websites for ideas. If you know the sex of your babies, you can focus exclusively on names that match their gender. Have some backups for the opposite sex, or some androgynous options, just in case there is a surprise!

Once you have a list of possibilities, consider how the names work in combination. Even if you want to avoid matching names, you will probably want to select names with similar styles or a sense of balance—for example, names that are all very feminine, monosyllabic, or of comparable meaning. Keep in mind any potential nicknames for each choice.

Can't come up with anything? There's no rule that you have to choose names before the babies arrive. Brainstorming names can be a fun diversion during labor. Or you may wait until you meet them to make a decision. Laying eyes on your precious newborns might provide the inspiration to make the perfect choice.

The Home Stretch

- **The final months of a multiple pregnancy may bring some discomfort.** Staying comfortable becomes the focus of the final trimester, as the strain of a multiple pregnancy exerts both physical and emotional pressure on mom. As she enlarges to accommodate two or more growing babies, she'll need to outfit herself in comfortable clothing and may even outgrow her shoes.
- **Work winds down.** Depending on the circumstances of your employment environment, it may be necessary to take a break during the final months of a multiple pregnancy. Extra rest is required as more and more of mom's energy is expended on the pregnancy. However, it's not a good time for a getaway. It's best to stick close to home with ready access to medical care in case of an early delivery.
- **Multiples have their own timetable.** Although much attention is focused on preventing a preterm birth, plenty of multiples take their own sweet time to arrive. The final months of a multiple pregnancy may come to an abrupt halt if preterm labor strikes, or may drag on endlessly if the babies stay safely ensconced until their due date.
- **The third trimester is a time of preparation and planning.** If you haven't already, it's time to develop a birth plan, pack for a hospital visit, choose names for the babies, and be the center of attention at a baby shower.

CHAPTER 7

Having a Healthy Pregnancy

Having multiples puts extra demands on the mother's body. In order to ensure the vitality of both mom and babies, it's important to make health a priority. There are many steps you can take to preserve and even improve your overall health while you're pregnant with multiples. You know you should be eating right and getting enough sleep, but do you know exactly what that means? It's also important to be aware of the things you should avoid during pregnancy.

What Should You Eat?

With so many facets of a multiple pregnancy beyond your control, your diet is one way that you can directly contribute to your babies' healthy development—after all, what you eat is passed along to the babies through the placenta. It's important not only to eat the right foods but also to consume enough food to satisfy everyone's nutritional needs.

Plenty of Protein

Research has suggested that protein plays a vital role in fetal development. The amino acids found in animal proteins, such as meats, milk, and eggs, are important components in the creation of human cells. These essential acids cannot be produced by the body but are consumed through the food you eat.

ALERT

Be careful—not all sources of protein are the same. Some sources of animal protein have the disadvantage of being high in fat. Lean sources of protein are a better option, especially those that also supply omega-3 fatty acids, such as seafood and fish. You can also eat a combination of other plant sources of protein to provide the essential acids that your body needs. These include rice and beans, peanut butter, whole grains, and soy.

It's recommended that the average woman consume about a quarter of her calories in protein, or about 100 grams per day. However, a woman expecting multiples needs an increased amount. While you should discuss your specific requirements with your doctor or nutritionist, many experts recommend that mothers of multiples consume at least double that amount. Protein is not stored in the body, so it's important to replenish the supply by eating adequate amounts throughout the day. Here are some protein-rich foods to stock up on:

- Eggs
- Cheese
- Yogurt

- Chicken breasts
- Fish
- Lean cuts of meat such as turkey, ham, or roast beef
- Nuts such as almonds, walnuts, or cashews
- Peanut butter
- Tofu
- Soymilk products
- Beans

Keep Eating Those Carbs and Fats!

When you're not pregnant with multiples, carbohydrates and fats may be "no-nos," something to be avoided in a healthy diet. But when you are pregnant with multiples, they are definitely a "go."

Your body needs an energy boost from complex carbohydrates. Carbohydrates help your body process the extra protein you're consuming and maintain your blood sugar. Just as with protein, it's important to choose the right source of carbohydrates.

There are two types of carbohydrates, simple and complex. Simple carbohydrates give a quick boost of energy from sugar, while complex carbohydrates release energy slowly over time. Fruit is the preferred source of simple carbohydrates, rather than sugary treats such as candy, cake, or cookies, because of the added vitamins and nutrients fruit contains. Many fruits also have high water content, so they provide hydration as well as nourishment. Complex carbohydrates are found in many starchy foods, such as bread, cereal, pasta, potatoes, and rice, as well as some vegetables and legumes, such as beans and peas. Choose whole-grain starches for the added B vitamins and fiber they provide. A fiber-rich diet prevents constipation and can reduce your risk of contracting hemorrhoids.

When you're not pregnant with multiples, fat can be a dirty word. But fat can be your friend during this time. Fat ensures that the other nutrients you take in are put to good use. It is calorie dense, helpful when you're trying to increase your caloric intake during a multiple pregnancy. As with carbohydrates, there are different kinds of fat. Omega-3 fatty acids are preferable over trans fat or partially hydrogenated oils. Omega-3s benefit your developing babies, promoting their physical and cognitive development, and may even reduce the risk of preterm labor and other pregnancy complications.

How can you promote these good fats in your diet? Seafood is a key source. Salmon, scallops, shrimp, and sardines all offer a healthy dose of omega-3 fatty acids. If you're not a fan of seafood, or are concerned about the harmful effects of mercury in some sources of seafood, consider walnuts, flaxseeds, or winter squash. Some food products are also enhanced with omega-3 fatty acids, such as eggs or milk. Review your diet with your caregiver or nutritionist to determine if your intake is sufficient or whether a supplement is advisable.

Don't Forget Your Minerals and Vitamins

As you make food choices during your pregnancy, you should consider foods that provide vital minerals, such as iron, calcium, and folic acid. While these substances are also available in the form of dietary supplements, you'll give your babies a better start if you ingest them naturally in the foods you eat. Calcium is essential in the creation of your babies' skeletal structures and also enhances their heart, muscle, and nerve functions. It may also be beneficial in reducing the risk of pregnancy induced hypertension and preeclampsia.

FACT

Although the most common source of calcium is dairy products, many green vegetables offer a generous helping as well. Arugula, kale, spinach, and collard greens are excellent sources of calcium.

Many expectant moms of multiples experience anemia due to their increased blood volume during pregnancy. Because iron helps transport oxygen in the blood, it helps combat anemia. The problem with iron intake is that you not only have to take it in, but your body also has to absorb it properly. Some foods enhance iron absorption and others inhibit it, so food combinations are important. Dairy products, bran cereal, antacids, tea, and soda products can hinder absorption. Wait about an hour after ingestion to eat iron-rich foods or take an iron supplement to reduce the inhibiting effects. Drinking orange juice may also help, since vitamin C helps convert iron into a form more easily absorbed by the body. Iron-rich foods include:

- Red meats
- Spinach
- Eggs
- Prunes
- Pumpkin seeds
- Soybeans

Folic acid is a B vitamin that is credited for dramatically reducing the risk of birth defects in the brain and spinal cord when taken prior to and during pregnancy. Folate, the natural form of the vitamin, is found in some food sources, such as black beans, asparagus, orange juice, spinach, peanuts, and romaine lettuce. Because of its benefits, some grain products, such as breads, cereals, and pastas, are now enriched with folic acid. However, to ensure that your intake is sufficient, pregnant mothers of multiples should also take a supplement or prenatal vitamin that includes folic acid.

How Much Should You Eat?

In addition to selecting the right foods to eat during pregnancy, you have to think about how much you're eating. Remember, you are not just eating for two, as in a singleton pregnancy. You have to consume enough calories to sustain yourself as well as the two, three, or more developing fetuses.

ESSENTIAL

Studies have confirmed the benefits of early weight gain in pregnancy, so it's important to start increasing your food intake as soon as your multiple pregnancy is confirmed. A simple way to start is by consuming small mini-meals at snack time—mid-morning, afternoon, and evening. Then increase your caloric intake at meals by having an additional serving of fruit, vegetable, or protein.

Most pregnant women are advised to increase their daily caloric intake by about 13 percent. For most women that's about 300–400 extra calories per day. That's not enough for mothers of multiples. Rather, they should aim for at least 300 extra calories *per baby* per day; some experts recommended even more of an increase. That means mothers of twins need an additional 600+ calories and mothers of triplets need to increase their intake by about nearly 1,000 calories. With higher order multiples, it can be difficult to eat enough food to meet the demand; there are only so many hours in the day! Expectant mothers of quadruplets or more should discuss their dietary needs with their physician to determine the optimum caloric goal. Your caregiver can also help you come up with strategies to meet that goal.

Specialty Diets

Your doctor or nutritionist may recommend that you follow one of the diets designed for optimal nutrition during a multiple pregnancy. There are various sources for these diets, and your doctor can help you decide which is most appropriate for your specific situation.

The Brewer Diet for Pregnancy was developed by Dr. Thomas Brewer and originally published in the 1970s. It claims to prevent pregnancy complications such as intrauterine growth retardation (IUGR), preterm labor, and preeclampsia. In general, the Brewer Diet for Pregnancy offers guidelines for the following daily requirements:

- 4 servings of milk
- 2 eggs
- 6 servings of meat or vegetarian protein
- 2 servings of fresh, leafy green vegetables
- 5 servings of carbohydrates in the form of whole-grain bread, starchy vegetables, or fruit
- 2 servings of vitamin C–rich foods, such as citrus fruit or tomatoes
- 5 servings of fat or oil (butter, oil, mayonnaise)
- 1 serving of vitamin A–rich food (orange-colored fruits or vegetables such as sweet potatoes or apricots)

Dr. Barbara Luke is an obstetrician, professor, and author who specializes in multiple birth. She advocates a high-calorie diet based on the principles of a diabetic diet to stabilize blood sugar and promote weight gain. She recommends generous quantities of dairy, lean protein, fats, and other foods in order to optimize weight gain, especially in the first half of pregnancy.

Nutritional Supplements

In order to obtain maximum nutritional benefits, your doctor may prescribe dietary supplements. Most experts agree that it is easiest for the body to utilize nutrients, vitamins, and minerals when they are obtained through foods, but during a multiple pregnancy, it may be necessary to ingest them in other forms. Your doctor or midwife will be able to advise you on the appropriate dosage and schedule; don't take any vitamins or supplements without consulting a medical professional.

Most women are advised to take a prenatal vitamin daily during their pregnancy, and many begin this regimen even before conception in order to give their baby an optimum start in life. Prenatal vitamin products are specifically designed to provide an extra boost of the vitamins and minerals that are most difficult to obtain through food, while minimizing the elements that can be dangerous to a developing fetus. Regular daily vitamin supplements may be too high in vitamin A, an excess of which has been linked to birth defects, or too low in important nutrients like folic acid and iron.

ESSENTIAL

Folic acid, a B vitamin, is essential for the healthy development of a baby's spinal cord and brain. Taken prior to and early in pregnancy, it can help prevent up to 74 percent of neural tube defects, such as spina bifida and anencephaly.

Many expectant mothers of multiples experience iron deficiency, or anemia. It is difficult to obtain sufficient amounts of iron, even with a healthy diet. Mothers of multiples are especially susceptible to this condition, so your doctor may routinely recommend an iron supplement, or an increased dosage in the second or third trimester.

Unfortunately, supplemental iron can have some uncomfortable side effects. Constipation is a common complaint, but you can overcome the effects of it by increasing the amount of fiber in your diet. Drinking plenty of water helps, as well. Vitamin C enhances your body's ability to absorb iron, so wash down your daily dose with a glass of orange juice.

Your doctor may also prescribe other supplements, such as calcium, magnesium, zinc, DHA/EP (essential fatty acid), vitamin B, vitamin C, or vitamin D, depending on your individual needs. Of course, you should never take any dietary supplements without discussing them with your physician first. And always follow the recommended dosage amounts. Too much of a good thing is not good!

If you are underweight, or if you are not gaining weight at an adequate pace, your doctor may advise you to augment your caloric intake with nutritional supplements. These products are available in a variety of flavors, usually in the form of a beverage or pudding snack. They are nutritionally balanced and calorie dense. If your doctor believes they are appropriate for your situation, he may recommend either a high-protein or high-calorie supplement, or perhaps a combination of both. They are not intended to replace food, but rather to increase your nutritional intake in order to maximize the healthy development of your babies.

The Importance of Fluids

Eating right is a good start, but you also have to think about what you drink. Dehydration poses risks to the babies, including preterm labor, as well as causing constipation and other complications for mom. Getting your fill of liquids is every bit as important as fueling up on food.

During pregnancy the blood volume in your body increases, nearly doubling its nonpregnant amount. Your body needs fluids to produce all that extra blood. Thus, good hydration improves your circulation, making you feel better and enhancing the development of your babies. You also require fluid to replenish the amniotic fluid surrounding the babies in your womb. If you're not drinking sufficiently, your body will leach the fluid from other systems. Ultimately, you can end up feeling lethargic; have dry, itchy skin; and become constipated.

Dehydration can also prompt the onset of preterm labor. In fact, rehydration is often one of the first lines of defense against early contractions. You can minimize the risk of preterm labor, and possibly keep yourself out of the hospital, by drinking plenty of fluids.

Most pregnant women are advised to drink six to eight glasses of liquid a day. However, that's if they are having one baby! Moms of multiples should strive for twelve to sixteen eight-ounce glasses a day, or in excess of 100 ounces. You may find it difficult to fill up on fluid. Try these tips and tricks:

- Drink a glass of water before each meal, then refill a glass to sip while you eat.
- Add slices of lemon or lime to flavor plain water.
- Try sparkling waters; the bubbles make them as refreshing as soda.
- Keep a full water bottle next to your bed so that you can sip in the night and first thing in the morning.
- Carry a bottle of water in the car and take a drink at every stoplight.
- Size up: Pour larger glasses or purchase larger bottles.

QUESTION

Are any fluids okay or do I have to drink water?
Water is the best choice. It provides all the elements your body needs without the high calories and added sugars of soda or juice. Sodas also contain phosphorus, too much of which can interfere with the body's ability to process calcium and iron. Caffeinated beverages can actually serve to dehydrate you as you drink them, and alcoholic beverages should be avoided entirely during your pregnancy.

If you aren't sure whether you're drinking enough, check your urine. The lighter the color of your urine, the more hydrated you are. If it's a dark yellow color, you could be dehydrated.

Exercise and Activity

Regular exercise is a vital part of a healthy lifestyle, but during a multiple pregnancy, it can sometimes cause extra stress and strain on your body. You should work with your health care provider to determine an exercise plan that will incorporate the benefits while minimizing the risks.

Should You Exercise?

If you were active prior to your pregnancy, you may be able to continue your routine with your doctor's permission. However, pregnancy is not the time to start training for a marathon. Your body is simply too busy building babies to undertake strenuous activity. You should focus your exercise effort on activities that enhance your circulation, strengthen your muscle tone, and help you relax.

ALERT

It's a different game plan when you're expecting multiples. Even if you exercised regularly in a previous singleton pregnancy, the risks are too great when you're carrying twins or more. Expect to modify or cease your athletic endeavors during this time.

Follow your doctor's advice. During the first trimester, your normal, pre-pregnancy fitness routine may be acceptable, as long as you're aware of your need for extra supplemental calories and hydration. Make sure you're exercising for the right reasons during your pregnancy. Don't let weight management be the motivation behind your workout. Instead, focus on overall health for you and the babies. However, as the weeks pass, you will likely be advised to avoid exercise that compromises your pregnancy or puts you at risk for complications. Strenuous exercise can cause you to overheat or become dehydrated. You should avoid any high-impact activity that puts extra pressure on the pelvic floor, such as running or aerobic dancing; it could induce preterm labor. As your uterus grows, your body's center of gravity changes. You may find that your sense of balance is affected, making you unsteady and at a higher risk for spills and tumbles.

Exercise Options

With your doctor's blessing, swimming can be an ideal exercise during your pregnancy. If you have access to a pool, take advantage of it! Swimming provides a cardiovascular workout and feels very refreshing. If swimming laps isn't appealing, consider other water-based activities. The buoyancy of the water allows you to move comfortably and reduces strain on your body, creating a gentle exercise environment for a pregnant woman.

Walking is another excellent exercise option. It's free, doesn't require any special equipment, and is easily accessible. You can set your own pace and adjust your level of intensity according to how you're feeling. You can walk outside in fair weather or head inside to a shopping mall when it's too hot, too cold, or rainy.

Gentle stretching exercises are also beneficial. Pregnancy yoga classes are available in many locations. The mental relaxation fostered by yoga can be especially soothing. Of course, check with your doctor before participating in a yoga routine; even if it is touted as "prenatal," the routines are designed for women carrying one baby.

Rest and Relaxation

Even as you realize that sleep will be a precious commodity after the babies are born, you may be surprised at how difficult it is to sleep through the night during pregnancy. Between the physical discomforts of heartburn and leg cramps, and anxiety about what's ahead, you may have trouble settling down at night. However, a good night's rest is one of the best gifts that you can give your body—and your babies.

Overcoming Sleep Disturbances

Throughout your pregnancy, there are a variety of issues that cause physical discomfort or otherwise interfere with sleep. To combat sleep disturbances, or outright insomnia, try to pinpoint the cause of your restlessness. Do you wake up because you need to urinate? Are you unable to find a comfortable sleeping position due to your growing girth? Are you plagued by leg cramps, snoring, or heartburn?

ALERT

Sleeping pills are not recommended for pregnant women. They can cause birth defects, such as cleft palate. Talk to your doctor before taking any sleep aids, even herbal remedies.

In the first and last trimester, your pregnancy may impose on your bladder. In the early weeks, pressure from your expanding uterus may send you running to the bathroom frequently throughout the day—and night. In the final days, no matter how far you grow out and around, things are pretty crowded inside you, and your bladder has nowhere else to go. Unfortunately, there's not much you can do to alleviate the condition when it wakes you up at night, except to reduce the amount of fluid that you drink as it gets closer to bedtime. You'll still need to drink plenty during the day, however.

Leg cramps and backaches are also uncomfortable side effects of pregnancy. Your muscles are working overtime because of the added weight of the babies. They can protest loudly—and painfully—by seizing up in the night. A lack of calcium or phosphorous in your diet can make the problem worse. A hand-held massage unit may help alleviate the tension in your legs, but if the problem persists, you may wish to consult your doctor. She may be able to recommend a pain relief product that is safe to take during pregnancy.

Heartburn

It's not just your drinking habits that can keep you up at night; what you eat has an effect as well. Heartburn is a common complaint among the sleepless. As your uterus expands to accommodate two or more babies, digestive acids from your stomach are forced northward, causing a burning sensation in your digestive tract. It won't hurt the babies, but it can make you uncomfortable, especially when you're lying down.

To combat heartburn at night, avoid common triggers like spicy, fried, or fatty foods. Don't eat large quantities of food close to bedtime. Drink plenty of water with and between meals. Altering your bed's incline can also help. Raise the head of your bed by about 6 inches to allow gravity to keep your stomach in check. If all else fails, talk to your doctor about over-the-counter heartburn remedies. Many moms find that keeping a bottle of chewable tablets on the nightstand provides quick access to relief when heartburn strikes in the middle of the night.

Tossing and Turning

Even if you're exhausted, it can be nearly impossible to get comfortable enough to fall asleep when you're pregnant, especially if you are accustomed to sleeping on your stomach or back. You may feel like a beached whale in bed, floundering to find a comfortable position. Your expanding body needs support, and extra pillows can provide it. There are specially designed pregnancy pillows on the market, but if you want to spare the expense, experiment with extra bed pillows or throw cushions. Many women find that sleeping with a pillow between their knees or at the small of their back provides comfort. Others use pillows to prop their belly.

FACT

The recommended sleeping position in pregnancy is lying on the left side. It prevents your body weight from settling on your liver and optimizes the circulation of blood from your heart to your lower body.

If you simply can't get comfortable in bed, head for the living room. Many mothers find rest in a large reclining chair. It's easier to get in and out of when they need to use the bathroom, and they don't have to worry about disturbing their partner. And it can simply be easier to relax in a reclined position than lying flat in bed. Another option is to rent a hospital-style bed; it can be adjusted to a comfortable position to help you rest. It is possible that the cost may be covered by your insurance.

The Need to Nap

Pregnancy can wreak havoc on your sleep habits. There may be occasions, especially in the first trimester, when the sedative effect of progesterone makes you incredibly sleepy during portions of the day when you need to be wide-awake. Likewise, you'll sometimes find yourself wide-awake and alert in the middle of the night if the babies or your bladder are particularly active.

Take advantage of opportunities to nap when you can. Short periods of rest do provide some restorative benefits. You'll never have a better excuse to lounge around than during this period of pregnancy with multiples. You may find it refreshing to catch a catnap the day after a restless night. Or it may be necessary to schedule a quiet rest into your daily routine. Listen to your body's cues. Give it a rest when you feel tired. Fatigue is a sign that you are overdoing it.

Things to Avoid

While there are certain things that you can do to enhance your health during pregnancy, there are many things that you should *not* do in order to assure the safety of your developing babies. Certainly, there are some activities, such as excessive drinking and smoking, that are inadvisable at any time, but the potential harm to two, three, or more developing individuals makes these actions inexcusable during pregnancy. However, other seemingly harmless things that were part of your life before you were pregnant may pose a danger now that you are expecting twins or more.

For example, soaking in a hot tub should be avoided during pregnancy. Studies have shown a connection between hot tub use and miscarriage in the first trimester. In addition, soaking in a 100-plus-degree hot tub can cause a body's internal thermostat to rise and overheat, a dangerous condition for the fetuses.

That morning jolt of caffeine from coffee may be a cherished routine when you're not pregnant, but you may want to consider cutting back or going without while you are. Although moderate amounts of caffeine aren't necessarily harmful, some studies show an association with stillbirth, birth defects, and other complications. Other studies contradict the evidence, but at any rate, caffeine can cause heartburn, increase your blood pressure, or keep you awake. That can put stress on your body, and your babies.

Your doctor can advise you as to how much is too much, but if you simply can't go without your morning cup of "joe," try to limit it to just one cup. Less than 200 mg of caffeine per day is generally considered safe.

Medications and Herbs

Usually you wouldn't think twice about taking aspirin for a headache or a decongestant for a cold. However, you would never give these drugs to an infant, which is basically what you're doing when you take medications during your pregnancy. Your doctor or midwife should approve any over-the-counter drugs. If you are taking prescription drugs, your health care provider will review your situation and make a recommendation as to whether it is safe to continue their use during pregnancy.

The popularity of herbal remedies to treat common ailments has risen in recent years. Be wary about their use during your pregnancy. Don't be misled into thinking that "natural" or nonmedical approaches are necessarily neutral; they may have harmful consequences. Always consult a medical provider before taking any kind of herbal product, including herbal teas, when you're pregnant.

Unsafe Foods

Listeriosis is an infection caused by eating foods that contain the *Listeria* bacteria. It's not a terribly dangerous condition for most adults but can have devastating effects on fetuses or newborns. You can reduce your risk of contracting such an infection by avoiding certain foods. Soft cheeses, including Brie, Camembert, feta, Roquefort, and asadero, should only be eaten if they have been cooked by boiling or broiling until they are bubbly. You can also minimize your risk by properly handling other foods that are likely to be contaminated with listeria. These include any foods that have been precooked and then refrigerated, such as hot dogs or deli-style luncheon meats. Cooking these foods will kill the bacteria, so they are safe to eat after they have been thoroughly reheated.

Despite its reputation as a delicious source of nutrition, some seafood is also potentially dangerous during pregnancy with multiples. Toxic levels of mercury or polychlorinated biphenyls (PCBs) can be found in some types of predator fish, including swordfish, king mackerel, tilefish, tuna, and shark. Check with your doctor or midwife about the types of fish to avoid, and enjoy other varieties in moderation.

ALERT

You don't have to give up your kitty while you're expecting, but stay away from the litter box. Toxoplasmosis is a parasite that can be contained in cat waste. Always wash your hands after holding your pet, and have someone else clean the litter box while you're pregnant to minimize the risk. It's not likely to be a chore that you relish doing anyway!

Secondhand Smoke

Even if you don't smoke, the dangerous effects of tobacco can still impact your babies. Secondhand smoke, also known as passive smoke, is the combination of exhalations from a smoker and smoke from their burning cigarettes, and it can be harmful to developing fetuses. Babies exposed to secondhand smoke are smaller and more likely to be born prematurely; with your multiples already at risk for these conditions, you don't want to heighten the odds. Passive smoke increases the risk of asthma and cancer, and children of smokers often exhibit increased irritability.

Stay away from smokers while you're pregnant. Avoid the smoking section when you're out in public. Keep your home smoke-free; if you have family members who smoke, ask them not to smoke inside while you're pregnant. (Better yet, ask them to stop altogether!)

Here's to Your Health

- **Eating right is everything.** With so many factors of a multiple pregnancy outside your control, your diet is one way you can actively contribute to babies' well-being. Eating plenty of healthy food and gaining weight according to your doctor's recommendations will help ensure that your babies have the healthiest possible start to life.
- **Don't just eat more; make smart food choices.** Quantity and quality count; after all, what you eat nourishes you and the babies, too! Be selective about what you eat, including plenty of protein, healthy fats, and complex carbohydrates in your diet. Choose foods that are rich in nutrients like iron, folic acid, and calcium.
- **Fluids are important also.** Staying hydrated has so many benefits in a multiple pregnancy. You need extra fluids to keep things flowing smoothly, and dehydration raises your risk of preterm labor. So drink up!
- **Exercise your options.** Discuss your exercise options with your medical caregiver. In a multiple pregnancy, the risks and benefits of exercise must be evaluated carefully. You want to stay fit, but don't want to endanger the babies, so choose an exercise routine that meets both goals.
- **Rest up.** Your body is working hard during a multiple pregnancy and needs plenty of rest in order to function effectively. Unfortunately, some of the side effects of pregnancy, such as heartburn, muscle cramps, and anxiety, make it difficult to get a good night's rest. You may have to seek creative solutions for sleeping arrangements in order to ensure that you get enough rest.
- **Avoid harmful substances to protect your babies.** There are several others you should strive to avoid because they pose a risk to developing babies such as soaking in hot tubs, taking herbal medications, eating certain foods, and changing cat litter.

CHAPTER 8

Your Medical Care

During your pregnancy with twins, triplets, or more, your medical care is crucial to ensuring a healthy outcome for you and your babies. If you have led a relatively healthy life up until this point, you may find the medical interventions somewhat overwhelming. Throughout the course of your pregnancy, you will be poked and prodded and probed. Educating yourself about the medical aspects of multiple birth will help you cope, and prepare you for an optimal pregnancy and birth experience.

What's Different When There's More Than One?

When you discovered that you were having twins, triplets, or more, you probably realized instantly that your pregnancy would be in a different category. Pregnancy accords a special status, but now you are more than "just pregnant." You have been elevated to an entirely different status.

But what is really different? When all is said and done, the ultimate difference between having a singleton and having multiples is extra babies. There may be problems and complications along the way, but for the majority of cases, the end result is healthy children. While you can't ignore the increased risks inherent in a multiple pregnant, you have to recognize them for what they are—they are possibilities, not certainties.

FACT

According to one study, the medical costs of a twin pregnancy were found to be five times higher than those of a singleton pregnancy. The costs escalate with each additional baby.

However, because of the risks, you are likely to receive more attention and intervention from your medical caregivers. You will be scheduled for more frequent checkups and assessments with your doctor or midwife. That is not necessarily a bad thing. The extra monitoring means that you are more likely to catch potential problems and may have access to more effective treatments.

Finding the Right Medical Provider

Choosing a medical practitioner is one of the most important decisions that you will make during your pregnancy, affecting many aspects of your experience. You will spend many hours in this person's office in the next few months, and your choice will ultimately impact how, where, and when your babies make their entry into this world. You should examine all your options and put some thoughtful consideration into your decision.

Depending on how your pregnancy was initiated, you may already be under the care of a doctor, nurse, or midwife. If your multiples were conceived as a result of fertility enhancements, your reproductive specialist may have referred you to a caregiver. Or maybe you have already been seeing a family practitioner, doctor, or midwife during your pregnancy, but now that you know you are having more than one baby, aren't sure if you need more specialized care.

ALERT

Finding out that you're expecting twins or multiples may mean a change of course for your medical care. The right doctor for your singleton pregnancy may not be the best option for your multiples. Be flexible about the change to give your babies the best possible care.

Family Practitioner

Before you were pregnant, you probably had a family doctor that you visited when you were sick or hurt. It is wonderful to have a medical professional with whom you are comfortable and familiar, and who knows your history and background. Many doctors in family practice also provide prenatal care for pregnant women, and some even deliver babies.

While that is fine for routine pregnancies, having twins or more puts you in a different class of risk, and your family doctor may not be able to provide the best care for you and your babies. You will have to weigh your options; are you more comfortable in the care of a trusted physician with whom you have a prior relationship or are you better off with a specialist who is experienced in multiple birth? If you choose to remain in the care of your family practitioner, be sure that he has plenty of prior experience with multiple pregnancies. This is only a safe option if you are having twins (not more) and your pregnancy remains fairly free of problems, as family doctors don't usually have access to the kinds of specialized equipment required to treat complications.

Ob-Gyn

The most common choice for pregnancy and birth care is an obstetrician-gynecologist, or ob-gyn. This type of doctor specializes in the care of women. Obstetrics focuses specifically on birth and the associated issues of pregnancy, labor, delivery, and postpartum care, while gynecology is the branch of medicine dealing with diseases and routine care of the female reproductive system. The certification of ob-gyn covers both areas, but some doctors prefer to specialize only in gynecology and choose not to deliver babies.

After medical school and four years of residency training in women's health, ob-gyn physicians must pass written and oral tests to become certified by the American Board of Obstetrics and Gynecology. Some doctors pursue additional certification to become a Fellow of the American Congress of Obstetricians and Gynecologists; they are identified by the acronym FACOG after their title.

Specialists

Within the field, some ob-gyn practitioners specialize in maternal-fetal medicine; these individuals are most experienced with high-risk pregnancies and best equipped to handle the associated complications. Perinatologists undergo training beyond the regular obstetrics residency, spending three additional clinical years in research and patient care. They are the top professionals for diagnosing and treating medical conditions that threaten the health of the mother or babies during pregnancy. Because they deal with high-risk situations, perinatologists often have a richer depth of experience with multiple birth. In addition they are usually associated with leading hospital facilities and have access to the latest and greatest technology for diagnosing and treating the conditions that might affect your babies' health.

Midwives

For centuries, it was midwives, rather than doctors, that assisted women with the process of giving birth. Before the advent of medical technology, they delivered plenty of sets of twins and, although the rate of infant mortality was quite high, occasional sets of higher order multiples as well. Many women are returning to the use of midwives for care during pregnancy and childbirth, seeking a more natural, less medical experience.

A certified nurse-midwife (CNM) is licensed to practice after obtaining a degree in nursing and completing a specialized training as a midwife. Midwives generally provide a more individualized approach to care, focusing on the patient's goals for her childbirth experience.

ESSENTIAL

Some women would prefer to give birth at home. While it is not particularly advisable, and probably outright dangerous in the case of higher order multiples, it may be an option for delivery of twins. If this is your desire, your best approach is to locate a midwife who is supportive of your plans and who will work in conjunction with a doctor in the event of an emergency.

Midwives are not usually equipped to handle high-risk pregnancies and deliveries. Because of the risks associated with multiples, expectant mothers are often discouraged from considering a midwife. However, the advantages of utilizing the services of a midwife are underestimated. Many CNMs are fully capable of handling the needs of uncomplicated twin deliveries, and occasionally even higher order multiples.

Making the Choice

With many options to choose from, how will you know what is best for you during your pregnancy? Ultimately, that decision will be based on your comfort level and the conditions of your pregnancy. If you are in good overall health, are having twins, and are committed to eating right and taking good care of yourself, you may be most comfortable with a doctor or midwife. However, if you are having higher order multiples, you should probably receive care from a specialist.

Any midwife who truly values her patient's well-being will work in conjunction with an obstetrician or perinatologist who can offer specialized care in the event that it is warranted. If you are considering a midwife's services during your pregnancy with multiples, ensure that she can readily provide access to other health care professionals if you encounter any complications.

In some cases, you can have the best of both worlds. In many cities, group practices offer access to a variety of medical professionals within the same setting. You can visit a midwife or nurse practitioner for routine checkups, have your ultrasound screenings reviewed by a perinatologist, and have an obstetrician deliver your babies.

If your heart is set on a midwife but your body won't cooperate, a doula may be a good compromise. A trained professional birth assistant who acts as your advocate, a doula is trained in the physiology of birth and is equipped to help you cope with the emotional aspects of childbirth. Studies have shown that women who use the services of a doula have faster labors, decreased use of epidurals, and fewer C-sections. You can hire a doula to attend you during labor, delivery, and even after the babies are born. Many doulas are trained as lactation consultants and can assist with breastfeeding and baby care.

Questions and Answers

In choosing a doctor, you should consider several things. Many times, your options may be narrowed or limited by your insurance coverage. No one wants to put a price on their babies' well-being, but the fact remains that medical care for pregnancy and birth is extremely expensive, even more so with multiple babies. If your insurance will pay for care from one doctor, but not from another, and both are equally qualified, then by all means choose a doctor associated with your medical plan.

If you do have a choice among medical practices, or doctors within a practice, evaluate their individual policies and procedures and find the choice that best matches your personal preferences. What are their recommendations for nutrition and weight gain during multiple pregnancy? Do they advocate mandatory bed rest or work stoppage at a particular point in the pregnancy? What is their approach for monitoring for preterm labor and complications? Will they schedule a delivery at thirty-eight weeks or wait for labor to initiate?

FACT

Don't underestimate the importance of personality; while you may not like every doctor or nurse you deal with, you should have confidence and trust in their ability to treat you and your children.

When making your choice, consider the physician's practice in addition to the individual. Is the office conveniently located? You will spend quite a bit of time there; toward the end of your pregnancy you will likely visit at least once a week. Does it have facilities for sonography and lab testing or do you have to go elsewhere? What hospital is your doctor affiliated with? Is it the best choice in the event that you or the babies have to receive long-term care? Who will handle your case if your doctor or midwife is unavailable? These are all important questions. Make sure the answers to them satisfy your needs when considering your options. Finally, consider your personal intuition as you make your choice. While you want the best possible care for your pregnancy, you also want a medical setting where you feel enabled to ask questions, receive adequate answers to those questions, and participate in your care as a partner.

Your Prenatal Care

During your pregnancy with multiples, and even after your babies are born, you will spend plenty of time in your health care provider's office. Knowing what to expect during these visits will help you make the most of your time and ensure that you receive the best possible care for you and your babies.

The Initial Visit

Your first visit is a time to establish a relationship with your doctor and set the tone for the next nine months. You should call to schedule a visit as soon as you suspect that you are pregnant. If you've been receiving treatment from a reproductive specialist, they may continue to monitor you for a period of time after conception and advise you as to when you should arrange for prenatal care.

ALERT

Before you visit, spend some time investigating your medical background. Ask relatives about their healthy history so that you are fully prepared to answer any questions. Be especially aware of any genetic or inherited disorders, such as hemophilia or mental retardation, and any incidences of pregnancy loss or infant death.

During the first visit, the doctor, nurse, or midwife will spend some time obtaining your medical history. Be prepared to delve deep into your medical background and to answer plenty of questions about your past illnesses, your family history of disease, and your lifestyle. The father-to-be won't escape the interrogation, either. It is important to establish his history as well, as it could impact the babies.

You will be given a comprehensive physical exam, assessing your overall health. You will be weighed and measured, and your blood pressure will be monitored. You may receive a breast exam, and you will most likely be given a pelvic exam, complete with a Pap smear. You may be asked to give a urine sample for analysis. You will have blood drawn, or will be scheduled for a visit to a lab at another site. Analysis of your blood will assess many different elements:

- Presence of hCG (human chorionic gonadotropin), a pregnancy hormone
- Blood type
- Hemoglobin and hematocrit (red blood cell count)
- Rh factor (rhesus)
- Antibody screening
- Rubella titer (German measles)
- Hepatitis B

Some doctors will screen for other conditions as well, such as immunity to varicella (chickenpox), HIV, toxoplasmosis, sickle-cell anemia, cystic fibrosis, and Tay-Sachs and other genetic disorders.

Your initial visit can be an exciting experience. In some cases it is a confirmation that you are indeed pregnant, or a revelation that you are expecting more than one. Your due date will be ascertained so that you can start anticipating the arrival of your new family members.

Future Visits

Every doctor or midwife has her own prescribed schedule of care for pregnant mothers of twins or more. Generally, you can expect to see the doctor more often when you are carrying more babies, and the frequency of your visits will increase as you go further along in your pregnancy. A typical schedule would look something like this:

- Initial visit between six and eight weeks; an ultrasound may be performed
- Monthly visits throughout the first and second trimester
- Visits twice a month after twenty or twenty-four weeks
- Weekly visits after twenty-eight weeks

Depending on your progress, more frequent visits may become necessary until you deliver.

Ultrasounds and Tests

Throughout your pregnancy, you and your babies will go through several tests and assessments. Some are prompted by the extra risks inherent in a multiple pregnancy, requiring more intensive monitoring than a singleton pregnancy. Others are routine assessments that are recommended for all pregnancies. It's important to know what each test is measuring and how it will be performed.

Ultrasounds

Ultrasound assessments can be a very enjoyable and reassuring test for expectant parents, offering them a peek at the developing babies. There are no known risks associated with ultrasound technology, and it generates little discomfort for the mother, other than requiring her to lie flat during the procedure. You are more likely to have several ultrasounds with a multiple pregnancy, as it is a simple, inexpensive, and relatively noninvasive diagnostic tool.

Some doctors routinely perform an ultrasound on their patients during their initial office visit, about a month into the pregnancy. An early ultrasound or sonogram is often the method by which a multiple pregnancy is confirmed, and perhaps your own twins, triplets, or more were revealed in the shadowy blobs of an ultrasound image. Others recommend an ultrasound evaluation toward the end of the first trimester as part of a screening evaluation for chromosomal abnormalities. During the second trimester, a more comprehensive ultrasound can be performed to detect a wider range of issues.

ALERT

The American Congress of Obstetricians and Gynecologists is somewhat wary of gratuitous ultrasound use in a healthy pregnancy; however, diagnosing and monitoring multiple pregnancy is considered acceptable and is a recommended use of the technology.

Your ultrasound scans may be performed by a trained sonographer, or by your obstetrician or perinatologist. Advances in ultrasound technology continue to provide even more detailed and defined pictures of the womb. Doppler technology, familiar to many as a weather forecasting tool, makes it possible to monitor fetal blood flow. Three-dimensional (3-D) imaging uses a computer to process a series of images into an even more detailed and defined picture of your womb, while 4-D ultrasound incorporates movement in real time, providing a very lifelike look at the developing babies.

Sometimes a Level II ultrasound is recommended for multiple pregnancies. This is simply a more detailed assessment. The same equipment is utilized, but it is generally performed by a maternal-fetal specialist at a hospital rather than in your doctor's or midwife's office. It will likely take an hour or two, whereas a regular ultrasound lasts about thirty minutes.

In the second trimester, most physicians recommend a routine ultrasound, often called a structural ultrasound. Generally, this exam is scheduled at about eighteen to twenty weeks. At this point in the pregnancy, the babies' anatomy is developed enough to be assessed, yet the babies are still small enough to be seen individually. Later in the pregnancy, as the womb becomes more crowded, their body parts may overlap and become more difficult to examine.

The procedure provides much useful information. It helps to ascertain that the babies are developing on schedule, confirms their due dates, and rules out potential problems such as Down syndrome, spina bifida, and hydrocephaly. Often other details are revealed, such as the babies' genders (if you want to make them known) and perhaps even their zygosity. In addition to getting a good look at the babies, a second trimester ultrasound is also a good time to check the length of your cervix. A long cervix is tightly closed, an encouraging sign that preterm labor is not imminent.

During the procedure, your doctor will likely spend some time trying to identify and assess the membrane that separates the babies' sac. A discernible membrane or a triangular shape called the lambda sign may indicate that the babies are dichorionic, although it doesn't necessarily confirm that they are dizygotic—even monozygotic (identical) twins can be dichorionic.) A thin membrane or a T-shape where the membrane meets the placenta might identify monochorionic twins, while the lack of a membrane might be a clue that the babies are monoamniotic.

Screening Tests

Screening tests help to identify risks and determine follow-up treatment. There are several recommended screening tests throughout pregnancy; some are routine tests offered to all pregnant women, while others are to determine risks more likely to be encountered in a multiple pregnancy. It is important to realize that the results of screening tests don't necessarily indicate the presence of a problem or complication; rather, these tests are used to catch potential issues and will usually prompt follow-up for actual diagnosis.

In the first trimester, a sample of maternal blood is screened for chromosomal abnormalities, such as Down syndrome and trisomy 18. This screening is usually performed between the eleventh and thirteenth week of pregnancy, and may be accompanied by an ultrasound scan to measure the nuchal translucency of the tissue on the back of the fetuses' necks.

A similar screening occurs in the second trimester. The quad screen occurs between fifteen and twenty weeks, when an analysis of a blood sample measures for four substances that can indicate possible genetic disorders. Abnormal levels of AFP (alpha-fetoprotein), hCG (human chorionic gonadotropin), estriol, and inhibin-A may alert physicians to conditions such as spina bifida, anencephaly, or Down syndrome. Your medical caregiver may refer to this screening by another name. Alternative versions and combinations of this screening test may be presented as a triple screen test, multiple marker screening, Maternal Serum Alpha-Fetoprotein (MSAFP), or AFP Plus.

Late in the second trimester, you will likely be screened for gestational diabetes. The test measures the amount of glucose in your blood to determine whether pregnancy hormones have affected the way that your body processes insulin. In most cases, the glucose level is measured via a blood sample. Your doctor will provide you with a sweet, high-glucose beverage and instructions on when to drink it. About an hour later, blood will be drawn and sent to the lab. If your blood serum glucose is high, you may be at risk for gestational diabetes. Usually a second round of more intensive testing, called an oral glucose tolerance test, is prescribed. You may be required to follow a special diet for a few days or fast the night before. It can be a time-consuming test, since your blood will be drawn several times.

FACT

In a singleton pregnancy, gestational diabetes screening is usually performed early in the third trimester, but many doctors recommend earlier testing for moms of multiples. The risk of gestational diabetes is nearly doubled for moms expecting more than one baby.

Testing for Preterm Labor

Fetal fibronectin testing allows doctors to predict whether preterm labor is imminent, although it doesn't provide any guarantees unless the test provides a negative result. Fetal fibronectin (fFN) is a protein found in the membranes and fluid of the amniotic sac. A glue-like substance, it bonds the amniotic sac(s) to the lining of the uterus. It begins to break down naturally about the thirty-fifth week of pregnancy, as the body prepares to deliver. However, if its presence is detected in the area of the mother's cervix or vagina between twenty-four and thirty-four weeks' gestation, it could indicate the onset of preterm labor, even when other symptoms aren't apparent.

Fetal fibronectin testing is quick and simple, and carries no risk of side effects. A swab of secretions near the cervix is collected and analyzed in a laboratory. If a negative result is returned, your chances of delivering in the next fourteen days are low. A positive test doesn't mean that you're ready to deliver; rather, it simply alerts doctors to the possibility of the onset of preterm labor so that additional precautions can be instituted.

Your doctor or midwife may perform one or more fetal fibronectin tests in the third trimester to assess your risk of early delivery. Biweekly scans beginning at twenty-four weeks can screen for an increased risk of preterm labor and guide decisions about your medical care.

ESSENTIAL

A negative fibronectin test can be reassuring; your chances of delivering preterm are less than 10 percent. A positive is less conclusive. The detection of fetal fibronectin doesn't necessarily mean that labor is imminent, but it will probably require you to be closely monitored.

Fetal Assessment

During the last trimester, you're likely to have ample opportunity to keep tabs on your babies. Fetal surveillance during the last trimester is accomplished with ultrasound and heart rate monitoring, with a variety of tests that determine the babies' condition. A nonstress test is a painless way for you to participate in assessing the babies. It is performed by your doctor in the third trimester, usually at about thirty weeks. Testing is done with transducers that measure each baby's heart rate and an additional monitor to record any uterine contractions. You'll be asked to sit quietly or lie down and relax. Remember, it's called a *non*stress test, so don't be anxious!

As the transducers monitor the babies' heart rates, you may be asked to indicate your experience of fetal movement. The test measures the heart rate of the baby in response to its movement to assess oxygen levels. A healthy baby's heart rate will increase with movement and decrease with rest, so the results of this test can help determine how your multiples are faring in their current womb conditions.

A nonstress test is one component of a biophysical profile, a test that gives an overall assessment of the babies' condition. It's usually recommended midway through the last trimester, beginning at about week thirty-two. It includes evaluations of each baby's heart rate activity, respiration, body movements, muscle tone, and amniotic fluid volume. It may also include an assessment of the placenta. The nonstress test provides information about the fetuses' heart rate activity, while the rest of the elements are measured via ultrasound. If one or more of the babies scores low on a bio-physical profile, it may be cause for concern and may even prompt consideration of an early delivery.

Amniocentesis and CVS

Between the fourteenth and twentieth week of your pregnancy, you may be scheduled for an amniocentesis, perhaps in response to the results of a screening test. During the process of amniocentesis, or amnio, your caregiver uses an ultrasound-guided needle to withdraw fluid from the babies' amniotic sac. Analysis of the fluid sample, which contains fetal cells, provides a wealth of information about the babies.

Amniocentesis may elicit some cramping, and you'll probably be advised to take it easy after the procedure. There are some inherent risks; the needle's invasion of the uterus can trigger infection, preterm labor, or even miscarriage. In a multiple pregnancy in which each baby's amniotic sac must be sampled, the risks may be increased. Generally, this procedure is recommended for mothers over the age of thirty-five, or whose families have a history of chromosomal abnormalities or birth defects. It may also be warranted if there is an indication that you will deliver your babies prematurely, as it can be an effective tool for assessing their lung maturity.

An alternative to amniocentesis is chorionic villus sampling (CVS). It is generally performed earlier in pregnancy, in the first trimester. Chorionic villi are tiny tentacles of tissue projecting from the chorion that provide a sample of the babies' genetic material. A catheter is inserted through either the cervix or abdominal wall to extract a sample of the villi. Although it is an extremely accurate tool for detecting genetic disorders, the risk of miscarriage after CVS is even 1 to 2 percent higher than with amniocentesis. It can be a challenging procedure when there are multiples, especially if they share a placenta. Your doctor will advise you as to the risks and benefits of undergoing such testing.

Your Medical Care

- **You have a variety of options for medical care during your pregnancy, but choose wisely.** General practitioners, midwives, obstetricians, and perinatologists can all deliver prenatal care, but be sure that your provider is equipped to meet the challenges of a multiple pregnancy. In many situations, a specialist can offer the most comprehensive care and may be required if there are complications or higher order multiples.

- **Attentive prenatal care is vital when you're having twins or more.** Because of the additional risks, be sure to attend all prenatal visits with your medical care provider and carefully follow recommendations. From your initial visit until delivery, you'll be screened and monitored in order to identify and prevent any potential complications.

- **Ultrasound allows your doctors to peek inside and keep an eye on the babies.** Mothers of multiples can generally look forward to several ultrasound screenings to monitor the progress of the babies. Ultrasound reveals numerous pieces of information that can assess their condition.

- **Additional screening tests are a part of routine prenatal care.** Some are standard measures of care during pregnancy, while others help detect risk factors specific to multiple pregnancy. You will likely encounter screening tests for gestational diabetes, preterm labor, and Down syndrome. In addition, you may be required to undergo more specialized screening that utilizes amniocentesis or chorionic villus sampling.

CHAPTER 9

Setting Up the Nursery

One of the most exciting and fun ways that parents prepare for a new addition to the family is by creating the baby's room. For parents of multiples, who are expecting two or more, the process can present some extra challenges, but is every bit as rewarding. There is no specific formula to follow; depending on your home's space allocation you may choose to put each child in his or her own room, designate a single room for all of them, or even create a "nursery niche" in a section of an existing room.

Cribs: One, Two, or More?

One of the biggest decisions parents of multiples will make about their babies concerns sleeping arrangements. Cribs are a big-ticket item in the nursery; not only do they consume a lot of floor space in a room, but they can also consume a big chunk of the budget!

Initially, you won't necessarily need an individual crib for every baby. Two or even three infants can easily share a sleeping space during the first few months. Instead of a crib, you may prefer to keep the babies close at hand by having them sleep near you in a bassinet, cradle, portable crib, or Moses basket. Eventually, however, you'll want to provide a designated, segregated spot for each baby in order to ensure secure and uninterrupted sleep for everybody. Once the babies are old enough to roll or scoot around, they can disturb each other, and that's the time to invest in additional cribs.

FACT

There are some bed options designed specifically for twins, but their cost and space demands may make them prohibitive for most families. The Duetta Crib Mate is a dual round crib for twins or two babies that retails for thousands of dollars and requires special bedding products at an additional cost.

Crib Safety Considerations

When choosing cribs for your babies, follow established safety guidelines, such as those established by the U.S. Consumer Product Safety Commission. They recommend:

- A firm, tight-fitting mattress so babies can't get trapped between the mattress and the crib
- No missing, loose, broken, or improperly installed screws, brackets, or other hardware on the crib or mattress support
- No more than $2\frac{3}{8}$ inches (about the width of a soda can) between the rib slats so a baby's body can't fit through the slats; no missing or cracked slats
- No corner posts over $\frac{1}{16}$ inch high so a baby's clothing can't catch

- No cutouts in the headboard or footboard so a baby's head can't get trapped
- No cracked or peeling paint; all surfaces should be coated with lead-free paint

For mesh-sided cribs and playpens, look for:

- Mesh less than ¼ inch in size, smaller than the tiny buttons on a baby's clothing
- Mesh with no tears, holes, or loose threads that could entangle a baby
- Mesh that is securely attached to the top rail and floor plate
- Top rail cover with no tears or holes
- If staples are used, none should be missing, loose, or exposed

In 2011, the Juvenile Products Manufacturers Association introduced a new certification that restricts the production of drop-side cribs and requires manufacturers to comply with strict federal safety standards. Be cautious about purchasing products that are not covered by this certification and do not meet the new standards, especially those with drop-sides.

Choices, Choices

Another factor to consider when choosing cribs is longevity. Many families find it convenient to keep twins or more sleeping in cribs much longer than they would a singleton, perhaps even up to the age of three. In that case, the multiples may move right into—pardon the pun—twin beds. However, if you anticipate the need for intermediate sleeping arrangements, toddler beds—with their protective railings and smaller mattresses—may be a viable option. Some crib models covert to toddler beds, extending their usefulness.

Secondhand: Is It Safe?

Cribs and baby bedding can be expensive, with fancy solid wood items retailing for well over $1,000. When you're faced with buying two or more at the same time, it may make sense to investigate secondhand products. Local mothers of multiples clubs are a wonderful source for locating secondhand sets of cribs, as well as other baby equipment. However, be aware that products manufactured prior to 2011 do not meet current federal safety standards, and the resale of such products is not advisable and in violation of the Consumer Product Safety Act.

ALERT

Dozens of drop-side crib models were recalled in 2010 after malfunction incidents led to concern about their safety. Old-style drop-side cribs may be able to be secured with immobilizers in order to meet new standards; check the Consumer Product Safety Commission's website (*www.cpsc.gov*) for a full list of recalled products and approved immobilizers.

Changing Table and Diaper Stations

A safe, sturdy changing station makes diaper duty more efficient. This is one piece of furniture that infant multiples will only use one at a time, but you may want to consider setting up multiple stations in convenient locations throughout the house. Be creative. A diaper station doesn't have to take the form of a traditional changing table; any sturdy furniture with a flat top, such as a dresser, can be transformed to accommodate your needs. Whatever you choose, make sure that it's a comfortable height and that the location provides sufficient but easily accessible storage. Stock your space with plenty of diapers, wipes, extra clothing, powders, creams, and lotions. Everything you need should be within arm's reach so that you never leave a baby unattended on the changing table. Finally, designate a convenient location for sanitary disposal of dirty diapers.

When you set up your diaper station(s), be sure to provide a secure spot for the baby who's waiting her turn, since your hands and attention will be busy with the diaper process. In the babies' bedroom or nursery, it might be a crib. Other alternatives include a bouncy seat, bassinet, or playpen. Position it so that you can keep an eye on everyone and won't ever have to turn your back on the baby who's being changed.

Double Decorating

After the furniture has been purchased, new parents can look forward to the excitement of decorating the nursery. Just remember, by the time a baby is old enough to form an opinion about the décor, he is likely to have outgrown the blue bunnies that his parents chose before his birth. Don't be overly concerned about fashion, but rather focus your efforts on creating a functional room with an eye to the future.

With practicality in mind, use washable paint products on the walls. Choose floor coverings that are easily cleaned and comfortable to crawl on. Lighting in a nursery is also very important. Look for controls that will allow you to dim or brighten the amount of light, even if your hands are full of babies or middle-of-the-night supplies. Light-blocking shades, blinds, or drapes will help maintain a dark environment and minimize sleep disruptions.

Complete your babies' nursery with additional furnishings that provide comfort for your family and storage for your children's things. Dressers with drawers and cabinets are handy for holding baby clothing and linens. Shelves with pretty baskets can contain tiny socks, sleepers, and diapers—you can never have enough storage space for extra diapers! Put away playthings in a toy bin or box.

Equip your nursery for daytime and nighttime usage. A comfortable chair, such as a glider or rocker, is a must. Parents of multiples will spend many tender moments in it; be sure you can reside there comfortably with all the babies at the same time! If you have the space, a small sofa or love-seat makes a convenient spot for quick feedings or short snoozes while the babies sleep in their cribs.

Baby Monitors

Monitoring devices that allow you to listen to or watch your babies without being in the room are an essential for parents of multiples. They provide you the freedom to roam around the house and reassurance that your babies are safe and happy. It's almost like being in two places at the same time, something that parents of twins or more are often called on to be.

Baby monitors have two components: a base unit and a receiver. The base unit is the listening or watching device, which is stationed near the babies. These units usually require a power source, so you'll probably have to position it near an electrical outlet. The signals detected by the base unit, such as sound or motion, are then transmitted to the receiver. A product with wireless receivers provides additional mobility, allowing you to move throughout the house without losing contact. Audio receivers generally have greater range than models with video, so you may find a need for both products if you have a large home or yard.

ALERT

Keep all cords and wires well away from cribs and other areas near the babies. They can pose a strangulation hazard.

Some models have unique features such as motion sensors or remote controls. Some operate like walkie-talkies, allowing you to communicate with your babies through the base unit. This can be a helpful feature for parents of multiples. Even if you're not able to enter the room because you are busy with another baby, the sound of your voice may be sufficient to calm an upset sibling. Smartphone apps are also available that enable your phone or computer to function as a baby monitor, a handy option when you are traveling or away from home.

Outfitting the Layette

Now that you have furniture for your babies' room, it's time to think about what you'll fill those dresser drawers with—what you'll soon use to cover their little bodies. A collection of clothing, blankets, bedding, and other "soft" items for babies is called a layette, although in recent years the term has been expanded to include all baby products. There are many layette checklists available, and you may be tempted to multiple the recommended amounts according to the number of babies you will have. That's not necessary, however, because multiples can share so many items.

FACT

As a general guideline, count on one-and-a-half times the suggested amounts of clothing and supplies for twins. Double the recommendations to meet the needs of triplets. Quadruplets will require two to three times the amount recommended for one baby. For quintuplets or more, count on three to four times the recommendations.

Baby Clothing

The baby clothing business is booming! Babies can be dressed to resemble their fashionable parents with designer togs in high style. But the practical fact of the matter is that baby clothes should be chosen for function and usefulness, and not just for their looks. Chances are, those high-priced outfits will fall victim to spit-up stains, diaper disasters, or growth spurts before they've even cleared the credit card charge!

Clothing is a very popular gift for new families, and people especially like to buy cute ensembles for multiples. You'll likely be showered with outfits from well-meaning friends and relatives. Consider their generosity before you invest a great deal of your own money in clothing. When you do buy it, purchase with practicality in mind. Keep the tags attached until the babies are ready to wear each item, and save receipts so that you can easily return unneeded items.

You'll be surprised how difficult it can be to anticipate clothing needs within size and season changes. In general, multiples tend to be a bit smaller than their singleton counterparts. They may wear newborn (0–3 months size) clothing for a longer period of time, especially if they are born early. However, some catch up very quickly and move into larger sizes within a matter of weeks.

To make it even more complicated, your multiples might not even wear the same sizes at the same time. There is often a weight and size discrepancy between twins, and not just among fraternal twins. Monochorionic identical twins that shared a placenta or had twin-to-twin transfusion syndrome can be vastly different sizes. Or a baby that experiences medical complications may not grow as fast as her healthy twin.

Dressing two or more infants can be a time-consuming chore, so choose clothing options that are easy to put on and take off. Snaps are preferable to buttons. Avoid shirts that have to be pulled on over the head; look for wide necks, snap fronts, or wrap styles. Likewise, don't struggle to pull on pants over wiggly baby legs. Snap crotches make diaper changes a breeze.

ESSENTIAL

Used baby clothing is a bargain, and you'd be wise to seek out sources for it, such as consignment stores or multiples-club sales. Check clothing for stains and tears before you buy, and be willing to reject overpriced items. If you shop smart, you'll save a bundle. Better yet, chances are, you can resell the items once your babies are through with them!

Getting Organized

Here's a checklist to help you itemize and organize your layette. Remember that these are only suggestions; your babies may require more or less.

FOR TWINS, EXPECT TO USE:

- ❐ 8–10 T-shirts or one-piece bodysuits for layering or wearing alone
- ❐ 6–8 lightweight sleepers (depending on the season)
- ❐ 6 blanket sleepers (depending on the season; fewer for warm-weather climates)
- ❐ 4 going-home outfits/special occasion outfits
- ❐ 4 hats
- ❐ 3 pairs of soft cotton mittens
- ❐ 6 pairs of socks/booties
- ❐ 4 sweaters/sacks/warm layers for winter
- ❐ 10 bibs (select a variety, including some waterproof items)

FOR TRIPLETS, PLAN ON:

- ❐ 10 T-shirts or Onesies for layering or wearing alone
- ❐ 10–12 lightweight sleepers (depending on the season)
- ❐ 8 blanket sleepers (depending on the season; fewer for warm-weather climates)
- ❐ 6 going-home outfits/special occasion outfits
- ❐ 6 hats

- ❐ 5 pairs of soft cotton mittens
- ❐ 8 pairs of socks/booties
- ❐ 6 sweaters/sacks/warm layers for winter
- ❐ 15 bibs (select a variety, including some waterproof items)

Obviously, quadruplets or higher order multiples will require more clothing to meet their needs. Use the twins list as a base, and multiply the amounts to accommodate the number of babies.

Linens and Bedding

In addition to clothing and diapers, you'll need to stock your linen closet with several other items to accommodate your babies' needs for bedtime, bath time, and beyond. Soft cotton receiving blankets are invaluable for keeping young infants swaddled, providing warmth, or creating a comfortable place to lie on the floor. They are also useful as cushioning when your babies are small and don't quite fit comfortably within the space of their stroller, bouncy seat, or infant car seat.

For the most part, crib bedding serves more of a fashion role than a functional one. Dust ruffles, pillows, and quilts are pretty, but not necessary. It's best to keep the cribs simple and uncluttered. Stuffed animals should be kept out of cribs and reserved for playtime, not bedtime. Although crib bumpers were once the height of fashion, their use is now controversial. The padding that covers the lower half of slats around the crib is designed to protect babies from bumps and bruises and banging against the hard surfaces of the crib. But some argue that they pose a strangulation or asphyxiation risk and should be banned.

Mattress covers, on the other hand, protect your babies as well as your cribs! At a minimum, purchase at least one waterproof mattress protector per crib, plus one or two extras for quick changes. In addition, you'll want at least two sets of sheets per crib. If you're planning to use bassinets, cradles, or portable cribs, you'll need additional sheets for them as well.

Baby towels and washcloths are designed with babies' comfort in mind, but any kind of soft, absorbent cloth will work just fine when you bathe your babies. Hooded towels help keep babies' heads warm and dry after their bath. You'll also want an ample supply of burp or spit-up rags. Keep them handy during feedings and stash them throughout the house and in the diaper bag. Even if you're using disposable diapers, it pays to invest in a stockpile of cloth diapers for this purpose. They're soft, easy to clean, and inexpensive.

Nursery Essentials

- **Preparing your home is an exciting way to anticipate the addition of multiples to your family.** You'll need to acquire some basic equipment and make a few accommodations in your home and automobile in order to create a safe and efficient place to care for your babies.
- **Sleeping arrangements are one of the first things you'll want to consider.** You don't necessarily need two (or more) cribs right off the bat. New-born multiples can be perfectly content sharing a space. But ultimately, you'll want to be sure that each baby has a place to sleep undisturbed by his comultiples, ensuring that they—and therefore you—sleep more soundly. Be sure that the cribs you choose meet safety standards. Be wary of secondhand products; safety guidelines were recently updated after dozens of drop-side crib models were recalled. Cover crib mattresses with waterproof pads for protection, but avoid other decoration accessories in cribs to minimize risks to babies.
- **Decorate with an eye to function, not just form.** Remember that your multiples will soon outgrow the baby-themed décor that outfits their nursery. Keep an eye to the future—and your children's safety—as you decorate with items that are child-friendly, easy to clean, and comfortable for toddlers as well as babies.
- **You don't necessarily need double of everything.** As you accumulate items for your multiples to wear, factor a formula of approximately one-and-a-half times the requirements for one baby, while triplets and higher order multiples will require two to three times the amount of supplies.
- **Baby monitors are another important piece of equipment.** When you have more than one infant, you definitely need an edge to help you keep an eye (or an ear) on everyone. A baby monitor—whether audio or video—allows you to keep tabs on the babies even when you're not in the same room and can also help you gain a few precious extra moments of sleep.

CHAPTER 10

Buying Accessories and Equipment

The addition of twins or more to your family is going to have a big impact on your lifestyle, and your home must be ready to accommodate those changes. Any infant requires some specialized supplies and equipment, and you can bet that multiple babies need even more. But take heart. You don't necessarily have to double or triple all your supplies. There are some things that your babies can share, and some things that they won't need at all.

The Diaper Dilemma

The daunting task of diapering your babies is likely to be one of the most significant challenges you'll face as a parent of multiples. The good news is that it's only a temporary responsibility; eventually your kids will grow up and learn to the use the bathroom. In the meantime, your goal is to devise an effective diaper system that makes the chore tolerable for everyone involved.

FACT

A family with twins is likely to perform nearly 5,000 diaper changes in the first year alone! Triplet parents should expect to serve close to 7,000 episodes of diaper duty, and parent of quadruplets can look forward to 8,000 or more. In the first few months, each baby can go through as many as twelve diapers a day, so be sure to have at least a few dozen on hand before they're born.

Your first challenge is to confront the ultimate diaper dilemma: cloth or disposable? If you've already made this decision for previous children, there's no real reason to change your habits for multiples. Whatever satisfies your personal cost, conscience, and convenience qualifications is the right choice. For first-timers, here's an overview of the advantages and disadvantages of each option.

Disposable diapers offer the benefit of convenience. They are ready to use, easy to put on and take off, and require the diaperer to have minimal contact with the offensive contents. Used disposables go out with the trash and can be easily discarded when you're out and about. Absorbent materials mean that babies' bottoms may stay drier, cleaner, and more comfortable. The downside is that these diapers are costly (for both consumers and the environment). Even when bought in bulk at a discount, each diaper can take about twenty cents out of your pocket. When you tally the total over your babies' diaper lifetime, the cost easily reaches into the thousands of dollars.

Cloth diapers have their associated costs as well; namely, the water consumed to wash them. Unless you're willing to use organic cotton products and wash all the diapers yourself, your efforts have a negligible impact on the problem. The products and treatments used by professional diaper services arguably have just as many negative environmental consequences as disposable diapers. Likewise, a family's cost to use a diaper delivery and cleaning service rivals the price of disposables.

Cloth diapers do have several qualities to recommend them. New styles function much like disposables; the days of pinning bunches of cloth are long gone, and comfortable covers are available in a wide range of colors and fashions. The natural fabric of cloth may be more comfortable for babies with skin allergies or sensitivities, and may reduce occurrences of diaper rash in all babies.

ESSENTIAL

Traditional diaper pails or disposals may be too small to accommodate your multiples' diaper output. If you like the convenience of these odor-reducing products, you may need to invest in two or three. They're useless without the odor-reducing liners, so be sure to stock up on these products, too.

You'll need diapers on the go as well as at home. A well-stocked diaper bag will be your lifeline for managing your multiples out in the world. Keep it stocked with eight to ten diapers, a travel case of wipes, antibacterial hand cleaner, one change of clothes per baby, a blanket or pad, burp rags, and sealable plastic bags for disposing of dirty diapers.

Bottles and Feeding Accessories

Regardless of how you'll feed your babies, there are some basic supplies that you'll need. Even if you're not breastfeeding, you may find it useful to invest in a U-shaped nursing pillow or "Boppy." And even if you decide to nurse, it won't hurt to keep some bottles handy; they can be used to store pumped breast milk.

Bottle Basics

Bottles are available in a wide variety of shapes and sizes. Most bottles have three components: a vial for containing the fluid, a nipple that the baby sucks on to access the liquid, and a cap or ring that secures the nipple to the bottle. Infants, who only consume a few ounces of breast milk or formula during a feeding, require smaller containers than older babies or toddlers, who may drink eight or more ounces at a time.

The babies' age may also be a factor in choosing a nipple style. Newborns who are just learning to suckle may need a product with a slower flow to prevent the contents of the bottle from gushing out all over them. As they get older, hungry babies with a more powerful sucking reflex will prefer a nipple style that delivers the liquid more quickly. If you're using bottles to supplement breastfeeding, look for nipple styles that more closely resemble the human breast.

FACT

Make sure you buy products that are certified BPA-free. Bisphenol A (BPA) is a chemical used in the manufacture of hard plastics that is associated with some health concerns. Some parents prefer glass bottles as a more natural approach, but the risk of breakage makes others steer clear.

Ultimately, the best choice is determined by personal preference—both yours and the babies'. Just as some adults would rather drink out of a crystal goblet than a plastic tumbler, babies sometimes prefer the feel and flow of a particular mode of bottle. Even individual babies within a set of multiples will express a clear preference for one product over another. You may want to start off with a few varieties for your newborns, then stock up on supplies after you've established what works best.

Breast Pumps

Many mothers of multiples agree that a high-quality electric breast pump plays a valuable role when successfully breastfeeding multiples. Pumping immediately following a feeding or between feedings helps to establish a sufficient supply of breast milk for all the babies and allows you to store the surplus for future feedings. Although inexpensive manual pumps exist, most women find that they simply aren't worth the hassle when they're pumping breast milk for more than one baby. Look for a model with a double pump; it will allow you to extract milk simultaneously from both breasts, a precious time saver for moms of multiples. They are expensive, but worth the investment if you can afford it.

Some hospitals or medical suppliers rent professional-grade equipment, but you'll need to evaluate whether the rental costs over time outpace the purchase price. The market for secondhand breast pumps is extensive; investigate the availability of a gently used model through your local parents of multiples organization or online.

ALERT

Most other feeding accessories aren't needed right away. Your babies won't be able to sit up in highchairs until they're several months old; you can put off this purchase if you don't have the space in your kitchen or in your budget.

Seats, Carriers, and Swings

The market for baby products is jam-packed with gadgets and gizmos designed to contain, sustain, and entertain your babies. But since you'll end up providing at least two of each of these items, you'll need to focus on the ones that have been proven most useful.

Infant Carriers/Car Seats

Car seats are the one item that you absolutely can't share among your multiples. In fact, you won't even be able to bring your babies home from the hospital unless you have a car seat for each of them. State laws vary as to how long your children must sit in car seats, but they are mandatory. Babies up to two years or twenty pounds should generally sit in rear-facing seats; older babies and young children sit in front-facing seats. Check your state's child restraint law and the seat manufacturer's guidelines before investing in car seat products.

There are four basic categories of car seats.

- **Infant seats** are used from birth until babies weigh twenty pounds. They are designed for a rear-facing position in the car, and you'll use them for about a year. Most have a carrying handle, and so are often referred to as infant carriers. Used with a base that remains secured in the vehicle, they're a convenient option for transporting babies. Some are incorporated into a travel system, designed to work as a car seat and stroller seat.

- **Convertible car seats** can be used in the rear-facing position for younger babies, then switched to a front-facing configuration for older babies. While they lack the convenience of infant carriers, they offer greater longevity; depending on the model, they can accommodate babies from birth up to sixty pounds.
- **Combination car seats** are used forward-facing only, distinguishing them from convertible seats that can be used in the rear-facing position. Combination seats have a harness system that can be adjusted for babies but can also be used as a booster seat for older children in conjunction with the seat belt.
- **Booster seats** are designed to keep older children safe when using the vehicle seat belts. They're used for several years, until they are old enough or big enough to sit safely with the car seat belts. Check your state's child restraint laws to determine the age, height, or weight limits for booster seat use.

There's no one car seat type that will serve throughout childhood, so you'll have to determine which combination works best for your children, your vehicle, and your lifestyle. Even though it means buying multiple versions, purchasing a set of infant carriers and then convertible or combination seats may be worth the investment. The convenience of transporting babies via infant carriers makes the early months much more manageable, but as they outgrow them, another set of seats will transition them into the next phase.

Bouncy Seats

Bouncy seats, basically a sling covering a lightweight metal or plastic frame, are an inexpensive and convenient option for managing your multiple infants. They securely hold your babies when you need your hands free. Babies can eat in them, sleep in them, play in them, or wait their turn while their twin is being attended to. If you have a multilevel home, you'll want a set on every story.

Swing and Slings

Some babies enjoy passing time in infant swings, and they can be a life-saver when you have multiples. Don't invest in more than one, however, until you've established that your babies are comfortable in them. Borrow swings, or start off with one, and buy additional swings if it appears your babies appreciate them.

A sling is a comfortable way to carry a baby in a close, bonding manner while keeping your hands free. There are some models designed to accommodate twins and some single models that can be configured to carry twins, or you can use two single slings. Some parents find it too awkward or heavy to carry both babies, especially after they reach a certain weight. But they are relatively inexpensive, and if it affords a workable solution for a few weeks or months with infants, a baby sling may be a worthwhile investment.

Choosing the Right Stroller

The stroller is perhaps the most crucial piece of equipment you will buy as a parent of multiples. Unless you plan to remain confined to your home until your children can walk themselves to school, you will need a good stroller to maneuver them through the world. Many families find that their stroller remains a convenient and safe method of transportation for several years, so it is worth investing in a quality product that will withstand some wear and tear. Think of it as a vehicle for your babies and give your purchase as much consideration as you would if you were buying a family car.

The Stroller Style Debate

Ask any parent of twins about their stroller, and they'll likely give you a passionate response as to why their model is the best choice available. However, there is no one perfect stroller; if there was, everyone would own it! Your perfect stroller is the one that meets your family's needs. If may be that there isn't a single stroller that fits your requirements and you'll want to consider purchasing more than one for different types of outings.

There are two basic styles of strollers. Tandem, or stadium seating, strollers have seats arranged in a straight line, with one behind the other. The seats may both face forward or face each other. Side-by-side strollers, as their name implies, feature two adjacent seats. Each style has advantages and disadvantages, and according to informal polls, parents are pretty evenly split in their preferences.

Tandem Strollers

Tandem double strollers are more readily available because they aren't used exclusively for twins. Most models are actually designed for two singleton siblings. One seat may be a bit roomier or positioned higher to accommodate a toddler or preschool-aged child, while the other space is made for a smaller infant. Because they appeal to a broader market, they are more likely to come with handy accessories such as sunshades, drink holders, and snack trays.

◀ Tandem-style double stroller

Tandems are generally longer and more slender than side-by-side models. For this reason, some people find them easier to maneuver through narrow spaces, such as shopping center aisles and doorways. But there are also aspects of tandem strollers that don't work well with twins. In many models, one of the seats, designed for an older child, does not fully recline. Until your babies' neck muscles develop sufficiently to hold their head up, they need support. An upright seat is useless with younger infants and napping babies.

Side-by-Side Strollers

Side-by-side strollers are a more traditional type of twin stroller. They operate most efficiently with two children of equal weight and provide adequate leg-and headroom for both as they grow. One distinct advantage of the side-by-side style is that it positions both children with an equal viewpoint, which is the arrangement many twins seem to prefer.

Side-by-sides are wider than tandems, but have a shallower profile. That gives the stroller pusher more control and puts the babies in a closer arm's reach. Unfortunately, many parents find their width hard to deal with in crowded or constricted locations, or when they need to go through single doorways or down narrow passageways.

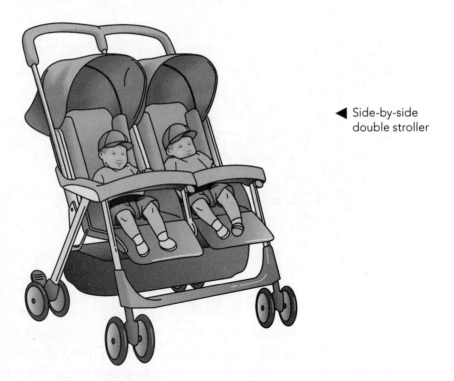

◄ Side-by-side
double stroller

One other potential problem to consider with side-by-side models: They put your twins in full view for the whole world to see. There is no chance of being anonymous! Twins, especially baby twins, attract a lot of attention when you take them out in public. It feels like everyone (especially perfect strangers) wants to look at them, compare their characteristics, interrogate their parents, and relate their own family's history of twinning. If you think that being the center of attention will bother you, minimize it by sticking with a tandem-style stroller. They are more efficient at keeping the babies out of the public eye.

A popular option for fitness-minded families is a jogger-style stroller. With pneumatic tires and heavy-duty frames, these strollers have a single front wheel and are designed for use while running or walking. They generally have larger wheels and perform well on uneven surfaces like trails or paths. Double—or even triple—models often can accommodate larger children, up to a combined weight of 100 pounds or more, giving them more usage years than other strollers. However, some families feel the rugged construction detracts from the practicality. They tend to be bigger and heavier, making them more difficult to store or transport.

Travel Systems

The ability to combine a stroller with an infant carrier has been a popular option in single strollers for years. However, the market has been slower to meet the demand for a travel system stroller for twins. Travel systems are sold as a package, with an infant carrier/car seat that snaps into a base in a vehicle and onto the stroller. With two or more babies and only two hands, the process of transporting babies is much more efficient. The babies remain in the seat from the house, to the car, to the stroller—a huge convenience for parents of multiples.

When evaluating travel system products, be sure that they are specifically designed to accommodate *two* infant seats. Many models are actually designed for an infant and an older child, and can only hold one seat. This small detail, of utmost importance to parents of twins, is not always explicitly advertised; be sure to read the fine print before making a purchase.

However, the concept is not without disadvantages. Because you are purchasing a combination of products, your choices for features are more limited than if you purchased seats and a stroller separately. Most models are tandem-style strollers, so if your heart is set on a side-by-side, you'll have to do some shopping research. Double strollers of this style tend to be bulkier and heavier to allow the frame to accommodate the base for the infant seats. And considering that the usage of infant car seat carriers is limited by weight, your babies will outgrow them in short order, but you'll still be using the stroller for many more years. Does the stroller portion of the travel system have the features you want in the long term? You'll have to decide whether the early convenience of a travel system for babies justifies the need to upgrade your stroller for your toddlers.

◀ Travel system double stroller

ESSENTIAL

Double Decker Stroller, Inc., a company started by a mom of multiples, makes an innovative stroller frame that accommodates infant carriers. The stroller is available in double and triple models. However, such products have a limited lifetime; when your babies outgrow the infant carriers (at twenty pounds or about one year of age), you'll need another stroller.

Choosing the Right Stroller for You

With advantages and disadvantages to all forms of strollers, how can you possibly decide what you need? Should you just get two? While that's often an effective solution to problems faced by parents of twins, it's not necessarily the answer when it comes to strollers. Consider the following when making your decision:

- **How will you use it?** Some strollers can accommodate infants; some are hardier for use with toddlers. Many families with twins find that they rely on a stroller long after their singleton counterparts; for longevity, select a model that is designed for children up to forty pounds.
- **Where will you use it?** All-terrain strollers are wonderful for jogging, hiking, or other outdoor activities, but they aren't very effective at maneuvering through tight indoor spaces such as office buildings or stores.
- **How will you use it?** Consider how your stroller will play a role in your everyday activities. Will you store it in your home? In the car? Will you use it to transport your babies to day care on a daily basis, or only for occasional jaunts to the park? Do you reside in a city location with crowded sidewalks and subways, or a rural environment with open, unpaved surfaces? Your specific circumstances will determine what kind of product will best serve your family.

Ultimately, your budget will also guide your decision. It is possible that your needs can only be met by a combination of multiple products. Perhaps you'll start out with a pricier travel system, but once your babies outgrow the infant seats, you'll find a bargain on a secondhand double jogger stroller. Or, you'll store a lightweight side-by-side umbrella stroller in the car and keep a more heavy-duty tandem stroller at home for jaunts to the park. Some families even make do with two single strollers—as long as there are two people to push them.

Strollers for Triplets or More

If you're expecting triplets or more, your stroller options are more limited, and more costly. You'll have to carefully evaluate how you'll utilize the equipment and anticipate whether the investment is worthwhile. You may wish to consider a combination of single and double strollers or a combination of strollers and other types of carriers, such as a sling or backpack.

Some stroller manufacturers do offer a triplet model, such as the Baby Jogger. This side-by-side model is best for open, outdoor spaces, with three seats that can also accommodate three children of different sizes. The Peg Perego Triplette offers stadium seating in a durable frame and fully reclining sets. Each of these products will set you back nearly $1,000 if purchased new.

Custom-made strollers from Runabout are popular with parents of higher order multiples for their durability and value-added features. They can accommodate up to five children, including infants over ten pounds, with fully adjustable seats and a lightweight frame. They are individually made in the United States, but difficult to locate, and can retail for more than $1,000. But they have excellent resale value and are very much in demand within the multiples community.

More Handy Items for Your Multiples

Other products are a must for multiples, but aren't useful until the babies grow up somewhat. These include walkers or exercise saucers, which are useful for babies older than three months. You can wait to buy these until the babies become more mobile. Bath seats keep older babies secure in the tub; it saves time and effort to bathe multiples together, so plan to have one per child.

Even if you've outfitted your nursery with beautiful cribs, a portable crib, such as a Pack and Play, is a handy item to have when there are more babies than hands. Some products are equipped with bassinettes; you can create a mini-nursery in another part of the house for naptime or quiet time. Use for travel, visits to grandparents, or day care providers. At first, one will suffice, but you may find the need for two as your multiples get older and need their own space, especially if you travel frequently.

Finally, a large playpen or play yard is one of the most recommended pieces of equipment for homes with multiples. A playpen could be used as an alternative to a portable crib if you need a temporary or secondary crib. However, multiple babies soon outgrow the weight limit, just about the time they become mobile and need them the most!

A play yard or designated gated room provides a secure location so that parents can relax and catch their breath. A play yard is a freestanding enclosure, usually composed of sets of interlocking panels. It can be expanded by adding additional panels, accommodating five, six, or more children. Although it's not needed for infants, down the road it will serve many uses and bring much peace of mind.

Before You Buy

- **You're going to need a lot of things for your babies!** But before you invest in double—or triple—of everything, consider what can be shared and what you can borrow. Some things are used only for a short time, while others aren't really necessary until your babies are older and more mobile. There's no need to buy out the baby store right away.

- **Stock up on diapers.** Whether you decide on cloth or disposable diaper options for your babies, you're going to need plenty of them. With multiple babies needing multiple changes every day, diapers are an important commodity. You'll also need to establish an effective system for processing dirty diapers.

- **Whether you breastfeed or bottle feed the babies, you'll need to shop for supplies.** Bottle-fed babies require bottles and formula, but bottles are also necessary for nursing moms who wish to pump and store milk. For both feeding approaches, a Boppy pillow or bouncy seat can prove an effective tool when trying to feed multiple babies at the same time.

- **Car seats are a vital piece of equipment, and every baby needs their own.** Unless you plan on walking and carrying the babies, you'll need car seats to get home from the hospital. There are several varieties, designed for infants, babies, toddlers, and kids, so do your research and carefully consider your safety recommendations as well as manufacturer guidelines before choosing a product.

- **If you're planning to get out and about with your multiples, a good double stroller should top your shopping list.** Double strollers come in two basic styles—side-by-side or tandem—with a few other varieties for special situations. Before you buy a double stroller, which can cost hundreds of dollars, evaluate how and when you'll use it, and find the product that will best suit your lifestyle.

- **Other equipment makes life more manageable as your babies become mobile.** From swings to slings and play yards to portable cribs, there are many baby products that will prove to be a lifesaver when you're juggling multiple babies. Swings and bouncy seats are a pleasant, comfortable place to situate babies when your hands are busy, while walkers and baby gyms provide a source entertainment.

CHAPTER 11

Complications

Sometimes things go wrong. There are a number of complications associated specifically with multiple birth, as well as an increased risk of other disorders that impact pregnancy. Fortunately, if diagnosed in time, many of these conditions can be remedied before the babies are even born, or shortly after birth.

Twin-to-Twin Transfusion Syndrome

Twin-to-twin transfusion syndrome (TTTS) may sound like a plot from a science fiction movie, but it's an actual phenomenon that can occur during a twin pregnancy. Undetected or untreated, it can have devastating consequences for the babies. However, new treatment options give doctors the ability to correct the situation and offer new hope to parents impacted by the disease.

What Is TTTS?

TTTS, also known as feto-fetal transfusion syndrome, parabiotic syndrome, or stuck twin syndrome, is a disease of the placenta. It doesn't make the mother sick, and its effect on the babies is environmental, not direct. In other words, the babies will begin to develop perfectly normally, but because the placenta they depend on to supply oxygen and nutrition malfunctions, they risk heart failure, brain trauma, and damage to their organs.

The placenta circulates blood and nutrients from the mother to her babies. Within a shared placenta, blood vessels called chorioangiopagous vessels may develop, connecting the circulatory systems of both babies via the placenta. This causes an unequal exchange of blood flow between the babies. Essentially, one fetus becomes a donor, pumping blood into the second, recipient fetus. This situation causes problems for both babies, with the donor twin not getting enough blood and the recipient receiving excess.

FACT

As the amount of fluid surrounding the recipient twin increases, the donor twin may be pushed to one side of the uterus. As her fluid levels decrease, she may appear to be stuck to the wall of the womb. Thus, the term *stuck twin syndrome* has been used to describe this condition.

The donor twin is at risk for anemia, intrauterine growth retardation, and restricted amniotic fluid (oligohydramnios). While the donor's growth is stunted, the recipient twin grows larger and larger. The extra blood overloads his circulatory system and puts him at risk for heart failure. As he struggles to process the extra blood, his urine production results in an excess of amniotic fluid (polyhydramnios). Eventually, polyhydramnios can trigger the onset of preterm labor, leaving both babies at risk of being born too early to survive outside the womb.

The timing of the disease ultimately determines the prognosis for the babies. It is easier to overcome later in pregnancy, when the simplest solution is to deliver the babies. Although they may face the consequences of a premature birth, they will escape the threat to their survival that exists if they remain in the womb. However, if the onset of TTTS occurs earlier, before the babies are viable, the situation is more dire, although there are treatment options. There are five stages of TTTS:

- **Stage I:** Small amount of fluid in donor baby, large amount in the recipient
- **Stage II:** Symptoms of Stage I, along with undetectable bladder in the donor twin
- **Stage III:** One or both babies will have evidence of poor blood flow
- **Stage III:** Characterized by hydrops fetalis in either baby (a fluid accumulation that signifies heart failure)
- **Stage IV:** One or both babies have succumbed

When TTTS is detected in the second trimester, it is usually termed chronic or severe. After twenty-four weeks, it is defined as moderate. When it occurs later in the third trimester, it is labeled mild or acute.

Who Gets TTTS?

Not all twins are at risk for the condition. It only affects a percentage of monozygotic twins, those individuals resulting from one egg. Depending on when the egg splits and implants, monozygotic twins may develop individual placentas or share a single placenta. TTTS only occurs when there is a single, shared placenta.

The term *monochorionic* describes twins that are joined in a single chorion, the membrane that attaches to a single placenta. Only monochorionic twins are at risk for TTTS because they are the only type whose circulatory systems may connect through the placenta. Although there has been some speculation that two fused placentas could develop a circulatory connection susceptible to TTTS, researchers of the disease confirm that is simply not feasible.

ALERT

According to the TTTS Foundation, TTTS only affects monozygotic twins. It occurs in about a third of monochorionic pregnancies, or less than 10 percent of all identical twins. If untreated, it has as much as an 80 percent fetal mortality rate.

How Is TTTS Diagnosed?

One of the reasons that a multiple pregnancy is subjected to closer scrutiny is so TTTS can be detected. Doctors use ultrasound to assess the risk by determining the number of placentas. If there is just one, subsequent ultrasounds will follow the babies' growth and development, as well as the amount of amniotic fluid to confirm that it remains equalized.

Doppler ultrasound can study the flow of blood from the placenta through the umbilical cords as well as the circulation through the fetal hearts.

What Can Be Done?

In the past, babies affected by TTTS were doomed. Without ultrasound technology to detect the disorder, it was likely that one or both of the babies would die in utero, or that they would be born too early to survive. Now, not only does sonography enable doctors to diagnose the condition, new treatments allow it to be cured.

Previously, the primary treatment approach was to stave off preterm labor until the babies were viable and could be delivered. This was accomplished by draining the excess fluid surrounding the recipient twin. Amnioreduction, a procedure similar to amniocentesis, was performed at regular intervals to remove fluid from the recipient baby's amniotic sac. While it was generally effective in stabilizing the situation, it carried the same risks as amniocentesis, including infection and miscarriage. It also did not compensate for the damage occurring to the donor twin.

In the 1980s, Dr. Julian De Lia developed an amazing procedure that allows doctors to correct TTTS by using a laser to seal off the connections in the placenta. The procedure is performed while the babies are still in utero, using a fetoscope, a powerful telescope allowing a surgeon to see inside the womb through a tiny incision. A 2004 study confirmed that this procedure, fetoscopic laser coagulation, produces a better outcome for the babies.

Treatment for TTTS depends on how far along you are in your pregnancy and to which stage the disease has progressed. Fetoscopic laser surgery is available in numerous facilities in the United States and throughout the world. The resources listed in Appendix A include contact information for TTTS support and treatment.

"Mo-Mo" Twins: The Danger of Being Monoamniotic

While TTTS is inflicted upon monochorionic twins, another class of monozygotic twins is subjected to even more dangers. Monochorionic/monoamniotic ("mo-mo") twins share not only a placenta, but an amniotic sac as well. They float together in a single encasement of fluid. They develop this way due to the delayed splitting of the egg, usually about eight days post-fertilization, after a single yolk sac has begun to develop.

FACT

Mo-mo is an extremely rare type of twinning, affecting less than 1 percent of all twin pregnancies. It's also a very dangerous situation, as every time the twins move, they jeopardize each other's survival.

Cord entanglement is the primary risk associated with mo-mo twins. Nearly all will experience some tangling of the umbilical cords as they move around in the womb. Entanglement by itself does not harm the babies. However, if the intertwining results in compression of either cord, the babies' supply of blood and nutrients from the placenta can be cut off, resulting in fetal death. Unfortunately, most of the ensnarling occurs in early pregnancy, when the babies still have plenty of room to move around in the uterine environment. And the longer the cords remain entwined, the greater the risk of damage or death to one or both babies.

How Is It Diagnosed?

Like many other conditions in multiple pregnancy, this type of twinning is detected by ultrasound. The presence of a single yolk sac in early pregnancy, same-sex twins, or the lack of a dividing membrane could indicate mo-mo twins. Even a thin or vague membrane could be cause for concern; sometimes late twinning can create a membrane that is so thin or full of holes that the babies are able to breach it. Mo-mo twins are often misdiagnosed if a dividing membrane is not confirmed by ultrasound until the third trimester.

What Can Be Done?

Ultimately, the cure for this condition is to deliver the babies. Parents of mo-mo twins will play a waiting game throughout pregnancy, constantly monitoring the situation until the babies are viable and can be delivered, at some point after twenty-four weeks. While they may suffer the consequences of prematurity, they will no longer be under threat of death in the womb.

Fortunately, cord entanglement usually happens gradually and can be monitored using a Doppler sonogram to measure the blood flow in the umbilical cords. The frequency of scans will depend on your situation; in some cases, constant monitoring requires the mother to be hospitalized for the duration of her pregnancy. Other times, scans will be scheduled at regular intervals, perhaps weekly.

ESSENTIAL

Fortunately, the survival rate for mo-mo babies has increased dramatically in recent years. Improved monitoring techniques allow doctors to respond more quickly in the event of a problem, improving survival rates to nearly 90 percent.

In this situation, delivery by cesarean section is required; even minimal tangling of the cords produces a risk of cord prolapse, a serious condition where the cord of the second baby is extruded as the first baby is delivered. The risks are so high that doctors aren't willing to attempt a vaginal delivery.

High Blood Pressure (Hypertension)

While many complications in multiple pregnancy put the babies at risk, one in particular jeopardizes the mother. Mothers of multiples are particularly susceptible to a group of diseases associated with elevated blood pressure.

Pregnancy Induced Hypertension (PIH)

Increased blood pressure—generally measured as higher than 140 over 90—is common in mothers of multiples. It is treated by reducing activity even to the point of bed rest, and sometimes with medication. Generally, hypertension associated with pregnancy will dissipate as soon as the babies are born, but these women may be at risk for high blood pressure later in life, especially in subsequent pregnancies.

Preeclampsia/Toxemia

A more serious condition affecting mothers of multiples is preeclampsia, also known as toxemia. Less than 10 percent of singleton pregnancies are impacted by preeclampsia, but it is much more common in mothers of multiples. About one in three women expecting twins, triplets, or more will suffer from it during pregnancy. While it is often confused with hypertension, two other symptoms must be present in order for a diagnosis of preeclampsia to be confirmed: edema and elevated protein in the urine.

There is evidence to suggest that a diet rich in certain vitamins, such as vitamin D, can reduce the incidence of preeclampsia in pregnancy. You should discuss the possible benefits of this with your health care provider before taking any dietary supplements.

The elevation in blood pressure inflicts damage to small capillaries, which leak fluid into surrounding tissue and cause edema, or swelling. Most pregnant women experience some degree of swelling, especially in the later months of pregnancy, but edema associated with preeclampsia is characterized by a sudden onset that persists throughout the day. In addition to edema, preeclampsia is characterized by proteinuria, the presence of significant amount of protein in the urine (this signifies kidney malfunction). Preeclampsia can precede a more serious condition, eclampsia, which can lead to seizures, stroke, kidney failure, a ruptured liver, and problems with blood clotting.

Preeclampsia usually affects women in the latter half of pregnancy, but the longer a woman combats it, the greater the potential for complications. There is no cure for the condition; the only remedy is to deliver the babies. Medical caregivers have to weigh the deterioration of the mother's state against the babies' outlook for survival if born early.

Notify your doctor immediately if you experience the symptoms of preeclampsia, including sudden swelling in the hands or face, rapid weight gain, blurred vision, seeing spots, intense headache, or abdominal pain. Generally, at the first sign of symptoms, you'll be advised to restrict your activity or may even be assigned to bed rest. Sometimes medications may be administered, such as antihypertensives or corticosteroids.

HELLP Syndrome

Fifteen percent of women with preeclampsia will develop HELLP syndrome, an abbreviation for hemolysis, elevated liver enzymes, and low platelets. This condition is due to disturbance of the liver's normal function, and mothers with HELLP can die from a ruptured liver if they are not treated. Sometimes the syndrome progresses before the symptoms of preeclampsia are identified, because women can develop HELLP in the absence of hypertension, edema, and protein in the urine. Be sure to report any unusual symptoms to your doctor, such as abdominal pain on the right side, fatigue, nausea, vomiting, or headache. These can be signs of HELLP syndrome.

Gestational Diabetes

Gestational diabetes in pregnancy is not the same as a diagnosis of diabetes outside of pregnancy. Although the disorder is similar—the inability of the body to process glucose (sugar) in the blood—the cause is directly related to pregnancy, and the condition should disappear after delivery. However, it is important to get treatment, because when glucose backs up in the bloodstream, it can damage the mother's organs, and possibly the babies' as well.

Gestational diabetes occurs two to three times more often in multiple pregnancy than in singleton pregnancies. The increase is likely due to the additional hormones produced when there are extra babies; hormones can interfere with the body's ability to process the insulin produced by the pancreas.

ESSENTIAL

Most health care providers routinely screen for gestational diabetes during pregnancy. A glucose challenge test is usually administered toward the end of the second trimester or early in the third.

If you are diagnosed with gestational diabetes during your pregnancy with multiples, you will need to alter your diet. In some cases, gestational diabetes may be controlled with lifestyle and nutrition management, but if your case does not respond, you may require injections of insulin for the duration of your pregnancy. Gestational diabetes may increase your risk of preterm birth or put the babies at risk for jaundice, respiratory distress, or hypoglycemia after birth, so it is important to manage it.

Placenta Problems

The placenta plays a vital role in pregnancy, delivering nutrients and oxygen to the babies and removing their waste. In a multiple pregnancy, each baby may have his own placenta, or two babies may share a single placenta. Either way, if something goes wrong, the babies' survival is at stake.

Placenta Previa

When the placenta implants low in the uterus, covering the cervical opening, it's called placenta previa. The chances of this happening are increased when a uterus has to accommodate two or more placentas. While placenta previa does not pose a risk to the babies' development, it may cause vaginal bleeding toward the conclusion of the pregnancy, as the cervix begins to dilate and open. Bed rest may help the bleeding subside by decreasing the amount of pressure on the placenta. In extreme cases, the mother may require a blood transfusion to prevent excess blood loss. Usually she will have to deliver the babies via cesarean section.

Abruptio Placentae

Sometimes the placenta begins to detach prematurely from the wall of the uterus, a condition called abruptio placentae. While it can be caused by trauma to the abdominal region, it can also be instigated by other conditions that are common in multiple pregnancy, such as high blood pressure. The detachment may be mild and partial, happening slowly over time, or complete and sudden. Pain and bleeding usually accompanies complete abruption; this requires immediate delivery of the babies by C-section. In more mild cases, doctors will closely monitor the pregnancy to determine the best option for the babies, weighing the consequences of early delivery. Bed rest may be recommended.

FACT

Placental abruptions are three times more common in a multiple pregnancy due to the increased stretching of the uterus as it expands to accommodate the extra babies.

Hemorrhage

Mothers of multiples have an increased risk of hemorrhage, or uncontrolled bleeding, during their pregnancy or following delivery. Several factors contribute to the risk:

- A uterus that is stretched and strained by accommodating additional babies
- A greater portion of the surface area of the uterus is covered by placental tissue
- An increased chance of undergoing cesarean section

Usually, the only consequence is heavier postpartum bleeding following delivery, but occasionally severe, uncontrolled bleeding puts the mother's health at risk. If postpartum bleeding is so heavy that you soak through a sanitary pad in less than an hour, seek medical attention. Additional signs of hemorrhage include bright red bleeding that lingers a week after delivery, vaginal discharge with a foul odor, or discharge that includes blood clots larger than an inch in diameter.

Intrauterine Growth Restriction (IUGR)

Multiples are particularly at risk for intrauterine growth restriction (IUGR), also known as intrauterine growth retardation. Essentially, this very wordy terminology is used to describe a small baby, a baby that is not growing at a "normal" rate according to standardized charts. Babies with IUGR are identified when they are below the tenth percentile on growth charts. IUGR occurs in more than a quarter of twin pregnancies, much more often than in the general population of singleton births, where the occurrence is only 6 percent.

What Causes IUGR?

IUGR can occur as a result of other conditions particular to a multiple birth, such as TTTS, preeclampsia, or a shared placenta. But sometimes just the fact that there is more than one baby competing for resources in the womb causes the restriction in growth. IUGR is the second leading cause of death in infants.

QUESTION

What's the difference between IUGR, SGA, and LBW?
IUGR refers to a baby who has not reached his growth potential because of some medical problem. An SGA (small for gestational age) baby is simply a small baby, growing to his full potential. LBW (low birth weight) is the term used to describe babies after birth, while IUGR and SGA refer to babies while they're still in the womb.

IUGR is defined in three ways:

- **Symmetric IUGR:** The baby's weight, head circumference, and abdominal circumference are all below the tenth percentile; usually attributable to an abnormality or infection.

- **Asymmetric IUGR:** The baby's weight is below the tenth percentile, but the head circumference and body length measure greater than the tenth percentile. It is usually caused by severe placental insufficiency.
- **Combined type IUGR:** The baby may have skeletal shortening and some reduction of soft tissue mass.

IUGR can impact one or all of the babies in a multiple pregnancy. When only one baby is affected, it is sometimes referred to as growth discordance.

What Can Be Done?

IUGR puts babies at risk for stillbirth and neonatal death. Often, the only option for treatment is to deliver the affected baby, or babies. They will be impacted by the usual complications associated with preterm birth, but can be treated for them. The effects of IUGR can follow the babies, even after birth. They're at risk for many long-term neurological and behavioral handicaps that may not surface until many years later. They are often hypoglycemic, and have weak muscle tone and poor circulation. Thirty percent of babies who succumb to SIDS (sudden infant death syndrome) had IUGR.

You can take some steps toward preventing IUGR from impacting your babies. Maternal nutrition is crucial. Eating healthy foods, and plenty of them, provides the energy that your babies need to grow adequately. Maternal tobacco use is a leading cause of IUGR, so it goes without saying that you should stay away from cigarettes. Finally, getting plenty of rest can also help. When you rest, nutrients will pass more easily to the babies, who utilize every calorie to grow and develop. While you can't absolutely prevent IUGR in a multiple pregnancy, there is no doubt that taking tiptop care of yourself is the best way to protect your babies.

When Things Get Complicated

- **A multiple pregnancy is vulnerable to numerous conditions that can cause complications for mom or babies.** The condition of carrying more than one baby causes an increased risk for some medical issues, but with careful monitoring and medical attention, a positive outcome is generally possible.

- **Twin-to-twin transfusion syndrome is a disease of the placenta that impacts monochorionic twins.** Crossed signals between blood vessels in a shared placenta causes one twin to become a "donor" to the other, putting both at risk. Fetoscopic laser surgery can help resolve the problem, but ultimately delivery of the babies is the only cure for TTTS.

- **Monochorionic/Monoamniotic ("mo-mo") twins share both a placenta and an amniotic sac.** This risky condition affects monozygotic twins when the egg splits later in the gestational cycle. Encased in a single sac of fluid, every movement puts the twins at risk for cord entanglement, potentially cutting off their supply of oxygen and nutrients. The condition can be monitored via ultrasound, and the babies can be delivered early if conditions deteriorate dangerously in the womb.

- **In a womb designed for one baby, the demands of a multiple pregnancy can restrict the babies' growth.** Intrauterine growth restriction (IUGR) can affect one or all the babies in a multiple pregnancy, and can result in developmental problems even after birth. However, pregnant mothers can reduce the risk of IUGR by optimizing the uterine environment with good nutrition and ample rest and avoiding harmful substances like tobacco.

- **Some of the complications of a multiple pregnancy put mom at risk as well as the babies.** Gestational diabetes and hypertension that results from carrying multiples can be potentially harmful to a woman. Routine screening for these conditions should be a part of standard prenatal care in a multiple pregnancy.

- **The placenta is an important structure in pregnancy, providing a lifeline of nutrients and blood as the babies develop in the womb.** In a multiple pregnancy, there may be a single, shared placenta or one placenta for each baby. The placenta(s) in a multiple pregnancy covers a greater area of the interior wall of the uterus, creating greater risk for conditions such as placenta previa (covering the cervical opening) or abruptio placentae (detachment of the placenta).

CHAPTER 12

Bed Rest

One of the greatest ironies of multiple birth is that you spend most of your pregnancy trying to avoid bed rest, but once the babies arrive, you crave it! Some form of bed rest is a reality for the majority of mothers of multiples during their pregnancy. It can be an important tool in keeping the developing babies healthy and preventing preterm labor. In the event that your doctor recommends bed rest, it's important to understand the ramifications of your situation.

What Bed Rest Accomplishes

Historically, bed rest has been a common treatment for a variety of pregnancy ailments. With fewer side effects than drugs, it can prevent or diminish many problems that would otherwise result in the loss of one or all of the babies. When you're carrying multiples, the goal is to keep them in your womb as long as possible in order to ensure optimal health and development. Usually women carrying higher order multiples have a greater chance of going on bed rest, have to stay on bed rest for a longer period of time, and have to endure a stricter regimen of bed rest than mothers of singletons.

As the pregnancy progresses, the combined weight of the babies strains the cervix. Gravity increases the pressure. Alleviating the pull of gravity and the pressure on the cervix can help prolong the pregnancy. Both of these goals can be accomplished by staying off your feet and lying horizontally in bed.

At one time it was considered prudent to routinely prescribe bed rest in a multiple pregnancy; bed rest at twenty-eight weeks was the standard recommendation for moms of multiples. Fortunately, that's not the case now. Most doctors acknowledge the emotional and psychological toll on the family of a pregnant woman, as well as potential physical deterioration for the mother.

FACT

About 20 percent of pregnancies require bed rest, or about 700,000 women per year. However, it's much more likely in a multiple pregnancy.

Blood Pressure Benefits

Another common problem in multiple pregnancy is hypertension, or high blood pressure. It can be a symptom of preeclampsia, a serious disorder that, if left untreated, can be fatal for the mother and the babies. Bed rest can be effective in lowering pregnancy by taking the pressure of the uterus off the vena cava, a large vein that runs along the right side of the body. Usually mothers who are undergoing bed rest to reduce the blood pressure are advised to lie on their left side to improve circulation.

Placating the Placenta

Dizygotic or multizygotic multiples each have their own placenta, maximizing the surface area of the uterus that is covered by placental matter. This increases the chances of complications, including placenta previa, a condition that occurs when the placenta covers the cervix. The resulting hemorrhage can be dangerous for the mother and impede development of the babies. Bed rest and reduced activity can help diminish the bleeding.

Bed rest also allows more blood and oxygen to flow to the placenta(s), enhancing the growth of the babies. If you're experiencing complications such as preterm labor or placenta previa and your babies will likely be delivered early, a period of bed rest accompanied by treatment with steroids may give them a developmental boost.

ALERT

Be wary if your doctor routinely prescribes bed rest at a particular point in the pregnancy without regard for your individual circumstances. Except in the case of extreme higher order multiples, bed rest should not be mandated without specific conditions that necessitate it.

Good for Mom

Although bed rest is usually prescribed to benefit the babies, it can be just as beneficial to the mother's well-being. A multiple pregnancy places a tremendous strain on the mother's organs, which work overtime to keep up with the demands of nurturing multiple fetuses. Sometimes rest and relaxation in bed is required to minimize a mother's activity and give her body a break. Often, bed rest becomes a last resort for women who can't seem to slow down otherwise.

What to Expect

Every expectant mother of multiples should be aware of the possibility of bed rest during her pregnancy. Although there are plenty of women—especially mothers of twins—who never have a reason to go on bed rest during their pregnancy, you should still be prepared for the eventuality. Awareness and preparation will make the experience much more manageable if it does happen.

Suddenly Finding Yourself in Bed

Often confinement comes unexpectedly. Perhaps you visited your doctor for a routine checkup and were ordered to bed. Or you rushed to the hospital with symptoms of preterm labor and were admitted. Once you're assigned to bed, it may be too late to make arrangements, and you'll have to scramble to provide coverage for work, family, and other commitments. Usually bed rest becomes a reality later in the pregnancy, but don't assume that it only happens in the third trimester. Many mothers of multiples may experience bed rest in the second, or even first, trimester.

Bed rest may be a temporary measure to stabilize a condition, or it may be prescribed for the duration of your pregnancy. The level of confinement may be adjusted as your condition changes. Your restrictions may even be lifted if you surpass the crucial number of gestational weeks and are able to deliver full-term babies.

Bed Rest for Preterm Labor

If you are experiencing preterm labor, your rest may be combined with uterine monitoring to detect contractions. You may also be given medication to reduce contractions and/or accelerate the babies' development.

FACT

The evidence is mixed as to whether monitoring is an effective tool for preventing premature birth. Some feel that it is useful in identifying patterns of contractions, while others argue that it causes needless inconvenience and worrying over false alarms.

It's important to fully understand what your doctor expects of you so that you can comply with the orders. Ask questions to clarify anything that you're unsure about. Rebelling against your doctor's advice only endangers your babies, or even your own health. Don't be a martyr. Pushing the limits at home may result in bed rest at the hospital where your doctors can enforce the limitations.

Lying Low

Lying around isn't exactly a bed of roses. Being inactive for an extended period of time can have a negative impact on your body. Weight loss, weakened muscle tone, loss of muscle mass, bone deterioration, and blood clots are all common consequences of bed rest. The general weakness that results may hinder your recovery after delivery and leave you ill-equipped to care for the babies when they arrive.

The psychological toll of bed rest is also a factor to consider. Feelings of anxiety, frustration, and depression are common. Boredom is rampant. Isolation from family, friends, and the workplace only increases the emotional distress. Because a mother's emotional state has a great bearing on her physical well-being, these feelings must be acknowledged and dealt with as conscientiously as her medical condition.

Partial Versus Full Bed Rest

There are various levels of bed rest. Your condition will determine which type is most beneficial for your babies. Recommendations for your situation may vary throughout your pregnancy, depending on your health and the status of the babies.

Often the first stage is decreased or reduced activity. Your doctor may recommend this regardless of condition, simply to give your body a chance to rest from its work of nurturing multiple babies. Or you may voluntarily cut back on your schedule as your pregnancy progresses and you start feeling more tired or out of sorts. You'll probably be advised to avoid heavy lifting, strenuous exercise, or anything that causes you to exert yourself. This is a time to slow down and take it easy. Spend some time each day with your feet up, or fit a nap into your daily schedule.

Partial Bed Rest

The least restrictive form of actual bed rest is partial bed rest, also called modified or moderate bed rest. The amount of time spent lying down can vary widely. You may be advised to spend a certain number of hours in bed each day or, conversely, you may be allotted a specified amount of time out of bed. Every individual's circumstance is unique; some women are able to continue working and running the household, but most will need to make adjustments to their lifestyle. Your doctor will advise you as to your exact limitations.

Be sure you check with your doctor about allowable activities when you're out of bed. They may be restricted to basic necessities, such as bathing or eating. Other situations may permit short errands and quiet activity around the house. Depending on your condition, you may need to spend the majority of your lying-down time on your left side. If you prefer, you may be able to fulfill this type of bed rest on a couch during the daytime hours, rather than a bed, so that you can be more accessible to the household.

ALERT

Because partial bed rest leaves you with a lot of freedom to control your activity, it's important that you not overdo it. Ask your doctor for explicit instructions as to what is allowed or discouraged.

Complete Bed Rest

Complete bed rest is the strictest level. You'll be required to remain in bed twenty-four hours a day. (If you're lucky, you'll be allowed to get up to use the restroom.) Spending all your time in bed can be a grueling experience. Not only are you prevented from caring for your family, but you will require assistance for your own basic needs. It is likely that you will have to give up work for the time being, unless your job is such that you can work exclusively via phone or laptop computer. Even that may prove difficult if your condition necessitates that you lie in a particular position. Visits to the doctor for checkups are the only respite from this type of bed rest, and even those may be restricted.

Know Why You're in Bed

Whichever level of bed rest that you are assigned, be sure that you understand the reason behind it, and the goal or outcome. Are you trying to maintain your blood pressure? Minimize contractions? If you feel that your doctor is being overly cautious in prescribing bed rest, discuss your concerns. You may be able to negotiate a compromise that satisfies your doctor's conditions but still allows you freedom to do the things you want to do.

Hospitalization for Bed Rest

In extreme situations, you may find yourself confined to bed in the hospital. Sometimes this occurs at the onset of symptoms, before even needing home bed rest. Other times, it is the final result of a bed rest trial at home that simply isn't working. While a period of hospitalization may be stressful and inconvenient, there are also some advantages to being cared for in a professional setting.

It's Not All Bad

Being admitted to the hospital during your pregnancy with multiples can be terrifying. It may feel like a prison sentence. You'll likely feel a disturbing loss of control over your life, anxiety about the outcome of your pregnancy, and a fair amount of panic about the responsibilities you've left undone at home or work.

On the other hand, being admitted to the hospital can be reassuring. You can turn over responsibility for your babies' health to professionals. It is comforting to know that you are in the best possible place if anything goes wrong. If you've been on bed rest at home, it may be a relief to have caregivers available to attend to your needs, such as bringing meals or helping you use the toilet. With external circumstances out of your control, you can just lie back (or however you're instructed to lie!), relax, and focus on nurturing the babies inside you.

ESSENTIAL

You'll need to inform your place of employment about your hospital confinement as soon as possible. Depending on your job situation, your absence may be covered by maternity leave, disability leave, or sick leave. Be upfront and honest with your employer about your situation. Pass along any information you have from the doctors as to the timeline of your confinement.

The Comforts of Home

In most cases, you won't have a lot of time to plan for hospitalization. You'll have to rely on your partner, friends, or relatives to cover the details you've left behind until you can make arrangements. Ask someone to bring some things from home that will help make your stay more comfortable.

- Loose-fitting, comfortable maternity clothes for daytime
- Loose-fitting, comfortable pajamas for nighttime
- Slippers or socks
- Comfort items from your bed at home, such as a pillow and blanket
- Toiletries and hair care items
- Pictures from home that make you happy
- Water bottle
- Entertainment: books, magazines, puzzles, crafts, laptop or tablet
- Cell phone charger
- iPod or music player

If you have other children at home, you'll have to arrange for their care in your absence. If the designated caregiver is your spouse, this can be a difficult position for both parents. Fathers may feel torn between their obligations at home and their desire to comfort their wife in the hospital. There may be financial concerns if both parents have to miss work due to the hospitalization.

Surviving Off Your Feet

For the sake of your babies, you have to make the best of bed rest in order to endure it. There are many ways to make the experience more tolerable as you pass the time. It can even be a productive and enjoyable time as you await the arrival of your babies.

Attitude Adjustment

With your physical self temporarily out of commission, you'll have to rely on your mental abilities to gain control of your situation. Your attitude toward your situation can make a huge difference in how you tolerate it.

Stress, frustration, and anxiety only serve to make physical problems worse. Adjust your mindset by accepting your circumstances and acknowledging that this temporary confinement will provide the best possible start in life for your precious babies.

Put your situation in perspective. Remember, this is temporary. No one remains pregnant forever. Eventually, the babies will be born and you'll be back on your feet. It may seem unbelievable now, but there will come a day when you'll wish for a few hours alone in bed.

FACT

Prayer, meditation, and relaxation techniques will help you cope with the anxiety and worry. Fill your mind with peaceful, positive images. Play pleasant background music, read lighthearted material, or watch funny movies.

Finally, view your bed rest as an assignment, or a goal, that can be accomplished one step at a time. Get through just one hour at a time, and eventually the hours become days, and the days become weeks. Every extra moment that you give your babies in the womb is beneficial to their development.

Creating a Restful Environment

Once you have your mindset in the right perspective, enlist some help in setting up your "workstation"—the place where you'll perform the work of surviving bed rest. Designate a spot in the house where you can position all your supplies within arm's reach. You'll want plenty of healthy snacks and water on hand. Books, magazines, and craft projects help pass the time, if you can concentrate on them. Electronic equipment, remote controls, and chargers should be easily accessible.

ESSENTIAL

A cooler is a very handy accessory next to your bed. Keep it stocked with nutritious snacks and drinks. Even though your body is not physically active, you need to keep your calorie and fluid intake high.

Creating structure within your day will make the time pass faster. Stick with a routine similar to your normal daily schedule. Get cleaned up and dressed every morning. Brush your hair and put on makeup. Even though you're not going out, you might be welcoming visitors and you'll feel better physically if you look presentable. Wear comfortable maternity clothes, not ratty pajamas. Eat meals and snacks at regularly scheduled times; it will give you something to look forward to! Open the blinds or windows to let the sunshine in each morning and close them when it's dark to signal your body that it's nighttime and time to sleep.

Bed rest is not intended to be one long series of naps. Ask your doctor to define how much sleep you should be getting and try to keep yourself "active" the rest of the day. Talk to your doctor about any exercise that is safe for you to do in bed or, if you're on modified bed rest, appropriate exercise when you're out of bed. While you don't want to do any activity that would jeopardize your condition, there may be some allowable exercises that will help prevent muscle loss.

Exercise that involves the core muscles isn't advisable, since the stimulation may trigger contractions in the uterus. But light weight-bearing exercises can help maintain strength and flexibility in the arms and upper body. For the lower body, light stretching and movement can condition joints and help prevent blood clots. While many doctors discourage exercise during bed rest, others are acknowledging the benefits and may even be able to refer you for services from a physical therapist for specific assistance.

Staying Involved

Despite being confined to bed, you're not useless. Being productive will help you feel less incapacitated. Find ways that you can participate in your family's lifestyle or a way that you can contribute to chores. For example, you may be able to fold laundry, help children with their homework, research recipes for meals, pay bills online, or even shop for groceries via the Internet. Undertaking a responsibility will give you a sense of purpose and ease your frustration about not being able to care for your household in the normal manner.

Bed rest may cause you to miss out on some of the milestones of pregnancy: your baby shower, shopping for baby supplies, and childbirth education classes. If you weren't able to accomplish these earlier in your pregnancy, you may still be able to experience them. It just takes bit of creative planning. Find out if your childbirth educator can provide a video about labor and delivery that you can watch online or at home. Contact the local mothers of multiples club to find out what educational resources they can provide from their learning library. If you can tolerate the stimulation, you can even preside over a baby shower in your bedroom; you'll just have to ask your guests to bring the party to you!

Use your time wisely. Enjoy the relative peace and quiet that precedes the addition of multiples to a family. Bond with your babies before they're born. You can read to them and sing to them; studies have proven that babies hear voices from inside the womb. Compose a letter for each baby to be given to them at a later date. Organize your family's photos into albums or scrapbooks. Write a blog to document your experience and share your updates with friends and family (or a wider readership, if you don't mind a public audience). Start preparing baby books for each of the babies. If you have sewing or craft skills, create a gift for each baby, such as a crocheted blanket or hat.

FACT

The wonder of modern technology means that you can accomplish a great deal, right from your cell phone or laptop computer. The isolation of bed rest can be overcome with social networking, video chats, and access to a plethora of programming, for information or entertainment.

Although bed rest adds a frustrating and anxious element to a multiple pregnancy, it can be an important preservation tool for the babies. You'll all make it through just fine if you employ a positive outlook, rely on plenty of outside help, and comply with your doctor's orders.

Bed Rest Basics

- **There are two kinds of bed rest: partial and full.** In partial bed rest you may only have to spend a few hours each day lying down in bed and the rest of the day you can still do moderate activities. Full bed rest is more confining, requiring you to stay in bed twenty-four hours a day.

- **Being assigned to bed rest may come unexpectedly.** As a mother of multiples you should always be prepared for the possibility of bed rest. Your doctor may order you to bed after a period of fatigue or stress or you may have a sudden complication like bleeding. Have contingency plans ready for your work, home, and the care of your other children in the event that you are suddenly ordered off your feet.
- **Lying in bed all day will lose its luster pretty fast.** Being inactive can have a negative impact on your body and your mind. Boredom, isolation, anxiety, and frustration are common among moms on bed rest.
- **Try to stay as active and involved as possible.** Being stuck in bed doesn't mean you can't still be a part of your family. Perhaps you could fold some laundry or help one of your children with their homework, or do grocery shopping online. There are many tasks you can do safely from your bed that will help you feel like you are still a contributing member to the family.
- **The key to surviving bed rest is adjusting your attitude toward it.** Stress and anxiety will only make the situation worse. Remember that pregnancy and bed rest are only temporary and your sacrifice is for the good of your babies.
- **Fight isolation with technology.** Unlike mothers of the past, you have the ability to stay connected with your friends, family, and even your job through the power of technology. Chat with friends on social networking sites, blog about your babies or even your bed rest, join support groups for mothers of multiples. Technology can help you feel more useful and less alone, so take advantage of it.

CHAPTER 13

Preterm Labor

From the moment you found out you were having multiples, you were likely warned about the risks of preterm labor. It's a problem that affects more than half of twin pregnancies and nearly all higher order multiples. While not every mother-to-be will experience the symptoms of preterm labor, it's very important for everyone to understand the signs in order to get effective help in the event it occurs.

Why Preterm Labor Is a Concern

Preterm labor, or the onset of cervical dilation before a baby is considered full term, is a major source of concern because it can lead to premature delivery. The fact that preterm labor is more prevalent in multiple pregnancy makes it a focus of concern for any expectant mother of twins or more. It's important to look at the true definition of preterm labor in context. Preterm labor is defined as labor that begins before a baby is thirty-seven weeks old. A normal singleton gestation is usually considered to last forty weeks. However, opinions vary on the optimal gestation for multiples. Some define full term as thirty-seven or thirty-eight weeks for twins, and thirty-six weeks for higher order multiples. (There is even some evidence to indicate that carrying babies past thirty-eight weeks in a multiple pregnancy can pose risks to the mother's health.)

ESSENTIAL

Mothers of twins are almost five times more likely to experience preterm labor than a singleton mother. For higher order multiples, the chances are even higher. However, preterm labor doesn't always result in disaster. Learning about the reality of preterm labor and premature birth should be a lesson in preparation and prevention, not a source of alarm and worry.

So when you see the claims about the high percentage of multiple pregnancies that encounter preterm labor, realize that these cases occur over a vast period of time during the nine months of pregnancy. It may occur as early as the second trimester, with severe consequences, or relatively late in the pregnancy—up to thirty-seven weeks—producing full-term, completely healthy babies.

However, the dangers can't be denied. Preterm labor can lead to premature birth. Despite amazing advances in medical technology, babies born too early simply can't survive outside the womb. You'll find more details about the impact of prematurity in Chapter 16. The simple fact is that preterm birth is the leading cause of neonatal death, and preemies who do survive may face a lifetime of medical problems.

Medical providers focus heavily on raising awareness about preterm labor because, if caught in time, it can be stopped or delayed. Heightened awareness about the risks may prompt a mother to take action and get medical attention sooner rather than later. While it's not always possible to halt preterm labor, in some cases quick medical reaction can increase the chances of success.

Causes of Preterm Labor

The causes of preterm labor are varied and not always identifiable. Certainly if the exact cause was known, treatment to prevent it would be developed. In a normal pregnancy, hormones signal the body to go into labor when the baby is ready to be born. In order for labor to occur, two things must happen:

- Regular coordinated contractions of the uterus
- Changes in the cervix, including effacement (thinning) and dilation (opening)

With preterm labor, something triggers a physiological miscommunication, and the labor process begins too early. In a multiple pregnancy, any number of factors can ignite the process.

Physical Causes

There are several physical factors that contribute to the onset of preterm labor. One factor that can trigger the uterus to begin contracting is its size. Clearly, that's one reason why mothers of multiples are more prone to preterm labor. When a uterus contains more than one baby, it is going to expand to a greater size more quickly! But if that was the only trigger for preterm labor, then all mothers of twins or more would deliver early, and that's certainly not the case.

While we tend to think of a mother's womb as a tender and nurturing place, some factors can make it irritable or hostile. In response, it begins to contract, resulting in the onset of preterm labor. Some experts believe that a lack of circulation is a leading cause. Physical exertion, and even simply standing upright, causes the uterus to settle on top of the arteries and veins that exist along the pelvis. The increasing weight of the babies compresses the arteries, reducing blood flow and hampering circulation. This problem is obviously worsened by the added weight of multiple babies, but it can also be influenced by the shape of the uterus.

FACT

The daughters of women who took DES during their pregnancy are particularly plagued by a uterine deformation that can cause preterm labor. DES (diethylstilbestrol) was a drug given to women in the middle of the twentieth century to prevent miscarriage, but was found to cause birth defects.

Infection can also cause a response from the uterus. Expectant mothers of multiples need to be especially wary of infections of their genitals and urological system. Report any signs of kidney or urinary tract infections to your doctor.

The uterus isn't the only culprit in the battle against preterm labor. Remember, the cervix plays an equally important role in the labor process. The cervix is the opening between the uterus and the vagina, and if it malfunctions by starting its job too early, it can be the cause of preterm labor. During pregnancy, it should remain tightly closed, keeping the babies in and everything else out! But sometimes it starts the process of thinning out and opening up too early. This is referred to as an incompetent cervix, and although it can happen to any woman, the added strain of a multiple pregnancy can contribute to the condition. The good news is that an incompetent cervix can be treated. Unfortunately, however, it often isn't discovered until it's too late to prevent delivery.

ALERT

Don't let the scary statistics convince you that preterm labor is in your future. For a good proportion of twin pregnancies, it's not an issue at all. Be prepared and informed, but don't adopt a negative mindset by assuming that it will happen to you.

The womb is a complicated system. Sometimes, even though the uterus and cervix behave appropriately, other malfunctions may produce the onset of labor. Weakened amniotic membranes, problems with the placenta, or the presence of fibroids are a few of the more common conditions. In addition, one or all of the babies may be the source of the mixed signals. Congenital defects, more common in multiples than singletons, often trigger an early onset of labor.

Environmental Causes

In addition to the numerous physical conditions that exist, there are several environmental impacts that can trigger preterm labor. Some of them are modifiable or avoidable, while others are simply inherent risks of heredity or lifestyle. Sometimes these factors are intensified in a multiple pregnancy.

Preterm labor may occur as a result of an accident that causes trauma to the mother's abdomen. An auto accident or a fall down the stairs is always unfortunate, but during pregnancy such an incident can have a devastating impact on the babies. While you can't prevent accidents, you can minimize your risk by being extra cautious during pregnancy and avoiding dangerous situations.

FACT

Although it may cause contractions, sexual intercourse is not usually a cause of preterm labor. Unless your medical provider advises you to refrain from sex, don't let fear of preterm labor keep you from intimacy.

Opinions are mixed on whether stress causes preterm labor, but emotional upheaval has been proven to have a negative impact on pregnancy. Some theorize that emotional strain increases the level of corticotropin-releasing hormone (CRH), which can prompt the release of prostaglandin, ultimately triggering contractions. At any rate, studies clearly show a connection between stressed-out mothers and low-birth-weight babies. While reducing stress may not prevent preterm labor, it can enhance your babies' development, improving their odds in the event they do arrive ahead of schedule.

Many environmental risk factors associated with lifestyle can be modified or alleviated, especially if the mother makes changes before becoming pregnant. Women who are either overweight or underweight have an elevated risk of experiencing preterm labor, so good nutrition before conception is important. Smoking, drinking alcohol, and using illegal drugs all vastly increase the levels of risk, not just of preterm labor but also for a host of other problems and complications.

Ways to Reduce Your Risk

So you accept the fact that there's a chance that your twins, triplets, or more could come early. Is there anything you can do to improve your odds? Although no one can eliminate the risk, there are some things that you can do—or not do—to take control of your pregnancy.

What Not to Do

The duration of your pregnancy is less than a year, and you want it to last as long as possible to ensure the health of your babies. So during those months while you're expecting, take time off from any activities that might increase your risk of preterm labor. Certainly any strenuous or dangerous sports are out of the question. But even moderate activity can aggravate the conditions that prompt preterm labor when you're carrying two or more. Use good judgment about your behavior and avoid exertion.

As you go further along in your pregnancy, avoid lifting anything heavy. You probably won't mind being excused from hefting around the vacuum cleaner or toting packages, but this can be a difficult assignment if you have other children, especially young toddlers who want to be held or carried. When you do have to lift something, be sure to use proper posture to avoid strain. Keep your cool in the summertime, when heat and humidity run rampant. The risk of preterm labor increases with the temperature since your body is more likely to be stressed when it is overheated.

What to Do

Diet and nutrition can have a big impact on the outcome of your pregnancy. While there's no magic menu that will keep you out of harm's way, you can actively contribute to your babies' health by eating healthfully and amply. Sufficient calorie intake helps your babies grow and develop, preventing intrauterine growth restriction (IUGR) and low birth weight. In the event that they are born early, they'll stand a much better chance of survival.

Drink plenty of water. The link between dehydration and contractions is clear and unmistakable. Dehydration causes contractions. Rehydration can sometimes stop them. Drink your fill of water every day to keep the contractions at bay.

Give your body the rest it needs. In a multiple pregnancy, gravity is working against you. Taking time off your feet alleviates pressure on your pelvis. Follow your provider's guidelines for rest. Aside from physically resting, it's also important to relax mentally. Emotional stress can aggravate preterm labor. When you get angry or upset, your hormones go into high gear, elevating your blood pressure and heart rate. That diverts circulation from your uterus, which may start contracting in response.

Learn to monitor contractions. If you've had a previous pregnancy, you are probably familiar with the tightening sensation, but even so, they can be harder to discern in multiple pregnancy when the uterus is stretched more tautly. You may need assistance from a home uterine activity monitoring unit (HUAM), which your doctor must prescribe. Make it part of your routine to track and record the timing and duration of any contractions, and communicate with your caregiver about your findings, especially if you experience more than four contractions per hour.

Some doctors recommend weekly injections of progesterone, a female hormone, for the prevention of preterm labor. While studies have found this approach effective in reducing the incidence of preterm birth in singletons, the evidence doesn't support its effectiveness for twin pregnancies. Regardless, some doctors pursue progesterone therapy for their patients with multiples. If your doctor suggests this approach, be sure to discuss the risks and benefits.

Finally, education and awareness are two of your strongest weapons against preterm labor. Understand the signs so that you can recognize them if they happen to you. Stay in close contact with your medical provider. Attend all scheduled prenatal visits. Follow recommendations and don't push the envelope if you are assigned limitations. Report any suspicious symptoms, even if it's just a feeling that something's not quite right.

Signs of Preterm Labor

How will you know if preterm labor starts during your pregnancy with multiples? There are some clues, but they might not be obvious until it's too late to stop a delivery. That's why it is so vitally important to know the signals and to contract your medical provider as soon as you suspect something.

Contractions

Sometimes preterm labor is silent. Many women don't realize that their body is undermining their pregnancy until it's too late—or rather, too early for their premature babies. You won't feel an incompetent cervix dilating or effacing. You may not even feel contractions, especially if you've never been pregnant before.

The uterus contracts throughout pregnancy. These irregular, "practice" contractions are called Braxton Hicks contractions and they can start as early as the second trimester. As the body readies for labor and delivery, however, the timing, regularity, and intensity of the contractions will increase.

ESSENTIAL

It is the pattern and frequency of the contractions that can signal that labor is imminent. Occasional or irregular contractions are normal. Recurring contractions at a rate of more than four per hour are cause for concern and require further monitoring.

Know Your Body

Women experience contractions in different ways; they may produce a sensation of pain, hardening, pressure, heaviness, tightening, or cramping. They may be felt in the abdomen, pelvis, and lower back, or even the upper thighs. You'll have to spend some time getting to know your body to understand how the contractions will be manifested in your multiple pregnancy. The best way to tune into contractions is to lie quietly on your left side. Put your hands on your belly. You may feel protruding baby parts, such as a head, elbow, or rear end. These will feel hard and bumpy; feel for a softer spot so that you can feel your uterus and not the movement of the babies. At rest, your uterus will feel soft and fleshy, but when contracted, it will be tight and hard, like a flexed muscle.

Suspicious Signs

The following symptoms and situations should be reported to your caregiver:

- More than four or five contractions per hour
- Rhythmic or persistent pelvic pressure
- Cramps, similar to menstrual cramping
- Backache

ALERT

Don't ignore the signs. Your body may be trying to tell you that something is wrong. A prompt response may buy you extra time, crucial time for your babies to develop and grow.

While contractions are the main indicator of preterm labor, you can't count on them to let you know what's going on. There are some other signs that indicate that labor is already in progress. Should you experience the following, notify your doctor immediately:

- Diarrhea
- Vaginal bleeding or discharge
- Uneasy sense that something is wrong

Some of these symptoms can be unrelated to preterm labor, but they should still be reported. Diarrhea and stomach upset can result from something you ate, but they can also be preliminaries to labor. Vaginal discharge is not an uncommon occurrence during pregnancy, but a change in the amount or type of discharge can be a warning sign. Any vaginal discharge that is bloody or streaked with blood can indicate that the cervix is beginning to dilate.

If you experience a leaking or gushing of fluid from the vagina, it could be a sign of premature rupture of membranes (PROM). The fluid comes from the amniotic sac that contains a baby. If that sac breaks open, the fluid will escape through the vagina. It might come out as a trickle or a gush, and it is usually clear with a distinct odor. A pH test can determine if it is indeed amniotic fluid, but you'll have to visit the doctor to confirm this. Even a small leak can present a danger of infection, so it's important to notify your caregiver as soon as possible.

FACT

PROM occurs in about 10 percent of twin pregnancies, and more often in triplets or higher order multiples. Most multiples are in separate sacs, but some monozygotic twins are contained in a shared sac. One or all of the sacs may rupture prematurely, but it is usually the sac that is closer to the cervix.

Cerclage

If there is evidence that your cervix is shortening or dilating, an obstetrician may recommend a preventive procedure called a cerclage. Basically, cerclage involves sewing your cervix shut, keeping the babies inside until they're ready to be born. Sutures are inserted through the cervix to prevent it from opening; this can delay preterm birth and buy precious time for the babies to develop. It's common with higher order multiples and in women whose previous pregnancy experience indicates an incompetent cervix.

Generally, cerclage is most effective when performed earlier in pregnancy. It may require a short period of hospitalization, during which contractions are monitored. You will be given anesthesia; generally a spinal or epidural is used, but occasionally general anesthesia is warranted. After the procedure, you'll need to remain at the hospital for monitoring, perhaps for several hours or overnight. You may be given drugs to stave off infection or contractions. Once you return home, you should plan to take it easy for a couple of days, staying off your feet. There may be some mild bleeding, cramping, or vaginal discharge.

ESSENTIAL

Your doctor may advise you to abstain from sexual intercourse before and after the cerclage due to the risk of introducing infection. Ask for specific advice as to when it is safe to resume sexual activity.

The cerclage sutures must be removed in order for you to deliver the babies vaginally. If the procedure is effective in staving off preterm labor, the sutures may be removed in the doctor's office at a time when it is determined that the babies are old enough for delivery—for example, thirty-six or thirty-seven weeks. Otherwise, they will be removed in the event of infection, when there are contractions indicating the immediate onset of labor, or if your water breaks.

Cerclage is not without risks. Most health professionals recognize that the benefits of prolonging pregnancy outweigh the risks, but you should still be aware of the potential consequences. They include:

- Preterm labor (the very thing you're trying to prevent)
- Chorioamnionitis, an infection of the amniotic sac
- Premature rupture of membranes (PROM)
- Laceration of the cervix
- Reaction to anesthesia or medication
- Hemorrhage

There is some disagreement as to whether cerclage actually has a positive impact. Some argue that if it extends pregnancy even for a few weeks, then it benefits the babies. Others cite the associated risks and side effects and regard it as unnecessary intervention.

Treatment Options for Preterm Labor

If you are diagnosed with preterm labor, there are several options for treatment. Your doctor will first do an assessment of your condition. Your contractions will be monitored. Your cervix may be examined, and an ultrasound may be performed to update the status of the babies' development.

Rest and Relaxation

Often the first attempt to stop the progress of preterm labor is to assign the mother to rest. You may be encouraged to decrease your level of activity or may need to begin some level of bed rest. Contractions will be monitored to see if they respond to the change in activity. You may be given a monitor to use at home or be asked to report to the hospital or doctor's office for occasional monitoring. If dehydration is considered a factor, oral or intravenous fluid delivery may be required.

Treatment with Medication

There are a variety of drugs that can be used to counteract preterm labor and delay delivery. These medications, called tocolytics, act to relax the muscle of the uterus to stop it from contracting or to counteract the hormones that are initiating the onset of labor.

There is some controversy regarding the use of tocolytic drugs. There is no single drug that is a perfect remedy, and none are proven to stop preterm labor, only to possibly delay preterm birth. Most tocolytics are drugs approved by the FDA for other purposes, but may be prescribed to prevent preterm birth. None of the choices are without side effects, however. You and your doctor will have to review the options and weigh the risks against the benefits.

Drugs such as magnesium sulfate (MgSO4), nifedipine (Procardia), indomethacin (Indocin), and terbutaline (Brethine) have all been used in treating preterm labor, although they were originally intended as medication for other conditions, such as asthma. While they are not categorized by the FDA for use as tocolytics, they are the accepted standard of care in the medical field. Usually they are first administered intravenously, but are also available in the form of a pill or injection. In the past, ongoing treatment was continued with a subcutaneous pump that delivered small doses of medicine at regular intervals, but new warnings make the practice controversial. Be sure you fully discuss the risks and benefits of tocolytics with your doctor, and consider alternatives.

Magnesium sulfate is also commonly administered in the treatment of preterm labor. It's also used to treat preeclampsia and pregnancy induced hypertension. It relaxes the muscles of the uterus. You will most likely be hospitalized for a few days while you receive this treatment so that you can be closely monitored for side effects. Magnesium sulfate can cause nausea, headache, weakness, and heart palpitations. Many women who take it experience a sensation of flushing and their skin feels hot.

ALERT

All of these drugs have side effects and risks. Taking them is not generally a comfortable experience for the mother. Tocolytics can raise your heart rate, making you feel shaky and jittery. Headaches, dizziness, drowsiness, nausea, and muscle cramps may also result.

Often, it is more effective to administer medications for the babies, rather than the mother. Instead of slowing down labor, these drugs speed up the babies' development, increasing their viability at birth. The use of corticosteroid therapy has greatly improved the odds for premature infants when administered twenty-four to forty-eight hours before birth. Steroids such as betamethasone or dexamethasone are injected into the mother to speed up the development of the babies' lungs and intestines to give them a better chance of survival after delivery.

What You *Need* to Know about Preterm Labor

- **Preterm labor is cause for concern in a multiple pregnancy.** Early delivery is more prevalent when there is more than one baby, and with so many factors increasing the risk, the goal of a pregnant mom of twins or more is to prolong the pregnancy as long as possible to avoid the consequences of preterm birth for her babies.
- **Numerous factors contribute to the cause of preterm labor.** From simple gravity and increased size of the uterus, to environmental influences like dehydration and stress, many factors heighten the chances that labor will initiate before the end of the standard forty-week gestation period.
- **You can reduce your risk of an early delivery.** Follow your medical caregiver's recommendations carefully. Create an optimal womb environment by following a healthy diet that ensures sufficient weight

gain throughout the pregnancy. Stay hydrated by drinking plenty of fluids, preferably water. Avoid stress and exertion, as well as any other activities discouraged by your doctor. Get plenty of rest and stay off your feet if necessary.

- **Know the signs of preterm labor so that you can seek quick medical attention if it happens to you.** Contractions, pelvic pressure, cramping, backache, or vaginal bleeding can all be cause for concern. Educate yourself about preterm labor, and establish a protocol with your medical provider so that you will know what action to take if you encounter any of the signs.
- **There is treatment for preterm labor.** The early onset of labor is cause for concern, but measures can be taken to prevent or delay delivery. Sometimes rest or rehydration is sufficient, but in more critical cases, a cerclage procedure, hospitalization, or treatment with medication may be a preferred route.

CHAPTER 14

Labor with Multiples

After the long months of gestation, the onset of labor is the transition time marking the departure of pregnancy and the arrival of your babies. Whether your labor is long or short, weeks early or days overdue, it's an important process. It's the work your body must do to bring your babies to life.

Signs of Labor

Labor may come on suddenly, or it may take its time. Either way, you will want to know the signs so that you are ready to act at the appropriate time. Labor with twins, triplets, or more is not that much different than with a singleton; usually it starts out the same way, but requires more careful monitoring in case of complications. It also tends to happen earlier in pregnancy, so it may be unexpected. Being knowledgeable about the signs will give you confidence to act appropriately if you are surprised by early symptoms.

Contractions

The most important sign of labor is contractions. You may have been experiencing contractions earlier in your pregnancy, but labor contractions are different. You can distinguish them by their timing, regularity, and intensity. Productive contractions, those that are preparing your cervix for delivery, will come at regular intervals with increasing frequency. They will also increase in intensity.

ALERT

Painless, irregular contractions that fade away if you lie down or change positions may be Braxton Hicks, a form of "practice" contractions that ready your uterus for labor. With Braxton Hicks, the sensation is usually centered in the abdomen, while true labor contractions may radiate from the front to the back.

Unless it is early in your pregnancy and your contractions are associated with preterm labor, or if you are in a great deal of discomfort or pain, you probably don't need to panic and rush to the hospital just yet. Use a stopwatch to gauge the amount of time in between the contraction sensations. Contact your doctor or midwife; they will advise you whether to head to the hospital or relax at home. They may suggest that you wait until your contractions reach a designated frequency, such as fifteen or twenty minutes apart, or recommend that you come in for monitoring. Because of the risk of complications, most health care providers prefer to monitor multiple pregnancies more closely than singletons and want expectant mothers of twins or more to arrive at the hospital earlier in the labor process.

Ruptured Membrane(s)

Another sign of labor is the release of fluid as the amniotic membrane ruptures or breaks. Despite the TV and movie stereotypes, you may not be fully aware if your water breaks. Rather than a gush and a splash, you might experience a trickle, and it can be difficult to ascertain whether it is labor or just a dribbling bladder.

However, if you have any suspicion that your water has broken, you should contact your doctor or midwife without delay. If the membranes have ruptured prematurely, you could be at risk for infection if delivery is not imminent. Usually, however, contractions follow shortly thereafter.

FACT

Many doctors recommend an induction of labor if contractions do not start within twenty-four or forty-eight hours after a woman's water breaks.

Other Signs

While regular, productive contractions are the sure sign of labor, there are several other symptoms that some women experience when it is almost time. They indicate that the body is getting ready for childbirth. You may notice that your insides seem to be shifting around. In a singleton pregnancy, the baby's position shifts toward the pelvis in preparation for birth, and mom may experience more pressure in her bladder. This sensation of "lightening" or "dropping" into the lower belly can indicate that labor is imminent. But with multiple babies, who are already crowding mom's internal organs, the shifting sensation may not be as obvious.

Vaginal discharge that changes or increases could be a sign that your cervix is effacing or dilating, especially if it is accompanied by the bloody show, a plug of mucus from the cervix. It is sometimes accompanied by diarrhea. Discuss any of these symptoms with your medical caregiver if you suspect they are associated with the onset of labor.

At the Hospital: Examination and Preparation

When you arrive at the hospital, you will be examined to assess the progression of your labor. A pelvic exam will determine if your cervix is effacing (thinning) or dilating (opening). If it is determined that your contractions are "false labor" because your cervix is not opening, you may be sent home, a disappointing and frustrating experience after the excitement of arriving at the hospital. However, in a multiple pregnancy, many doctors prefer to keep a closer eye on their patients and may recommend you remain at the hospital for monitoring.

You will probably have an IV inserted in the event that medication or a hydrating solution is required. You'll change into a gown, either one you've brought from home or one provided by the hospital. Finally, you and the babies will be monitored. With one monitor per baby and one for your contractions, you may feel a bit overwired. Be sure to read the information on monitoring later in this chapter so that you understand all of your options.

Inducing Labor

There are some instances where labor doesn't start on its own and needs to be artificially initiated. There are many reasons why medical professionals recommend inducing labor, but ultimately the decision is made because the babies or their mother will be better off if the babies are born rather than remaining in the womb. Sometimes it is because one or both babies are in distress, perhaps due to cord compression, placenta malfunction, or infection. In other situations, the mother's well-being is at risk, such as when pre-eclampsia develops.

ALERT

Your doctor may recommend induction at thirty-seven or thirty-eight weeks if you have not delivered your twins prior to that date, or she may prefer to wait until forty weeks to provide additional time for you to start labor on your own.

Ways to Induce Labor

There are a couple of different ways to prompt labor, and the approach will depend on the reasons motivating the induction and on your physical condition. Induction serves to ripen the cervix and stimulate contractions. This can be achieved manually or by administering hormones.

Often, the first step is to apply prostaglandin, which contains a hormone associated with labor, to the cervix. It is applied in a fairly quick and pain-less procedure, and has the effect of softening the cervical tissue so that it can better respond to the contractions. Prostaglandin may be applied the day before a scheduled induction as the first in a series of treatments. Or it may be sufficient to prompt the onset of labor on its own.

In cases where the amniotic sac(s) remain intact, another way to induce labor is to manipulate the membranes. They may be manually "stripped" by loosening the bag of waters from the wall of the uterus. Doing so may help start labor by releasing prostaglandins and allowing the first baby to rest directly on the cervix, pressuring it to expand and open. Or the amniotic sac may be artificially ruptured by making a small hole, allowing the fluid to leak out. Neither method guarantees that labor will result, and if it doesn't begin once the water is broken, you may have to have a C-section.

FACT

Induction of labor is on the rise in the United States. More than 20 percent of babies were delivered after induction—that's one in five. The rate doubled from the late 1900s, when only 9 percent of women were induced before delivery.

Labor can also be induced by administering Pitocin, a synthetic form of the pregnancy hormone oxytocin, to start or strengthen contractions. For some women, labor induced by Pitocin may result in intensified contrac-tions. You'll be monitored closely to ensure that the contractions don't stress the babies.

There are also some natural methods of prompting labor. You should discuss these options with your medical caregiver before attempting them, but they may be worth considering before attempting a medical induction. Stimulating your nipples or having sexual intercourse to the point of orgasm may sufficiently raise your own hormones and prompt contractions. A less pleasant tradition is to swallow castor oil, a potent laxative, to activate your bowels.

Impact of Induction

Induction is not always a direct route to delivery. Induced labor may be longer or more intense than a spontaneous labor, or it may fail altogether. Induction is associated with a higher rate of cesarean delivery. Your doctor may recommend a C-section if your labor doesn't adequately progress after a designated trial, perhaps twenty-four hours.

Stages of Labor

The process of childbirth can be broken down into three stages. The first stage, the process of opening the cervix, is generally the longest and most uncomfortable stage. The good news about labor with multiples is that the hard work accomplished by the body during this stage accommodates both (or all) babies; you don't have to repeat this stage for each baby. Understanding the process, and knowing what to expect, can help you manage your expectations and create a more meaningful experience.

During the first stage, the cervix must fully open as a passageway for the babies. This stage can be broken down into three phases, which are covered in detail here. The final two stages of childbirth, pushing and delivery of the placenta, will be discussed in the next chapter.

First Phase: Early (Latent) Labor

Early, or latent, labor is the first phase of the first stage of labor. It is during this time that the cervix prepares to open and provide access for the babies' departure from the womb. This readying of the cervix is called ripening, and it requires the cervix to do two things: efface (thin out) and dilate (open).

You can be in early labor for several days, or even weeks, without really being aware of it. Gentle contractions and pressure on the cervix open it a couple of centimeters. They may happen as infrequently as once an hour, but will occur with increasing frequency and will intensify as the phase progresses. They can last as long as forty-five seconds each. Most women are fairly comfortable through this stage and are able to participate in light activity.

ESSENTIAL

Latent labor lasts, on average, for ten to twelve hours. For women experiencing childbirth for the first time, it can be longer. However, the extra weight and pressure associated with carrying two or more babies often expedites the process for mothers of multiples.

Second Phase: Active Labor

Early labor gives way to the active phase when the contractions are about five minutes apart and the cervix has dilated to three or four centimeters. The contractions are intense at this point, lasting up to a full minute, but with breaks in between. A mother in this phase of labor will become increasingly uncomfortable and will need assistance to manage the pain, either with medication or relaxation techniques.

While it may have taken twelve hours for the cervix to dilate a couple of centimeters during the latent phase, the increased contractions and pressure of the baby moving toward the birth canal speed up the process during active labor. It can take only a few hours or as little as fifteen minutes for the cervix to fully dilate to ten centimeters. If labor stalls during this phase, Pitocin may be administered to jump-start the process.

A doula, or labor coach, begins to play a very supportive role during this portion of labor, helping the mother to focus her energy during the contractions and keeping her comfortable and relaxed during breaks.

Phase Three: Transition

Just when you think that you can't take any more, the final phase of labor intensifies the discomfort. Contractions lasting more than a minute come fast and furious, as frequently as every other minute. The presenting baby's proximity to your fully dilated cervix places increasing pressure on your bottom. You may feel like you want to push, but will have to focus your energy on resisting the urge, according to your doctor's or midwife's direction. To make matters worse, your body may betray you, compounding your discomfort with nausea, vomiting, and pressure in your rectum.

In the midst of this discomfort, you will likely be moved to an operating room or a delivery room equipped for emergency surgery. That's a good sign; it means that the arrival of your babies is not far away!

Monitoring

With more than one baby in the mix, the risk of complications for one or all of them is heightened. To control the risk, the medical community is generally more comfortable with close monitoring of babies during the labor process. Therefore, you are more likely than a mother of a singleton to be monitored during your labor. You should be aware of your options for monitoring, discuss them with your doctor, and include references to your wishes in your birth plan.

Fetal Monitoring

There are two ways to keep an eye on the babies' condition while they're still in the womb: external and internal fetal monitoring.

If your babies will be externally monitored, electronic sensors will be attached to your belly with straps. Some models may have two or more sensors for multiples, or multiple units will be put in place. The sensors will be positioned directly over each fetus to monitor the beat of each heart. An additional belt will measure your contractions to produce a visual correlation of the babies' heart rates in response to contractions. If the heart rates are above or below the norm, it could indicate a lack of oxygen or other signs of distress.

As the babies wiggle around in your womb, they may move out of the range of their sensors, causing the signal to be lost. This isn't a sign of distress, but it may be necessary to reposition the sensors. Sometimes the monitor is connected to an alarm that sounds when the reading exceeds acceptable levels. This alarm can be an annoying disturbance, especially when it is triggered by a false reading.

Internal monitoring is more precise and avoids the false alarms of disrupted external readings. A small electrode will be inserted into your womb through an opening in the cervix and attached to a baby's scalp. This can only be accomplished if the head is accessible, so the bag of water will be broken if it is still intact. It requires the mother to be immobile for the remainder of labor, so it's usually reserved for situations where there is great cause for concern. Also, it can be difficult to monitor multiples with an internal monitor, as it only accesses the presenting baby—that is, the one closest to the cervix.

Monitoring Contractions

In addition to keeping a close eye on the babies, your contractions will be monitored. This may seem redundant to you; after all, you will probably be painfully aware of each contraction as it happens. But it is still important to assess the frequency and intensity of the contractions in order to determine how well labor is progressing. Even if pain medication dulls your perception, the monitor will help your caregivers keep track of the exact frequency and duration of each contraction. It is particularly important if you are induced, to ensure that the right dosage of Pitocin has been administered.

Contractions are monitored using a transducer that senses the changes in the surface of the abdomen. Like a fetal monitor, movement can disrupt the signal. A more accurate assessment can be obtained with an intrauterine pressure catheter (IUPC) to measure the actual pressure within the uterus.

ESSENTIAL

Wireless monitors provide continuous assessment without inhibiting movement. Called telemetry, this advanced technology combines the best of both worlds, giving mothers more control over their body during labor, but allowing doctors to keep a close eye on the babies.

Monitoring Alternatives

Continuous monitoring can be uncomfortable and inconvenient for a mother in labor. With her movement restricted by belts, straps, and wires, she's prevented from physically working through her contractions. If your pregnancy and labor have proceeded without complications, you may be able to consider some alternatives that would allow you more freedom to labor comfortably. Your doula can act as an advocate if you wish to pursue another option.

One alternative to continuous monitoring is intermittent assessments of the babies' heart rates. A nurse or midwife can take a reading of the babies' conditions using a fetoscope or hand-held ultrasound at designated intervals—for example, every fifteen minutes. With this method, it is important to ensure that each individual baby's heartbeat is able to be detected and receives equal attention.

Pain Management During Labor

There's no way around it: The process of labor can be quite painful. While labor with multiples is not necessarily more painful than with a singleton, there are some special concerns regarding the ways that pain is managed.

Medical Pain Management

Medications to dull or block sensations of pain may make the labor experience much more comfortable. While there are some risks associated with anesthesia, modern options for pain relief are generally very safe for both the mother and the babies.

Many women sing the praises of epidurals for the relief that they can provide during childbirth. In the event that a C-section is warranted, the epidural can also be used to administer anesthesia for the surgery. The only downside to epidural pain management is in the installation; once in place, an epidural delivers immediate, continuous pain relief to the lower half of your body without impacting your mental acuity.

FACT

An epidural is designed to provide pain relief (analgesia), not to completely block sensation (anesthesia). You may still feel contractions, but should not experience them as severe pain.

After an injection with a numbing solution, the anesthesiologist, obstetrician, or nurse-anesthetist will insert a catheter into the hollow space just outside the membrane surrounding your spine at your lower back. The procedure takes about fifteen minutes.

With the catheter in place, pain relief can be administered, usually by a combination of narcotics and local anesthetics. Although the cocktail blocks the sensation of pain, you'll retain control of your lower body. It may make you unsteady on your feet, however.

Early in labor, systemic medications, such as Demerol, Fentanyl, or Nubain, can help take the edge off the pain. They'll be administered through your IV or injected. They won't make the pain disappear, but can dull the sensation enough to help you relax. These drugs will probably make you drowsy, and the babies as well, since they can enter the fetal circulation through the placenta. For that reason, the effects are short-lived, and they should only be given in early labor, long before delivery is imminent.

Local anesthetics may be utilized at other points during labor. They are administered directly to relieve pain in a specific area, such as the pudendal canal or perineum in preparation for an episiotomy.

ESSENTIAL

If you attended a childbirth education class, you likely learned several nonmedical strategies for managing the pain and discomfort of labor. A doula or labor partner may be able to assist you in implementing them. Breath control, relaxation, massage, and other means of providing comfort can help reduce or delay your need for medical pain relief.

Unmedicated "Natural" Birth

A multiple birth free of medical intervention is fairly rare. Despite a trend toward "natural" unmedicated childbirth, few mothers of multiples deliver their babies without anesthesia. Many of those who do, do so unintentionally, either because their labor progresses too quickly or some other complications prevent the opportunity to administer it. If it is your goal to deliver without pain medication, discuss your wishes with your doctor. Hiring a doula to assist you through the experience may be a worthwhile investment.

You may wish to consider having a catheter implanted just in case so that regional anesthesia can be administered in the event of an emergency

C-section or if the pain becomes unbearable. Otherwise, you may miss the birth entirely due to being unconscious from general anesthesia.

Labor Day

- **Whether early, on time, or after your due date, eventually the time will come for your babies to arrive.** Your body's process of readying for delivery is called labor, and it is hard work. The good news about having multiples is that you don't have to undergo the entire process more than once.

- **Your body may go into labor on its own—sometimes earlier than planned—or you may require medical assistance to get things rolling.** Sometimes the onset of labor makes a surprise appearance, so it's important to know the signs and symptoms. But in other cases, labor is induced if there is motivation to deliver the babies due to deteriorating conditions in the womb. And some mothers of multiples never undergo labor at all if a scheduled delivery via cesarean section is determined to be the best course of action.

- **Labor is the first of the three stages of childbirth, and there are three phases of labor.** In a multiple birth, much of the work of labor prepares the way for both babies, so you don't have to repeat the entire process. During early (latent) labor, the cervix effaces and dilates, opening and widening to accommodate the passage of the babies. In active labor, uterine contractions increase in frequency and duration as the first baby prepares to exit the womb. Finally, during transition, the baby surges toward the cervical opening in anticipation of delivery.

- **Pain management and monitoring during labor ensure that the process is as comfortable, effective, and safe as possible.** Attend a childbirth class to educate and prepare you about the process of labor and delivery. You have several options for pain management during labor, from medication to breathing techniques. Although you may have a preference about how you want the labor to proceed, remain open to the recommendations of your medical team. Monitoring the labor process allows them to assess the condition of the babies and determine the best course of action for a healthy outcome.

CHAPTER 15

Delivering Your Babies

The time has come! Your babies are making their entry into this world. Whether you delivery vaginally or via cesarean section, delivering twins, triplets, or higher order multiples is an amazing event, leading up to the miraculous moment when you meet your babies face to face for the first time.

Presentation Combinations

An important factor in delivering multiples is *presentation*, the term used to describe the position of the babies within the womb. The presentation of the babies at the time of delivery will guide your doctors in deciding the best method of delivery. There are several combinations of positions that your babies can take.

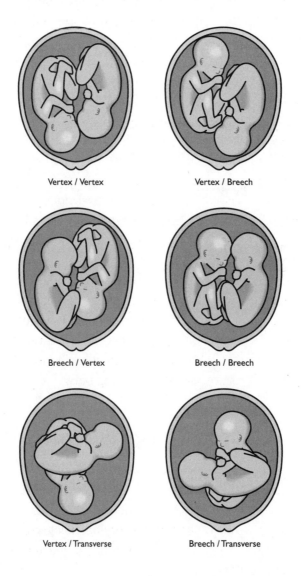

Vertex / Vertex   Vertex / Breech

Breech / Vertex   Breech / Breech

Vertex / Transverse   Breech / Transverse

▲ The babies may be in a variety of positions or presentations.

Vertex is the term to describe a baby that is resting head-down, the most common and safest option for vaginal delivery. Your doctor will be most concerned with whether the presenting baby—that is, the one closest to the cervix—is vertex, as this is the baby that would enter the birth canal first. A twin pregnancy where both babies are vertex is the best candidate for a vaginal birth.

A breech baby is the opposite of a vertex baby; his head is pointing upright. A breech baby may be arranged in one of three ways:

- **Frank breech:** The buttocks are positioned closest to the cervix, with the legs folded straight up toward the head.
- **Complete breech:** The buttocks are pointed toward the cervix, but the arms and legs are crossed in front of the body.
- **Incomplete or footling breech:** One or both legs are dangling down toward the cervix.

There is some controversy as to the best option for delivering a breech baby. Some doctors are more comfortable performing a cesarean section if even one of the babies is breech. Others are willing to attempt a vaginal delivery if certain conditions are met.

Transverse babies rest horizontally in the womb. A transverse baby lying at the bottom of the womb is not a good candidate for a vaginal delivery. Usually, however, the baby closest to the cervix is either breech or vertex, and the second baby rests in a transverse position higher in the womb, closer to the mother's rib cage. Your doctor will most likely base a delivery decision on the position of the presenting baby.

Is Vaginal Delivery an Option for You?

Delivery through the birth canal and out the vagina is generally the safest method of birth for mother and babies, and therefore it is the preferred approach, unless certain circumstances create risks that make a cesarean section a better option. Vaginal delivery carries less risk of hemorrhage or infection, requires less anesthesia, and has a quicker recovery time. It also produces less scarring.

FACT

Only about one quarter of twin pregnancies result in a vaginal delivery. Sometimes the first twin is delivered vaginally, but a C-section is required for the second because of complications.

Vaginal delivery is not an option if:

- You are having triplets, quadruplets, or other higher order multiples.
- Your twins are monoamniotic (share an amniotic sac).
- The presenting baby is transverse.
- You have active genital herpes.
- You have placenta previa or another medical condition.
- Your pelvic structure makes it difficult for your babies to pass through.

Vaginal delivery may be discouraged if:

- One or both babies are breech.
- You have preeclampsia.
- Your twins are premature.
- One or more of the babies are in severe distress and cannot tolerate labor.
- Previous cesarean delivery or abdominal surgery puts you at risk for uterine rupture.

ESSENTIAL

Your babies may also benefit from a vaginal delivery. As they travel through the birth canal, their lungs are compressed, forcing out fluid and preparing them to breathe air.

Vaginal Birth After Cesarean (VBAC)

At one time, a previous cesarean section automatically ruled out a vaginal delivery. That is not the case these days, however. The danger of labor and delivery after cesarean surgery is that the incision site could rupture.

New techniques make that less likely now. Most doctors are willing to attempt a TOLAC (Trial of Labor After Cesarean) in the hopes of achieving a VBAC (Vaginal Birth After Cesarean), assuming certain conditions are met.

It's important for your doctor or midwife to review your case if you have had a previous C-section, so be sure they are aware of your history.

Breech Babies

Breech babies are the source of some contention among the medical community. Only a small percentage of singleton babies are presenting breech at delivery and, in most cases, a decision is made to schedule a cesarean section to deliver those babies. However, opinions differ on the appropriate approach for breech twins. Believing that most multiples are smaller than singletons of the same gestational age, some doctors are actually more willing to deliver a breech twin than a singleton. It is only rarely favorable to deliver vaginally if the presenting baby is breech. However, a breech baby following a vertex twin may be a candidate for vaginal delivery.

Sometimes a doctor or midwife will make an attempt to turn the breech baby. If unsuccessful, consideration will be given to the baby's status. Is he tolerating the labor well? Does he appear to be in any distress? Is he frank breech, the least difficult position to deliver? Fetal monitoring and ultrasound will give a picture of the baby's condition.

ALERT

Even identical twins can look very different at birth when one is vertex and the other is delivered breech. A vertex baby's head is rounded by its headfirst passage through the birth canal, while a breech baby's head is more pointy and cone-shaped. After birth, the soft skull tissue reforms into a normal shape and they will look more alike.

One of the most important criteria to consider in determining whether a baby should be delivered breech is how her size compares to her co-twin. If the second baby is smaller than the first, she is more likely to be a successful breech delivery, as the doctor can be fairly assured that she will pass through the birth canal.

Your doctor's previous experience will determine his comfort level with breech delivery. If your baby meets the criteria to attempt a breech delivery, your doctor will reach into your womb and grab the baby's feet. You'll push and he'll pull, and the baby will slip feet first through your cervix and into the world.

Vaginal Delivery

The process of labor, described in the previous chapter, prepares the mother's body for a vaginal delivery. After the first stage of labor completely opens the cervix to provide a gateway for the baby's exit from the womb, it's time for the second stage of labor: pushing the presenting baby through the pelvic bones and out the vaginal opening. This stage can last for five minutes or several hours. Usually, it lasts about an hour. On average, it takes three to five pushes to move the baby out.

After the fast and frequent contractions experienced during the transition part of the first stage, this second stage of labor provides some relative relief. However, while the contractions may subside somewhat in frequency, they won't lessen in intensity, and they will be accompanied by an overwhelming urge to push or bear down. Your doctor or midwife may guide you to coordinate your pushing efforts with your contractions, or you may be encouraged to bear down when it feels right. If your epidural is still effective, you should probably receive some coaching, as your sensation will be dulled.

ESSENTIAL

The bad news: You have to experience this stage of labor separately with each baby. The good news: Twins are usually a bit smaller than singleton babies, and most mothers of multiples don't have a difficult time pushing them out.

The force of your uterus's contractions will continue to guide the baby through your pelvis toward the vaginal opening. If necessary, an episiotomy will be performed to prevent tearing of the perineum. The doctor will make a small cut to the tissue that stretches between your vagina and rectum.

The clean cut heals faster than ripped tissue. Or perineal massage may help stretch the tissue to accommodate the oncoming baby.

Once the head crowns, or bulges through the perineum, the excitement really begins. Your doctor or midwife will slowly coach the first baby's head out of your vagina. You may be instructed to stop pushing for a moment while her nose and mouth are suctioned. After the head, the largest part of the baby's body, has exited, the arms, torso, and legs slip out without much exertion. The umbilical cord will be clamped and cut, and your first twin will be handed off to a waiting attendant. Sometimes, if the baby's condition is not critical due to preterm birth or other complications, mom or dad will have an opportunity to greet and even hold the first of their new children.

It's done! The first baby has arrived! You can bask in the joy of this moment and relax for a few minutes. You're not completely finished yet, though. There's more to come.

The Intermission

If you were having a singleton, your childbirth experience would end here. But you're having another baby! While twins may be born within a few minutes of each other, most twins arrive in intervals of twenty to thirty minutes. This intermission between babies is a crucial time, during which both babies' conditions will be assessed.

With more room to move, the second baby may stretch out and change position—with luck, into a vertex presentation. His rearrangement will likely be monitored by ultrasound to determine the course of action. If the baby is in a breech or transverse position, your doctor may attempt to turn him. This process, called external cephalic version, can be uncomfortable, as the doctor pushes forcefully on your abdomen in an attempt to turn the baby head down.

This baby requires some careful monitoring during this time. If her bag of water remained intact during the delivery of her co-twin, it will need to be broken now. With her brother or sister out of the way, her situation poses some risk. The previous contractions and pushing activity may have caused the placenta to detach, reducing the amount of oxygen delivered to the remaining baby. And there is always a concern about cord compression or prolapse, if the umbilical cord enters the birth canal before the baby does.

FACT

There have been some cases where twins or multiples experience an extended intermission between births. Usually this occurs when pre-term labor cannot be halted and one multiple is delivered extremely prematurely. In a delayed interval birth, the labor is stopped after the birth of one fetus, and a cerclage is performed to close the cervix. This gives the remaining baby or babies more time to develop and optimizes their chances for survival.

Your contractions will also be watched carefully during this time. If your uterus slacks off, you may receive a dose of Pitocin to reactivate the contractions to deliver the second baby. If everything is in place, it's time to push out the second baby. With a path already paved by her co-twin, the good news is that the second twin usually requires fewer pushes and is often born relatively quickly.

Final Stage: Delivery of the Placenta(s)

After both babies are delivered, there's one final step. You have to deliver the placenta(s). This important organ has been the source of nutrition and nourishment for your babies for the last few months, but now that it is no longer needed, it is time for it to depart your womb.

ESSENTIAL

Most hospitals do so as a matter of routine, but you'll want the placenta(s) sent to pathology for examination. An analysis may reveal your babies' zygosity. A monochorionic placenta will indicate that your babies are monozygotic, or identical.

When the doctor or midwife clamps each cord, request that they distinguish the cords—and the corresponding placentas—so that they can be identified for ownership. In the event that there is a problem with one of the babies, an examination of cord or placental abnormalities might help pinpoint a diagnosis.

With your hard work done, you can lie back and relax. If you were given an episiotomy or experienced any tearing, you'll be stitched up and cleaned up. Your epidural may be removed at this time if you don't require any follow-up care.

Cesarean Section

Nearly all triplets, quadruplets, and higher order multiples are delivered by cesarean section, and many twin pregnancies are also candidates for cesarean delivery. Your cesarean delivery may not be a surprise. With multiples, it is often a planned event, decided in advance based on your situation. Even if you prefer a vaginal delivery, you should consider the possibility of a C-section and prepare accordingly.

Why Cesarean?

A cesarean section may be planned due to anticipated complications for you or your babies. This is the case when there are higher order multiples, monoamniotic twins, placenta previa, or other conditions that would make a vaginal delivery dangerous. Other times, your doctor may decide that a C-section is the best course of action after labor has started, perhaps because of the babies' presentation or because monitoring indicates that they are not tolerating the pressure of the uterine contractions. Finally, sometimes an emergency cesarean must be performed despite the mother's best efforts to deliver vaginally, because of fetal distress or other dire consequences that could result in the loss of mother or babies if delivery is not immediate.

You may feel conflicted about the prospect of having a cesarean section rather than a "natural" vaginal delivery. Perhaps you have a vision of the ideal birth experience and feel that a C-section will rob you of the opportunity to fulfill that dream. It's normal to feel frustration or disappointment that you can't control the outcome. But it's important to keep the situation in perspective. The priority is the health and safety of your precious babies, and your own well-being. Trust your medical providers to make the best decision for all involved.

Preparing for a Cesarean

If your C-section is planned, once being admitted to the hospital you will be prepped for surgery in the operating room. In most cases, your husband, partner, or birth coach can accompany you. Certified doulas are usually allowed to attend as well, but hospital policies vary on this issue. An intravenous line will be established and the area of your abdomen sterilized and possibly shaved. A catheter will be inserted to keep your bladder empty.

Except in the case of an emergency C-section, you will be given regional anesthesia, which will allow you to be awake and alert during the procedure without feeling any sensation in the lower half of your body. Anesthesia is generally administered with a spinal or epidural. A nasal cannula fitted in your nostrils will provide oxygen for you to breathe. The babies will be monitored with ultrasound and fetal monitoring, and your vital signs will be continuously checked.

A sterile environment is imperative in the operating room. Your body will be draped with sterile clothes. A screen will prevent you from viewing the actual procedure, but may be lowered to show you the babies as they are removed from the womb. Your husband or partner will also have to don a surgical scrub suit, mask, and hair and shoe coverings to accompany you in the operating room.

ALERT

Hospital policies vary regarding the use of cameras and electronics in the operating room. Be sure you investigate the rules beforehand to find out which aspects of the birth can be filmed. Check your supply of batteries, film, or memory storage ahead of time. You don't want to miss the big moment because of an equipment malfunction.

Emotionally, you may feel anxious, excited, terrified, and elated. Physically, while you won't feel the pain of the procedure, you may feel somewhat uncomfortable lying flat on your back. You may feel vulnerable and intimidated by the strange sights and busy activity surrounding you. You may feel nauseous from the effects of the anesthesia or your prone position and may even have to retch or vomit. Your anesthesiologist may be able to help you overcome this feeling with medication added to your IV.

The C-Section

Fortunately the procedure itself is relatively short. The doctor will make an incision low across the pubic area; this "bikini" cut creates a less conspicuous scar and reduces the risk of uterine complications in future pregnancies. After cutting through muscle and tissue to access the uterus, the doctor will make an incision through the uterine wall to access the first baby. As the baby is lifted out, you may feel some pressure and tugging, but no pain.

As the first baby is lifted out, ask to have the screen lowered so that you can have a look. The baby's cord will be clamped and cut, and the baby will be handed to an attendant for examination. In the meantime, the doctor will already be moving on to the next baby, reaching into your uterus and pulling out another multiple. Another attendant will be ready to receive her, and the process will continue until all the babies have been delivered. You may be able to hear your babies cry out as they take their first breaths. Your partner may have the opportunity to participate in the process, cutting the cords or holding the babies after they have been examined.

After the babies are removed from your womb, the doctor will deliver the placenta(s) and examine your uterus for fragments of placental tissue. A dose of Pitocin in your IV will help your overworked uterus start the road to recovery. Then the process of suturing and stitching begins, which often takes longer than the actual delivery.

FACT

During pregnancy, babies are often identified as "Baby A," "Baby B," "Baby C," and so forth based on their presentation, with the baby closest to the cervix termed Baby A. In a cesarean delivery, the babies may or may not arrive in order, depending on how they are arranged in the womb. The baby closest to the incision will be the first to be born.

Emergency C-Section/Combination Birth

Many mothers are very concerned about the prospect of delivering their first baby vaginally and then having a C-section to deliver the second baby, as it means experiencing the worst sensations of both methods: suffering through the discomfort of labor as well as surgery, and having to recover from both an episiotomy and an incision. While you'll probably hear plenty of stories about this unfortunate series of events in twin birth, statistically it's not likely to happen. Only a small percentage of twin births happen in this fashion.

No doctor prefers this combined method of delivery. If there is any doubt that the second baby can be delivered vaginally, a cesarean section would be recommended to begin with. Surgery to deliver the second baby is only performed when fetal distress is indicated and the baby's life is at risk. Although it is not the ideal experience, most mothers would agree that their baby's life is worth the added discomfort.

The Babies' First Few Moments

No matter how you deliver, your babies will spend their first few moments amid a whirlwind of activity. Most deliveries of twins or more will be attended by an array of medical staff. Often the babies are well outnumbered by their attendants, with at least one doctor and nurse caring for each infant.

Immediately after birth, your babies' condition will be assessed. After placing them on a warming tray and cleaning them up, the medical staff will be checking out several different aspects of their physical state. Your babies' first standardized test is the Apgar, which provides a general assessment of their health at birth. Apgar is assessed twice, when they are one minute old and then again five minutes later.

A score of ten is perfect, and anything above seven is considered average. If there is cause for concern based on a lower score, your baby will be treated according to his needs.

▼ INFANT APGAR ASSESSMENT

Characteristic	Measures	0	1	2
Activity Level	Muscle Tone	Limp	Some	Active
Pulse	Heart Rate	Absent	Slow	Above 100 bpm
Grimace	Reflex Irritability	None	Grimace	Cough or sneeze
Appearance	Skin Color	Blue or pale	Body pink, extremities blue	Pink
Respiration	Breathing	Absent	Weak	Good

In addition, your babies will be weighed and measured. Ointment or eyedrops will be placed in their eyes. Their footprints will be inked, and a blood sample will be taken for testing. They'll be given a dose of vitamin K to assist with blood clotting. Depending on their condition, as well as your recovery status, the babies may spend some time in your arms. This quiet period of alertness that follows birth is an ideal time to initiate breastfeeding.

If your babies are born early, the events of their birth may be surrounded by a bit more concern and immediacy. Neonatologists will be standing by to care for them as they make their entry. Quick action will be taken to ease their transition from the womb to the world, especially to help them breathe. They may be whisked away to the NICU (neonatal intensive care unit), and your opportunity to spend time with them may be limited as the medical staff strives to stabilize them.

The abrupt end to your pregnancy can be a very difficult experience. Your babies may be facing several months of critical care. However, many premature infants survive their ominous start in life; only time will tell your babies' stories. Have faith in the medical staff's ability to care for them. You'll find much more information on parenting premature multiples in Chapter 16.

Postpartum Care and Recovery

Just as your body—and mind—took some time to adjust to the idea of being pregnant, you'll need some time to recover after giving birth. Your recovery period will be determined by how you delivered; cesarean moms have undergone major surgery and will need more time to heal, although a vaginal delivery also takes a toll on a woman's body.

After Vaginal Delivery

After delivery, your uterus will begin to shrink back to its prepregnancy size. You may feel some mild cramping during this process, but you should not experience extreme discomfort. If you do, notify your doctor. You'll have some bleeding, which may be heavy at first. For the first few days you may find that you soak a sanitary napkin in a couple of hours. If you've had a previous pregnancy, you won't find this surprising, but it may be heavier than you experienced in the past. That's because your uterus stretched and expanded further to accommodate the extra babies. You may want to be prepared with some supersize sanitary napkins from home; they'll work better than those provided by the hospital.

ALERT

Drinking plenty of fluids is vital after delivery, especially if you intend to nurse your babies. An increased fluid intake will speed your recovery and keep you healthy as you begin to care for your newborns.

The bloody discharge, called lochia, can last for several weeks after delivery. It should taper off, however, and should not include any large clumps or clots. If it increases, or is accompanied by pain, fever, or a foul odor, notify your doctor right away.

You will need to wear sanitary napkins to accommodate this discharge for up to six weeks after you deliver. Tampons are not recommended. If you experienced anemia during your pregnancy, it's important to continue supplementing your iron intake, either by eating iron-rich foods or by taking pills prescribed by your doctor.

If you had an episiotomy or any tearing of the perineum during your delivery, you may be somewhat sore. Ice packs, sitz baths, and witch hazel pads can relieve the discomfort. You may also be plagued by hemorrhoids as your distended veins return to normal capacity. Discuss their treatment with your caregiver.

Although you'll probably be ready to leave the hospital soon after your delivery, it will take a couple of weeks for your body to return to full strength. After the strain of pregnancy, the process of labor is intense—your body worked hard!—and you need to give yourself time to recuperate. It's not realistic to expect that you will get plenty of rest and relaxation; the weeks following the delivery of multiples are hectic, to say the least. But you should definitely consider lining up plenty of help so that you can minimize your responsibilities and focus your energy exclusively on caring for yourself and the babies.

After C-Section

A cesarean section is major surgery and necessitates more intensive recovery. You'll probably have to remain in bed for at least twelve hours, after which time you'll be encouraged to move around or at least get out of bed. It may be unpleasant; the effects of the surgery and the anesthesia may leave you feeling like you've been hit by a truck. Rely on the nurses and caregivers to assist you. You may have a great deal of pain or discomfort, but relief is available. Discuss your options for pain medication with your doctor.

QUESTION

Will pain medications affect my breastfeeding plans?
You can still initiate breastfeeding, even if you are taking pain medication. Your doctor will advise you if the medication will impact the babies. Even if it prevents you from feeding the babies, you can still begin the nursing process using a pump.

A cesarean section does not exempt you from the other aftereffects of delivering a baby. You will still have some cramping as your uterus returns to its normal size, and you will have a vaginal delivery of lochia as your body expels blood and tissue. As with a vaginal delivery, you'll have to wear sanitary napkins for several weeks after your babies are born.

As you recover from a C-section, you'll have to avoid strenuous activity for a period of time. That may include driving, stair climbing, and heavy lifting. Depending on your circumstances, it may be difficult to obey some of these restrictions. However, it is important to follow your doctor's recommendations during your recovery. You cannot effectively care for your newborns if you are unwell. Arrange for extra help and give your body the time and nurturing it needs to heal.

Emotional Impact

No matter how much you read, study, and prepare for the arrival of your babies, their birth will be nothing like you expected. You may feel overwhelmed by emotions: relief, anxiety, elation, despair, fear, and love. Your conflicting feelings may stir up some unusual reactions. Remember that this is a time of transition. You're not pregnant with multiples anymore; rather, you are the mother of two, three, or more infants. You are all settling into your new roles as a family and will require some time to adjust.

Postpartum depression (PPD) is characterized by feelings of hopelessness that last most of the day and don't diminish after several weeks. It's normal to feel overwhelmed or out of control, but you need to seek medical attention if your feelings are preventing you from properly caring for your babies or yourself.

FACT

Fifteen percent of women experience postpartum depression after giving birth, and mothers of twins are particularly at risk. A 2004 study by the National Organization of Mothers of Twins Clubs found that nearly 40 percent of moms of multiples experienced depression.

Have some strategies in place for coping with the stress of multiples. Line up plenty of help to see you through the rough times. Maintain a sense of humor. Find the joy in your amazing babies. Establish priorities and give yourself permission to temporarily release any nonessential responsibilities.

Communication is key. Talk to your spouse or partner about your feelings. Share your experience with fellow parents of multiples; they will understand what you are going through. Down the road, you will recall the rush of emotion that followed the birth of your babies with amazing tenderness.

Special Delivery: The Birth Day

- **How the babies are arranged in your uterus may determine how they are delivered.** Presentation describes how the babies lie, and they can be arranged in several combinations. Babies can be vertex (head down), breech (head up), or transverse (lying sideways). Vertex babies are the best suited for vaginal delivery.
- **While many multiples are delivered by cesarean section, a vaginal delivery is a safe option for twins if the situation is free from complications.** Vaginal delivery is preferred as the safest approach, but some

circumstances make it risky for multiples. If you are having triplets or more, if your twins are monoamniotic, or if there are problems with the placenta, vaginal delivery may not be an option. Vaginal delivery may be discouraged if one or both babies are in a breech presentation, the babies are premature, or the babies or mothers are in distress.

- **In the second stage of childbirth, the babies are pushed out of the womb.** The baby that presents closest to the cervical opening will be born first, and after a short interval (usually within thirty minutes in normal circumstances), the second multiple arrives. The intermission between births is a critical and chaotic time. The second baby will be closely monitored for signs of distress, and medication may be administered to ensure that the labor process does not abate.

- **The final step is delivery of the placenta—or placentas—followed by a time of assessment.** As mom gets cleaned up, the babies are weighed and measured and their condition is evaluated. If the birth is premature, the babies may be whisked away for medical treatment to stabilize them for life outside the womb. But if circumstances permit, you may have an opportunity to meet and greet your new arrivals.

- **Many multiples are delivered by cesarean section.** A surgical delivery—whether scheduled or the result of urgent circumstances—is performed while the mother is anesthetized. Although it requires a more difficult recovery for mom, it may be the safest option for multiples who are at risk or in distress. Although doctors generally try to avoid a combination delivery in which mom must undergo—and recover from—both labor and surgery, it does occur on occasion.

- **After giving birth, mom's body needs some time to recover.** Even though the focus is on the new arrivals, attention must be given to mom's postpartum condition. Both vaginal and surgical deliveries require some recovery time, as her body repairs any damage from pregnancy and childbirth. Consult with your medical caregivers about any causes for concern and be prepared for some emotional, as well as physical, reactions.

CHAPTER 16

Premature Multiples

Prematurity is a reality for many multiples. While it's not the ideal way to begin life, these babies are remarkably adaptive and can usually overcome their early start after a few weeks in the hospital. Premature babies will require specialized medical care. It's not the most pleasant experience for babies, or their parents, and it's a difficult topic to talk about. Nevertheless, it's vitally important for parents of multiples to understand the ramifications of prematurity in the event that their babies do arrive early.

The Impact of Premature Birth

Normally, human babies require about 270 days to fully develop in the womb, after which they are usually ready to make the transition to life on the outside. When babies are born too early, many of their body's organs and systems are immature, unable to function properly on their own. Fortunately, medical science has the ability to help those babies stay alive until they can sustain themselves.

The consequences of premature birth vary from short-term to long-lasting. Some are major disabilities while others are minor inconveniences. Some are manifested immediately while others may not surface until later in life. How prematurity will affect your babies depends a great deal on just how early they were born. For example, cerebral palsy, mental retardation, and blindness are all major complications that result from premature birth. At the other end of the spectrum are minor conditions that can be corrected or overcome later in life, such as asthma, vision deficiencies, hyperactivity, or orthopedic irregularities.

▼ PREEMIE VIABILITY

Weeks Gestation	Survival Rate Estimate
22 weeks	1–7%
23 weeks	2–26%
24 weeks	16–55%
25 weeks	33–77%
26 weeks	54–84%
27–30 weeks	95%

Birth is the transition point between development in the womb and life on the outside. Premature babies simply aren't ready to exist in the outside world. Fortunately, medical intervention makes it possible to sustain their vital systems while the babies adapt to the conditions of life and finish developing outside the womb. However, their immature functioning can often cause irreparable damage to vital organs.

One of the most difficult aspects of having premature multiples is not knowing where they will land within the spectrum of severity. There is simply no way to know what the future holds. Only time will reveal the full impact of prematurity on your multiples.

FACT

Twenty-five years ago, babies born prior to twenty-eight weeks were not considered viable. However, advances in medical technology now make it possible for some infants as young as twenty-two weeks to survive. For each week that the baby is denied development in the womb, the chances of catastrophic complications increase.

Medical Issues of Premature Birth

Preemie babies face such a daunting array of challenges. Nearly every physical system is affected. Some of the issues can be addressed medically, with drugs, treatments, and even surgery. Others simply require the passage of time and will resolve with maturation.

Respiratory Problems

Breathing is the biggest problem for premature infants. Without breath, the intake of oxygen and outflow of carbon dioxide, a human simply can't live. Designed to function in the fluid-filled environment of the womb, preemie babies' lungs just can't make the immediate transition to air; they're almost like a fish out of water.

Helping your babies breathe is a critical step in stabilizing them after birth. Initially, a hand bag can be used for artificial respiration until the babies are intubated, or placed on a ventilator. The ventilator, also called a respirator, essentially does the breathing for them, forcing air in and out of their lungs. Some babies will need to breathe air with a higher concentration of oxygen until their lungs mature enough to tolerate the air around them. The ventilator may mimic the physical process of breathing for your babies, but eventually their brain must take over the operation, reminding them to breathe on their own.

One of the major causes of respiratory distress in premature infants is the lack of surfactant, a component in the lungs that makes breathing easier.

Just as stretching out a balloon makes it easier to blow up, surfactant makes the lungs more elastic and easier to fill with air. Administration of synthetic surfactant greatly enhances your babies' ability to breathe on their own.

ALERT

Many premature babies suffer permanent lung damage due to the time spent on the ventilator and must cope with chronic lung problems throughout their lives. It is crucial that they avoid exposure to cigarette smoke after you bring them home.

Apnea, or the temporary cessation of respiration, can occur in babies born prior to thirty-four weeks, and even up to thirty-six weeks. Medication can help overcome the problem. Just as a cup of coffee wakes up an adult in the morning, caffeine is used to jolt the baby's immature respiratory system back into action.

ESSENTIAL

The deficiency in a preemie's lungs also affects the heart. Apnea is often accompanied by bradycardia, an abnormally low heartbeat defined as less than 60 beats per minute. If you have preemies in the NICU, you'll often hear the medical staff refer to "Aps" and "Bradys," nicknames used to describe the occurrence of apnea and bradycardia.

Some babies don't require a ventilator but still have trouble taking in enough air to fill their lungs. Continuous positive airway pressure (CPAP) helps accomplish that by keeping the lungs inflated via small tubes inserted into the babies' nostrils. CPAP can also be an effective transition step between the ventilator and unassisted breathing.

Cardiovascular Conditions

The heart is also profoundly affected by prematurity. Many preemie babies have heart problems. An atrial septal defect (ASD) is essentially a hole in the heart that doesn't completely close over during development.

Depending on the size of the hole, the heart can still function normally, and the defect can be easily repaired without surgery when the infant is stronger. Patent ductus arteriosus (PDA) is a shunt malfunction that causes blood to divert from the lungs.

Neurological Impact

One of the most frightening and uncontrollable effects of premature birth is on the brain and nervous system. Unfortunately, there is little that doctors can do to treat these problems, and it can be excruciating for parents to endure a "wait and see" approach.

Premature infants often suffer a variety of brain injuries. The consequences of the injuries can be mild, such as hyperactivity or learning disabilities, or much more serious, including epilepsy, cerebral palsy, mental retardation, or, ultimately, death. Fortunately, the risk of these injuries subsides after thirty-five weeks' gestational age.

Gastrointestinal Problems

In the womb, the placenta(s) delivered nutrients to your babies via their umbilical cords. The babies' gastrointestinal systems didn't need to take in food, digest it, derive the essential nutrients, and move it through their intestines to be excreted as waste. Once the cord is cut, however, they're out of luck. They have to take in nutrients in order to continue growing, yet their stomach and intestines aren't ready to function.

Among the many tubes and lines emanating from a preemie baby is likely to be a feeding tube to supply nutrition. These come in several forms, depending on the baby's specific feeding problems. In the most severe cases, a parenteral intravenous line bypasses the intestines to administer nutrition directly into the blood. When the stomach is able to tolerate it, the babies will be fed enterally, either through a nasogastric tube slipped through the nostrils or through a tube inserted directly into the stomach through the abdominal wall. The babies' gastrointestinal systems can atrophy if not utilized, causing permanent damage, so it's important to attempt enteral feeding as soon as possible.

Unfortunately, enteral feeding has its own unpleasant consequences. Some premature infants are afflicted with a devastating gastrointestinal disorder called necrotizing enterocolitis (NEC). Essentially, tissue in the bowel dies due to infection or inflammation. It usually occurs in preemie babies about a week after birth or after enteral feeding is initiated. In some cases, a small area of dead tissue can repair itself, but large areas of NEC will cause the bowel to rupture, allowing the septic intestinal contents to spill into the intestinal wall and eventually into the bloodstream.

Surgery can be performed to halt the progress of NEC by removing the affected portion of the intestines. In severe cases, when the entire bowel dies, transplantation is an option. In mild cases, the condition can be treated with "intestinal rest" (returning to parenteral feeding), antibiotics, and naso-gastric drainage. Babies usually recover from NEC, and it does not usually produce any long-lasting gastrointestinal disorders.

ALERT

Breast milk has been proven to help prevent NEC in premature babies. Even though they can't directly nurse their babies at first, mothers of multiples are strongly encouraged to provide milk by pumping their breasts.

Premature infants are also quite susceptible to constipation and are often treated with medications, such as glycerin or laxatives, to stimulate their bowels. Because breast milk is generally gentler on premature diges-tive systems, providing expressed milk is one way that you can help alleviate your babies' suffering.

Delicate Skin

A premature baby does not look like a normal newborn. If you look past the tubes, contraptions, and devices surrounding them, one of the first things that you'll notice is the appearance of their skin. Discolored and shiny, it may be covered with fine downy hair called lanugo. Babies in the watery womb don't need the same kind of protective covering that they require in an air environment and don't develop the "thicker" skin that we're accustomed to seeing on full-term infants until thirty-four to thirty-six weeks' gestation.

Their thin skin and lack of body fat also inhibit a preemie's ability to regu-late his body temperature. Many premature infants are housed in incubators or isolettes, clear plastic boxes, to help them keep warm. Because they create a barrier around the babies, they may feel intimidating to parents who want closer contact with their children, but they serve an important purpose in helping babies adjust to life outside the womb.

Premature skin can be very sensitive to touch. Your doctors, nurses, and caretakers will advise you on how to interact most comfortably with your babies. It is frustrating and disheartening not to be able to hold and caress your eagerly awaited infants. Give them time to grow and develop, and stay focused on the time when you'll have the opportunity for closer contact.

ESSENTIAL

Kangaroo care is a pleasant procedure that not only helps your baby maintain her temperature but also promotes parental bonding. Babies are positioned skin-to-skin on your chest, allowing your body to radiate onto them. It's a warm, cozy experience that fathers can participate in as well as mothers.

Additional Complications

Numerous other complications are associated with prematurity. Sometimes during the NICU experience, it may seem that every improvement is accompanied by one or more additional problems. Because your premature babies have missed out on crucial development time in the womb, they are being forced to adjust to life in a harsher environment, and the impact of that is manifested in many different ways. Oftentimes, the very treatments that are intended to preserve their life cause damage and further complications.

Some of the other conditions that your babies may have to contend with are:

- **Jaundice:** This condition, characterized by yellow skin tone, is caused by excess bilirubin (a by-product of red blood cells) in the blood. Preemies are more susceptible to jaundice because lower levels of bilirubin are toxic to their immature livers, meaning that they reach the level of "excess" more quickly. Jaundice is usually treated with phototherapy, a special type of light that helps to break up the bilirubin.

- **Retinopathy of prematurity (ROP):** Retinal damage to the babies' eyes may cause temporary blindness and permanent vision damage. Your preemies may have to wear glasses when they grow up and should receive follow-up care from an ophthalmologist.
- **Anemia:** Preemies develop anemia for many reasons. The deficiency of red blood cells necessary to carry oxygen throughout the body may require a transfusion to correct.
- **Reflux:** Stomach acid backs up into the digestive track, causing discomfort and vomiting. Medications can control the problem and alleviate symptoms.

Other medical issues may not be apparent until months, or even years, later. They include cerebral palsy, chronic lung disease, learning disabilities, and hyperactivity.

Surviving a NICU Stay

It's up to the medical team to help your babies survive. But what about your survival? An NICU experience can be every bit as excruciating for parents as it is for the actual patients. Having one child in the hospital is stressful, but having two, three, or even more critically ill preemies can push parents to the edge. There are some coping strategies that make the situation more bearable and may indirectly help your babies' progress as well.

Changing Emotions, Changing Relationships

Don't be surprised by irrational reactions or unexpected emotions. Becoming a parent of preemie multiples is a tremendously stressful ordeal. You are likely to experience a whirlwind of feelings: frustration, anxiety, loneliness, elation, hope, despair, guilt, anger, and grief. Many mothers mourn for the loss of their "normal" pregnancy; they may feel as if they've been cheated out of the last few months. You may exhibit the classic stages of grief: denial, anger, bargaining, depression, and acceptance.

You may be surprised by how the NICU experience changes every aspect of your life. Your relationships with others may take on a new dynamic. The strain of having multiples in the NICU can take a toll on marriages, as well as relationships between family members and friends. You may feel resentful toward your friends who have "normal" pregnancies and babies. You may feel irritable with well-meaning friends and relatives who are constantly asking for updates or offering to help. You can't let your emotional state affect your care and handling of the babies, and you may be called on to make vital life-or-death decisions regarding their care.

FACT

Many hospitals assign families with preemies a social worker or advocate to guide them through the maze of medical terminology, insurance claims, and other issues. A counselor may be able to help you sort through your feelings so that you are better equipped to handle the situation.

Getting Through the Tough Times

In addition to counselors and social workers, the doctors, nurses, and staff that are responsible for caring for your babies are also an invaluable resource. Everyone has personality quirks and bad days, but for the most part you will find them as a group to be incredibly knowledgeable, caring, and responsive to your questions and requests. Don't be afraid to speak up. Ask questions. Ask for clarification if you don't understand the answer. If you forget the answer, ask again. You are your children's best advocate.

Many NICU hospitals have a support network for parents of preemies. Many of the members will be fellow parents of multiples. Talking to other parents who have experienced the NICU can be very reassuring. You'll realize that you are not alone in your journey and that other babies have survived more severe challenges than yours. If your hospital does not have a parents' network, contact your local parents of multiples club. They are likely to have members who have experienced the challenges of a NICU stay.

Because a NICU stay can extend for weeks or even months, it's important to establish a routine. You can't spend every moment at the hospital; allow yourself to take breaks to relieve stress, eat healthy meals, and get plenty of rest. If you have other children at home, you'll need to spend time with them as well.

ESSENTIAL

Create some structure within your day, allocating time with the babies at the hospital and time to lead your life. You can easily get burned out by worry and exhaustion if you don't. Many parents find it helpful to return to work in order to keep their mind occupied. It is not disloyal to the babies to do so.

Your spirituality may be of great comfort during your family's NICU experience. NICU nurses have observed that parents who have faith in a higher power have an easier time coping with the stress. Attending religious services, praying, talking to a clergy leader, and relying on the support of a church network may provide comfort and a sense of peace amid the crisis.

Contribute What You Can

One of the most frightening and frustrating aspects of parenting preemies is a feeling of loss of control. With doctors, nurses, and medical staff in charge of your babies, it can be difficult to determine your role. You have to get permission to even touch your own children. It can be difficult to bond with your babies under these circumstances. However, there are many ways that you can participate in your babies' care. Anything you can contribute will provide a sense of control over your situation. Medical science does not underestimate the importance of parental nurturing of preemies. Here are some things to consider, provided they are approved by your hospital's NICU policies:

- Make a tape of your voice talking, singing, or reading to the babies.
- Put up pictures of loved ones in the babies' incubators.
- Do the babies' laundry.
- Take lots of pictures of your babies. (You may not think that you'll want to remember this trying time, but you will!)
- Put stuffed animals or other comfort items in the babies' beds.

Perhaps one of the most important ways that mothers can contribute to their babies' progress is by pumping breast milk. Many NICUs have pumping facilities, or you may also want to rent or buy a pump for use elsewhere. A little breast milk is better than none; more breast milk is even better. The earlier you start and the longer you can keep it up, the better. The composition of breast milk from a mother of preemies is different than from a full-term mother. Its special properties benefit the babies in many ways, helping to prevent infection and promote growth.

ESSENTIAL

As your babies progress, talk to the staff about positioning them near each other. Most hospitals require that multiples be separated in order to reduce the risks of infection and mix-up, but they may be willing to consider your requests when the babies are older and healthier. Although there is no scientific proof, some theories support the idea that multiples receive comfort and strength from the close proximity.

The Road to Home

Once your babies have stabilized and conquered some of the more acute medical challenges mentioned earlier, their main requirement will be time: time to grow and develop. NICU staff often calls babies in this phase "feeders/growers." Usually babies require hospitalization until the time of their original due date, so it could be many weeks or months until your babies are big enough and strong enough to go home with you.

Discuss the standards of release with your doctors, but in most cases each baby will have to be able to do all of the following before going home:

- Suck and swallow to take in food (some babies are allowed home with a feeding tube, however)
- Urinate and defecate (in mommy language, that's "pee and poop")
- Maintain body temperature

In all likelihood, one of your multiples will accomplish those developmental milestones before the other(s). Doctors usually observe that the first-born multiple progresses faster, while the second-born faces more challenges and complications. With higher order multiples, the pattern continues, with the last born usually exhibiting the most problems.

Although graduating from the NICU is a joyous accomplishment, it is not the end of your journey. If you have to leave one or more babies in the hospital, it can be a rather bittersweet occasion. Your routine may become more complicated as you try to balance caring for your released multiple with visits to the hospital.

Caring for Preemies at Home

Hooray! The long-awaited moment has finally arrived, and your whole family is reunited at home. Although it is a happy occasion, some parents are surprised to discover that caring for their babies at home presents its own set of challenges. Some experience a sort of delayed depression, similar to postpartum depression.

ALERT

Parents of preemies should receive instruction in infant CPR so that they are able to resuscitate their babies in the event of an emergency. The staff at the NICU should be able to recommend a training program.

Hospitals acknowledge that while they are very good at caring for babies in intensive care, they are not as effective at preparing parents to care for the babies at home. Some facilities do encourage parents to care for their babies in the hospital for a night or two before they are sent home, but not much else is offered in the way of formal training.

ESSENTIAL

Although prematurity is a very frightening subject for parents, it's also an area of medicine associated with countless stories of miracles and hope. Advances in technology make it possible for even the tiniest of babies to survive. And despite their fragile appearance, don't underestimate the strength of premature infants, described by one neonatologist as "the strongest creatures on earth."

Some of the specialized equipment that kept your babies alive in the hospital may accompany you home. Breathing monitors sound an alert if a bout of apnea occurs. Some babies may remain unable to take in food by mouth and will require feeding tubes, while others will require oxygen tanks. Be sure that you understand how to operate and maintain any specialized equipment.

As happy as you are to leave the hospital environment, it won't be long before you have to schedule a round of follow-up appointments. Your babies may require follow-up care with specialists in ophthalmology, cardiology, or pulmonology, as well as occupational therapy, physical therapy, or other specialties. Transporting the babies to and from appointments can be complicated, and during such times, an extra set of hands will prove invaluable. Your babies will also need to receive regular checkups from a pediatrician. Be sure that the doctor you choose has some experience in treating children who were born prematurely and is aware of the special challenges they may face later in life.

Some families find it awkward to accept help from others when the babies return home. After weeks or months of relinquishing control to the hospital staff, they feel compelled to control the babies' care when they come home. Don't fall into the trap of denying help when you need it. Accept offers of help, but be specific in designating which forms of help are most comfortable for you. You may be wary about letting others handle the babies for fear of spreading germs and infection. Instead, ask for help with meals, errand running, and other chores so that your time is freed up to care for the babies.

Preemie Pointers

- **Many multiples are born early and require extra care to transition to life outside the womb.** The severity of the impact of prematurity on your babies will depend upon how early they were born. The closer they come to a full gestation, the less severe the consequences of prematurity. Some of the effects cause short-term complications, while others result in long-term disabilities. There's really no way to predict the ramifications for your babies, but advances in medical technology mean that preemies have a better outlook than ever.

- **Preterm birth affects every system of the body.** The respiratory and cardiovascular systems are some of the more critical processes that aren't quite ready to function outside the womb, but prematurity impacts babies in many other ways. Premature babies may have difficulty eating and maintaining their body temperature. In the long term, prematurity may impact their eyesight, muscle development, or cognitive abilities.

- **Your babies may require specialized care in the hospital.** Because your premature babies missed out on critical development time in the womb, they may require special treatments—such as phototherapy, being housed in an incubator, or medications to help with digestion—to help their bodies adjust to their new harsher environment.

- **Having premature infants is a stressful experience.** It is understandable to feel overwhelmed, helpless, and anxious about your babies. You're concerned about the condition of not just one, but two or more individuals. During this difficult time, it can be helpful to find ways to be involved in the babies' care. Pumping breast milk, kangaroo care, doing the babies' laundry, and holding them when you can are all ways that you can contribute to their improvement. The support of family and friends will be meaningful in this experience, and the hospital may also offer counseling or a community of parents that can be helpful.

- **In order to be released from the hospital, your babies will have to meet some goals.** Once they overcome any critical challenges to their wellbeing, premature babies simply need time to develop the skills for survival in the "real world." Often, preemies will remain in the hospital until their original due date, so it can be a period of days, weeks, or even months. Once at home, premature infants may require some additional care, such as monitors or feeding tubes.

CHAPTER 17

Breastfeeding and Bottle Feeding

As soon as your babies are born, you'll be faced with the first of many tough parenting choices: how to fill their hungry tummies. Instinct and scientific research confirm that breastfeeding is best, yet formula marketers offer assurance that their products offer healthy convenience. With more mouths to feed, efficiency is a priority, but not at the expense of the babies' health and well-being. Ultimately, there is no right or wrong choice, only what works best for your family.

Making the Decision

To make an informed decision about feeding your multiples, it's important to understand the advantages and disadvantages of each method. Each approach naturally has benefits as well as drawbacks, not to mention its own set of outspoken supporters who will make their opinions well known to you as soon as you announce your pregnancy.

No matter what you choose, you are likely to experience opposition about your choices. Breastfeeding advocates will try to make you think you're sacrificing your babies' well-being if you give them bottles. At the other extreme, your friends, family members, and even some medical professionals may call you crazy and try to dissuade you from exclusively breastfeeding your multiples. Ultimately, you have to do what's best for your babies; that may be breastfeeding, bottle feeding, or a combination of both.

Take the opportunity during your pregnancy to research the issue. Books, including this one, magazines, and websites will reveal useful factual information. Fellow parents of multiples are also a valuable resource.

ALERT

As you talk to other mothers about their experience, ask them how they arrived at their choice and why it worked best for them. Pay particular attention to circumstances that resemble your own—for example, previous nursing experience (or lack of it), working or stay-at-home parents, or supertwins.

Whatever you decide during your pregnancy, leave yourself an opportunity to change your mind once the babies arrive. You simply have no way of knowing what the future holds. Ruling out one option or the other may create more difficult circumstances for you in the long run. Even the most experienced breastfeeding advocate may find it overwhelming to nurse triplets, while the most reticent may feel compelled to nurse if her premature twins would benefit from breast milk.

Breastfeeding Multiples

Many people wrongly assume that breastfeeding twins, triplets, or more is impossible. Not only is it possible, but it can be a very rewarding experience for the entire family. You might be surprised by how many mothers exclusively breastfeed their twins and, with higher order multiples becoming more commonplace, even mothers with triplets or more have great success with nursing their babies.

The Benefits of Breastfeeding

The numerous benefits of breastfeeding are undeniable. For multiples, who are often at a developmental disadvantage due to low birth weight or prematurity, being breastfed can provide a wonderful boost. Consider the following benefits:

- Nursing aids teeth, jaw, and facial development.
- Antibodies in breast milk protect infants from illness.
- Breastfed babies have fewer allergies.
- Breastfed babies have fewer ear infections.
- Studies have shown that breastfed babies have higher IQs.
- Some studies suggest that breastfed babies grow up to have less incidence of obesity or hypertension.
- Nursing enhances bonding and helps the babies feel secure.

Breastfeeding also benefits the mother in several ways. For example:

- Nursing after childbirth increases the level of oxytocin in the mother, stimulating the uterus to return to normal quickly.
- Mothers who breastfeed generally lose weight more rapidly.
- There is some evidence to suggest that breastfeeding reduces the mother's risks of certain cancers and diseases, such as diabetes, osteoporosis, postpartum depression, breast cancer, and ovarian cancer.
- Breastfeeding mothers delay the onset of menstruation after pregnancy, decreasing the risk of iron-deficiency anemia.

Finally, breastfeeding brings several benefits to the family as a whole. First and foremost, it's free! Breastfeeding can represent a substantial savings for families with multiples. A researcher calculated that families who formula feed spend approximately $400 per month for supplies and equipment. That estimate only covers one baby; double it or triple it, and the costs skyrocket.

ESSENTIAL

Regardless of the final outcome, your initial attempts to nurse in the first few days after birth are extremely beneficial to your babies. Before your milk actually comes up, your body produces colostrum, sometimes called "liquid gold" because of its highly concentrated nutrients and antibodies. It helps develop the babies' gastrointestinal systems.

In addition, breast milk is readily available. There's no mixing or reheating. It doesn't require a midnight dash to the all-night market for refills when you run out. It doesn't have to be shaken or stirred. You don't have to wash and sterilize dozens of bottles, nipples, and accessories. And it's always the perfect temperature for your babies. Breastfeeding is the "green" choice, a renewable resource that does not impact the environment with demands for energy to package, transport, prepare, or dispose of it.

Your breast milk is the most desirable food source for your babies. However, breastfeeding is tremendously demanding on a mother of multiples, both physically and emotionally. It will be your primary activity during the first few months of their lives, requiring most of your time and consuming nearly all of your energy. To breastfeed exclusively requires determination, commitment, and a strong support system; it is not the right option for every mother.

Breastfeeding Twins

When breastfeeding twins, the first question to address is: together or separately? Since most mothers have two breasts, it is often convenient to nurse both babies simultaneously. It saves a great deal of time, but can be a tricky maneuver. The process of getting two babies on and off the breast sometimes requires an extra set of hands. In the beginning, you'll probably want some assistance in getting the babies arranged for nursing. A lactation consultant or maternity nurse can help while you're still in the hospital; once you are at home with the babies, enlist the help of your partner or someone you're comfortable exposing your breasts to.

For infant twins, the football hold works well, especially for mothers who have delivered via cesarean section. This position keeps the bulk of the babies away from the tender incision site. As the twins get bigger, the parallel, or "spoons," hold is convenient, while the criss-cross and front-V position are ideal for older babies who don't require as much head support. A good supply of pillows will support the babies so that you can use your hands elsewhere.

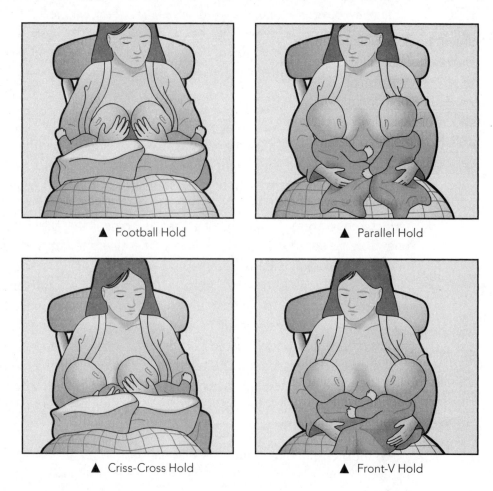

▲ Football Hold

▲ Parallel Hold

▲ Criss-Cross Hold

▲ Front-V Hold

Once the babies are in position near your breasts, it's time for them to latch on. One at a time, brush the babies' lips with your nipple to provoke them to open their mouths wide. As soon as there is an opening, quickly bring the baby to your breast. The babies should take the entire areola into their mouths, not just the nipple tip. Their lips should be turned out and their noses should be touching the breast. (Don't worry, they can still breathe!)

QUESTION

Can my body produce enough milk for both babies?
Breastfeeding works on a supply and demand system. The more you breastfeed, the more milk your body will produce. Nursing often and allowing the babies to empty both breasts will help you establish an ample supply of milk.

The frequency and duration of breastfeeding may vary, but most full-term newborns need to nurse ten to twelve times a day during the first few weeks. If you're feeding your babies simultaneously, it helps to keep them on the same schedule. If one baby is ready to nurse, put the other on the breast at the same time, even if you have to wake him up. Some experts decry the notion of ever waking a sleeping baby, but they probably don't have multiples!

Breastfeeding Triplets or More

If you have three or more babies, you obviously won't be able to nurse them all at the same time. It is still possible to nurse triplets, quadruplets, or higher; it just takes some organization and perseverance. Mothers of higher order multiples who want to breastfeed should assume that nearly all of their waking moments in the first few weeks at home will be spent with a baby or a pump at the breast.

Most mothers of higher order multiples find it easiest to use a rotation feeding schedule. For example, Babies A and B will nurse at the breast while Baby C receives a bottle of expressed breast milk. At the next feeding, Babies B and C are breastfed and Baby A receives a bottle. At the third feeding, Babies A and C are at the breast while Baby B takes the bottle.

Another approach is serial breastfeeding, or feeding each baby one after the other. It requires a lot of time and patience but allows each baby to have individual time with mom and ensures ample milk production. Be sure to alternate breasts as each baby feeds so that both sides will produce an equal supply.

Breastfeeding Preemies

If your multiples are born prematurely, you may not have the option to breastfeed them immediately. Preemies are often born without the ability to suck and swallow like full-term infants, so nursing may be delayed until they catch up developmentally. However, you can still provide the benefits of breastfeeding by expressing colostrum and breast milk. Whatever amount you provide will be incorporated into their feedings and will be a welcome boost to their nutritional needs.

Potential Pitfalls

If you expect that something as natural as nursing a child would come easy, you might be surprised by how difficult it can be at times. Even if you have successfully breastfed other children, you may find that nursing multiples presents some challenges. There are going to be times when you think you simply can't do it, and want to give up. Recognizing and addressing the potential pitfalls that you may encounter along the way can help you prepare to resolve any problems if they occur.

Many mothers give up on breastfeeding before they really get started by not giving their body time to recover from childbirth and set up for nursing. In the first few days following birth, your breasts produce colostrum, the clear, yellowish premilk substance that is so rich in vital nutrients for newborns. About three days later, your milk will "come in," the term used to describe the transition from colostrum to the milk, which is a bluish-white liquid. During this time, your breasts may become very full with milk. They may feel tight, uncomfortable, or even painful. It's important to remember that this is a temporary condition that usually lasts about a day, and that the best remedy is to nurse your babies or pump out the milk.

ESSENTIAL

You can relieve discomfort by applying cold compresses to your breasts in between nursing sessions. Bags of frozen peas work well for this purpose! Cabbage leaves also have some unknown but effective properties that alleviate breast discomfort. Try putting them inside your nursing bra.

Other signs of discomfort in your breasts, such as dry, cracked nipples or soreness after the first week, may be caused when the babies aren't latched on properly, but they can also be an indication of infection. If these problems persist, talk to your doctor or lactation consultant as soon as possible;

they can usually offer some solutions so that you can continue nursing your babies.

Sometimes women are tempted to forsake breastfeeding their multiples because it is too difficult to keep things straight. It's much easier to keep track of how many ounces each baby ingests when you can measure out the amount in a bottle. But remember, the mother's body will respond to her babies' demand for food; try not to worry as much about the exact quantity of intake, and concentrate more on your babies' behavior. Keep a chart to track each baby's nursing patterns. Establish a system that works for you; some mothers prefer to alternate the breast their babies feed from each time, others find that too complicated and assign each baby to the right or left side. Study and learn each baby's hunger cues, such as:

- Open lips
- Sucking on fist or fingers (or their co-multiple's body parts!)
- Rooting, or turning their open mouth toward the breast
- Fretful sounds

Although most experts advocate nursing on demand, especially in the first month to establish your milk supply, with multiples it's usually easier to follow a schedule. Early on, the babies may need to nurse every two hours, for as long as twenty minutes a session, especially since even full-term twins or multiples tend to be smaller birth weights. As they grow, the schedule will expand to every three or four hours. You'll know your babies are receiving sufficient nutrition by their output. Talk to your doctor or lactation consultant about what to look for in the first week, as stool frequency and appearance will differ from day to day and from baby to baby. After the first week, your babies should have at least six wet diapers and usually one soiled diaper per day. With more than one baby, don't rely on memory. Use a chart or log (see Appendix B for a sample) to help you keep track of who did what and when. If your babies exhibit any of the symptoms listed below, talk to your pediatrician, nurse, or lactation consultant to ensure that the babies are not dehydrated or malnourished:

- Listlessness, with a weak cry
- Sunken spot on the top of the head

- Dry lips
- Discoloration or yellowing of the skin, or skin that doesn't spring back when lightly pinched

Finally, the emotional and psychological burdens of breastfeeding multiples can discourage a mother from nursing. There's simply no private and discreet way to nurse two babies simultaneously, making it difficult to breastfeed them in public. It can be frustrating to be confined at home with little else to do but feed babies all day and night.

ALERT

Sometimes breastfeeding can be an issue of dissension between couples, especially if the mother's partner resents the breasts' functional change from sexual to nutritional. Open and honest communication about the issue, beginning during pregnancy, will help you work through the problem.

Any of these potential pitfalls, as well as a slew of others not mentioned here, may prompt you to abandon breastfeeding. It's important to make the decision with careful consideration, not in the midst of a hormone-crazed and sleep-deprived haze. Organize a support network that you can call on in times of trouble, including experienced mothers of multiples, your pediatrician, your lactation consultant, and trusted friends. They will assist you through the rough times, remind you of your commitment to give your babies the best possible start in life, and keep you on the path to breastfeeding success.

Getting the Right Nutrients

One of the biggest factors influencing the outcome of breastfeeding is maternal health. Just like a factory that relies on sufficient resources to manufacture products, the nursing mother's body requires proper caloric and fluid intake, as well as a nutritionally balanced diet, to produce breast milk. Remember, what goes into your mouth will be passed along to your babies via your milk. Just as in pregnancy, your health and well-being is of utmost priority while breastfeeding.

Throughout your pregnancy, your body experienced tremendous changes, including weight gain. After delivery, some of the extra pounds may decide to stick around. As tempting as it is to try to shed them immediately, restricting your diet while breastfeeding is not a wise approach. Fortunately, an added benefit of breastfeeding is that it utilizes some of the stored fat on your body, helping you to lose weight!

If you're trying to produce milk for two, three, or more babies, you'll have to eat enough to compensate. Experts recommend adding about 500 extra calories to your normal prepregnancy diet, approximately the amount found in a peanut butter sandwich or a cup of ice cream, but that's just for one baby! You'll have to adjust accordingly depending on how many babies you're feeding.

A healthful breastfeeding diet is more than just eating extra food. What food you eat has a big impact on the quality of the breast milk that you produce. Choose foods with nutritional power, not the empty calories of junk food. Good choices for a breastfeeding diet are:

- Lean meats
- High-fiber whole-grain cereals and breads
- Fresh fruit or 100 percent fruit juices
- Colorful vegetables, especially leafy greens
- Low-fat cheese or yogurt
- Eggs
- Beans

In addition to eating enough, you've also got to drink! It's much easier for your body to make milk if it's fueled with lots of liquids. Water is always the best choice, but juices and milk are also good options. You can also eat hydrating foods like fruits and soups. However, avoid caffeinated and alcoholic drinks. You don't want to pass along the effects of those drinks to the babies.

Sometimes certain foods the mother consumes can cause distress for the babies. Foods that cause gas, heartburn, or other digestive reactions for you will likely have the same effect on the babies, so avoid them while you're nursing. It takes about six hours for what you've eaten to have an impact on the composition of your breast milk. If you notice that a particular food item aggravates one or more of the babies, resulting in excess gas, spitting up, or fussiness, you'll want to stay away from that food until you have completed breastfeeding and weaned the babies.

ESSENTIAL

One way to ensure that you take in ample fluids is to drink a glass of water before beginning a nursing session. Then, refill the glass and keep it within reach so you can sip it while you breastfeed.

Alternative Feeding Using Breast Milk

Despite your best intentions, it may not be possible to immediately nurse your multiples in the traditional way. If you want to be sure that they receive all the benefits of breast milk, but are restricted from breastfeeding, there are some alternative methods you can employ.

Supplemental Nursing Systems

For some families, certain conditions may prohibit one or all of the babies from breastfeeding normally. As mentioned earlier, premature babies often haven't developed a sufficient sucking reflex. Or perhaps a baby's deformity, such as cleft palate, prevents nursing. Sometimes a mother is restricted from breastfeeding, either temporarily or permanently, but still wishes to pass along the benefits of breast milk. For any of these situations, devices exist that will allow you to simulate the experience of breastfeeding.

Finger feeding is an alternative method generally employed for short-term delivery of breast milk to a baby that is unable to nurse. The baby sucks on a tube attached to an adult's finger. Finger feeding can be instrumental in helping a baby develop proper nursing skills and also provides the intimacy of skin-to-skin contact.

A supplemental nursing system (SNS) delivers breast milk from a bottle via a tube connected to the mother's breast. A bottle containing breast milk hangs from the mother's neck, with tiny soft tubes that are taped to her breast, ending right at her nipple. The baby latches on to the mother's breast, including the tube, and receives milk just as if he were nursing.

Pumping

For moms of preemies or higher order multiples, pumping breast milk is a necessity; even mothers of full-term twins will find it to be a benefit. Expressing milk in the first few weeks enhances the supply of milk, ensuring that there is enough to go around. Meanwhile, building a stored surplus of expressed milk may also prove beneficial if mom needs a break—for example, if she is returning to work or wants to give dad a chance to feed the babies.

Breast pumps are available in two formats: hand-operated and electric or battery-operated. Hand pumps are useful for initial expressing of milk to establish supply in the first few weeks, but won't be very helpful for the mother who wishes to collect milk in greater quantities. The more powerful electric pumps are required for that job. You can buy a pump at any baby supply store, but might want to consider renting one. You'll get a top-quality piece of equipment designed for frequent use, and it may save you some money.

ALERT

Whatever equipment you use, be sure to select a product with double suction cups that allows you to pump both breasts simultaneously. It's a tremendous time saver and regulates milk production equally on both sides so that you don't end up lopsided.

To ensure a successful pumping session, follow these guidelines:

- Drink a glass of water before starting.
- Wash your hands thoroughly.
- Sit down in a comfortable, peaceful location.
- Look at your babies or a picture of your babies to encourage let-down of your milk.
- Use the proper collection receptacle for your breast pump model.
- Label the expressed milk and store it properly immediately after it is collected.

Breast milk should be refrigerated unless it is going to be used immediately. Refrigerated milk should be consumed within a week, but will keep in the freezer for months.

Dealing with Breastfeeding Guilt

While the benefits of breastfeeding are undeniable, sometimes it simply doesn't work out despite mom's best intentions and efforts. Nursing a baby is challenging enough; nursing multiples can be impossible and unfeasible for some families. The circumstances may be unfavorable if the babies are premature, or if the mother is recovering from a difficult pregnancy or delivery. Or the stress of having multiples may simply dictate that nursing is not an option, and bottle feeding is the most productive approach.

In such situations, the best solution is bottle feeding, regardless of the acclaimed benefits of breastfeeding. Mothers should not endure judgment for their feeding choices; each mother is capable of making the right decision for her multiples. If you find yourself unable or unwilling to breastfeed, do not allow criticism or anxiety to deter your confidence about mothering your multiples. Do not feel guilty, anxious, or inadequate about your decision; the right choice for feeding your babies is the one the works best for your family, whether by breast or by bottle.

Bottle Feeding

There are many reasons why families with multiples elect to bottle feed their babies. It definitely offers several advantages over breastfeeding, most notably that it allows someone other than the mother to be the primary source of food. Modern infant formulas, while not as perfectly nutritionally sound as breast milk, are able to provide a healthy alternative with the convenience of bottle delivery.

Bottle feeding requires a stockpile of supplies, and when there's more than one baby, all of the bottles, nipples, and formula may fill an entire pantry! It's always good to keep plenty on hand—running out when you have two or more hungry infants is not an option.

Before you leave the hospital, your pediatrician should advise you about the type of formula to feed your babies. Usually an iron-fortified product made from cow's milk is recommended for newborns because it most closely simulates human breast milk. However, your doctor may recommend other products such as soy formula for lactose intolerance or hypoallergenic products for allergy-prone babies. Don't give your baby alternative products unless instructed by your doctor.

Formula Basics

Formula comes in two basic forms. The most convenient—and most expensive—formulas are ready-to-eat. Some even come in their own disposable bottles! Others need to be dispensed into bottles. It's usually more cost-effective to use a formula product in a concentrated or powdered form; these are mixed with water before being served to the babies.

Some experts recommend sterilizing the water used for formula destined for infants under six months of age. Boiling the water removes impurities and kills potentially harmful bacteria. You may find it easier to skip that step and instead purchase bottled water. Discuss your local water supply conditions with your doctor to help you decide what's best for your babies.

QUESTION

Our water comes from a well. Is it safe to use in formula for the babies?
Well water often has a high concentration of contaminants and nitrates. Boiling it only increases the concentration of those elements. You should consider using bottled water for your babies' formula.

You may be puzzled by the diverse brands of formula on the market. The U.S. Food and Drug Administration (FDA) regulates the manufacture of infant formula to ensure that it is safe and nutritious. Both generic and brand-name products have to meet these federal standards. To your babies, the difference between one brand and the other can be equated to an adult's preference for Coke or Pepsi: a matter of taste. If you have strong preference for one, you may find the alternative unacceptable. Likewise, your babies may protest if you switch products on them!

Bottle Basics

Many bottle-feeding systems are available, and all have their own unique features. Ultimately, the best product is the one that works best for you and your family. Younger infants will need smaller four- or six-ounce bottles with low-flow nipple holes. As the babies grow, however, a feeding may average more than eight ounces, requiring larger bottles and nipples that allow a faster delivery of formula. You'll need at least one bottle per baby, but it's much more convenient to have a surplus.

Nipples are available in a wide range of styles, and it may take some experimentation to find the ones that work best for your babies. Some nipple styles mimic breastfeeding and are designed to reduce nipple confusion for mothers who choose to combine bottle feeding with nursing. Orthodontic nipples are shaped to properly develop a baby's gums and palate. Other nipple styles restrict the amount of air that babies intake as they suck formula, reducing (in theory, anyway) the discomfort of a gassy tummy.

FACT

In light of concern over the health effects of bisphenol-A (BPA), several states have enacted laws banning its use. The chemical, found in plastic products, is no longer used in the manufacture of baby bottles. Still, be sure that any baby bottle products that you purchase are certified "BPA-free."

There's no physical reason why babies require a warm bottle, but some do prefer it that way. Room temperature formula is usually comfortable for most babies, but since some formula products require refrigeration, you may find it necessary to warm up bottles before serving. If you choose to heat bottles, keep in mind that breast milk is delivered at body temperature, 98.6°F. Formula should never be served any hotter! Microwaving bottles is not recommended, since the liquid can heat unevenly. Despite that fact, many parents still do it. If you choose to, proceed cautiously. Always shake microwaved bottles thoroughly to disperse the heat, and test the contents to ensure they won't burn your babies' tender mouths.

To be safe rather than sorry, simply set the bottles in a pan of hot tap water for a few minutes to warm them. Electric bottle warmers are another option; they're probably not worth the cost for just one baby, but come in handy when you're warming multiple bottles.

Position Points

Proper positioning of the babies for feeding is important whether you are breastfeeding or bottle feeding. Be sure to support the babies' heads and bodies securely. Refer to the diagrams for nursing positions earlier in this chapter and emulate them for bottle feeding; the close contact and intimacy is important for bonding. Alternate sides and direction to enhance the babies' visual and cognitive development. Finally, holding a baby in a semi-upright position with the bottle at an angle helps prevent air intake.

Although it's tempting, and sometimes a matter of necessity, bottle propping is discouraged. Instead, consider a hands-free bottle, like the Podee products, for those times when you have more babies than hands. These bottles allow the container to rest upright by funneling the fluid into the nipple via a tube. It won't be long before the babies will be able to hold their bottles themselves! In the meantime, your infants should be held as much as possible during feedings. Use the time to cuddle and coo; make eye contact.

Combination Approach

Some families find that a combination of breast and bottle works best for feeding their babies, as this offers the advantages of both methods. Alternating between nursing and giving a bottle of either formula or expressed breast milk allows fathers and helpers an opportunity to feed a baby and gives moms a much-needed break. Each family has to find the system that best meets their needs. There are several ways to combine approaches:

- **Alternate babies:** One gets the breast, the other gets the bottle, and they switch at the next feeding.
- **Alternate feedings:** Breastfeed all babies one time, bottle feed the next.
- **Day/night rotation:** Breastfeed during the day, bottle feed at night. Alternately, working moms might try the opposite approach.
- **As needed:** Primarily breastfeed, but supplement with a bottle when mom needs a break.

Nipple confusion can be a concern when you combine the bottle and the breast. Sometimes babies prefer the relative ease of bottle feeding over a breastfeeding session where they have to work a little harder to suck milk. Other babies may prefer the closeness and comfort of breastfeeding and refuse to take a bottle if mom is nearby.

Whatever works for your family is the best option. Don't be swayed by well-intentioned but misguided advice from others. Have confidence in your ability to parent your multiples and to make the right feeding choices. Together, you and your babies will establish a routine that delivers optimum nutrition and convenience.

Feeding Facts

- **Feeding multiple hungry babies presents some challenges, and you'll have to choose the best method for meeting their needs.** The benefits of breastfeeding are many, but the challenges make it unfeasible for some families. Bottle feeding has its advantages, but can also be expensive and messy. Sometimes a combination approach provides the best solution; feeding pumped breast milk via bottles gives mom a rest while delivering the beneficial nutrients of breast milk.

- **Although challenging, breastfeeding twins or multiples is doable.** There are some ways to make it easier. Many mothers find success nursing both babies at the same time. A woman's body will produce breast milk in response to demand, so feed frequently to establish a supply. It's also important for you to maintain a diet of sufficient calories and fluids to fuel your body's milk production. Just as you took great care to eat right, drink plenty of water, and rest up during pregnancy, your responsibility to yourself—and the babies—continues as long as you're nursing.

- **Bottle feeding your babies takes some preparation as well and requires some supplies.** Stock up on formula, bottles, nipples, and caps, but don't invest too heavily in any one style or product until you're sure that they suit your babies' preferences.

- **Mom can pump milk from her breasts to store for later use, or to feed premature or higher order multiples.** Establishing a stockpile of refrigerated or frozen milk allows mom to get a break from feeding when necessary, whether she is returning to work or simply needs a rest. Pumping also helps increase the supply of milk to ensure that there is enough milk to go around. Moms of multiples are best served by a high-efficiency electric pump, rather than a hand-operated model, and may wish to rent equipment rather than purchase it.

CHAPTER 18

The First Few Months

Introducing twins, triplets, or more into a family demands some adjustments from everyone involved. The new babies are getting used to breathing, eating, and sleeping. The parents are juggling their work and home responsibilities while trying to meet the needs of two or more infants. Older siblings have to get used to sharing the spotlight with the new additions. Even the family pet has to adjust to the new smells, sounds, and schedules.

Getting Sleep

What's the hardest thing about having newborn multiples? Ask any parents and you'll likely hear a common lament: lack of sleep. With babies that need to eat every two to three hours around the clock, parents' normal nighttime sleep routine is out the window. Rather than retiring at 10:00 P.M. and rising refreshed at 7:00 A.M., they find themselves dozing for an hour in between feedings at 3:00 A.M., and catching a catnap at 3:00 P.M.

How Babies Sleep

Newborns need a lot of sleep. Unfortunately, the sleep patterns of young infants aren't concentrated during the nighttime hours, like adults'. Throughout a twenty-four-hour cycle, babies sleep, wake up to eat, and return to sleep several times. As they grow older, they'll start to extend the amount of time between feedings and thus stay asleep for longer periods of time. But in the meantime, parents have to adjust to a schedule of sleeping in short intervals.

Most full-term, normal-birth-weight newborns require between sixteen and eighteen hours of sleep a day. During the first few weeks, that time is spread throughout the day and night, in two- to three-hour bursts. Singleton parents can focus their attention on the baby when he awakes, then return to sleep when he does. The challenge for parents of multiples is that their babies' sleep patterns may not coincide, greatly reducing the amount of available rest periods in between feedings. In addition, multiples tend to be smaller; they often need to eat more frequently, and it may take more time for them to develop the ability to stay asleep for longer intervals.

Babies' sleep needs vary greatly. Some are able to stay asleep for five or six hours at a stretch as young as six weeks old. Others may take six months before they can sleep this long. There is no way to anticipate when that particular milestone will occur for each of your multiples; just rest assured that it will happen eventually.

Coping with the Lack of Sleep

So you've accepted the fact that having newborn multiples is going to be physically exhausting at times. There are some strategies that will help you survive the trying time until you can catch up on sleep.

From the very beginning, establish healthy sleep habits for your babies. The cozy, dark environment of the womb didn't distinguish between night and day, so newborns need some time to adjust to the new schedule. Many are born with their days and nights mixed up, being most alert in the middle of the night and sleeping soundly throughout the day. To encourage them to learn the difference, you can stimulate their senses when they are awake during the day and keep things still and quiet at night. For example, use bright lights, background music, and a cheerful voice during daytime feedings, but keep the lights dim and your voice low at night.

ESSENTIAL

Remember that infancy is temporary and fleeting. Your babies will grow older and stronger and they *will* sleep through the night. Rest assured that the day *will* eventually arrive, and take comfort in realizing that every new dawn brings you one day closer to that milestone.

Swaddling, the practice of wrapping babies "burrito-style" in soft blankets, is comforting to many babies and may help them to feel snug and secure while sleeping. It's most commonly used with newborns who are still accustomed to the close confines of their mother's womb. Research has shown that swaddled babies sleep more deeply and fall back asleep more readily when awakened. It's also been proven to reduce the risk of sudden infant death syndrome (SIDS) because it keeps babies in the safest position, sleeping on their backs. Babies usually outgrow the comforting effects of swaddling after a month or two.

ALERT

Don't allow young infants to sleep through their feedings during the first week or so, especially if they were born early. They need consistent nutrition in order to grow and develop. It may seem like a blessing, but sleeping for more than five hours at a stretch during the first few weeks may actually be a sign of a weakened state or even dehydration.

Some families find it helpful to take a tag-team approach in order to provide each parent with an opportunity for uninterrupted sleep. Mom might take the 9:00 P.M. to 2:00 A.M. shift, then dad takes over until the morning. If you have access to helpers, whether hired or willing volunteers, make the most of their assistance while you catch up on rest.

Finally, making resting a priority. Napping can be restorative when you can't get a full night's sleep. Sleep when the babies sleep; don't try to use that time to catch up on other things. Housework can wait!

Baby Care Multiplied

Leaving the hospital with the babies can be a terrifying event for new parents of multiples. With two or more tiny newborns dependent on you for their every need, it's no wonder that you feel anxious and overwhelmed! Don't let yourself worry too much—despite their fragile appearance, newborns are actually quite sturdy little creatures. Take confidence in your ability to parent your new multiples. With a little bit of creativity and organization, you'll be able to manage just fine.

For the first few months, your job is to keep the babies fed, clean, and clothed. That's not so hard, right? The challenge in caring for multiples is that they often have the same needs simultaneously, and you've only got two hands.

To keep your hands free, a baby carrier can be a lifesaver. Backpacks and front packs are great for babies who can hold their heads up, but not very effective for newborns. A sling-style carrier is a better option for newborns. Another option is to utilize the infant carriers that coordinate with your car seats. They make a comfortable resting place for the babies and are easy to transport through the house. Bouncy seats are another inexpensive type of equipment that fulfills this role.

Setting Schedules

Probably the most effective way to maximize your sleep opportunities is to get your babies on the same schedule. If you can feed them all at the same time and get them to sleep at the same time, then you've won the game. Because every infant is an individual, that is not always possible, but it is reasonable to establish a schedule that works out most of the time.

Ideally, feeding on demand is the most recommended approach for nurturing a singleton newborn. However, most parents of multiples find that it is more efficient to implement a more scheduled routine. That's not to say that you should ignore your babies' cues. You should never deny food to a hungry baby or ignore a baby's cries. Rather, you can gently encourage the babies to follow a complementary schedule by putting them to sleep together, changing diapers at the same time, and initiating simultaneous feedings.

Your schedule should be an organic plan that is constantly updated to meet your babies' changing needs, as well as the rest of the family's activities. You may encounter times when the babies appear to be hungrier more frequently. This behavior often precedes a growth spurt. During this enhanced period of growth and development, you'll need to adapt your schedule to meet their demand.

FACT

Growth spurts are good! They usually come before a period of increased sleeping. They frequently occur at about two weeks, six weeks, three months, and six months, but babies' timetables vary greatly.

Establishing a routine for other activities in your day will help keep the family organized and on track. The consistency provides a sense of security for your babies, because they know what to expect. For example, give the babies a bath at about the same time each day. As much as possible, schedule outings and errands during a designated time.

Easing your babies into a sleep routine will also help them to sleep longer and more soundly. Don't expect them to follow a sleep routine immediately, however. It will take some time to establish an acceptable routine, as the babies develop the ability to sleep for longer stretches at a time and concentrate their sleep hours overnight. But it's never too early to start constructing bedtime routines, using patterns of behavior that cue the babies that it's time to sleep. For example, an evening routine of a bath, followed by a feeding and snuggle time before putting each baby in his or her crib can help the babies recognize bedtime.

Bathing Basics

Because bathing a baby takes at least two hands, it's best to bathe multiples one at a time. This means bath time is one time where you can really make use of any available help. Fortunately, newborns don't get very dirty, so they only require a full bath a few times a week.

Perhaps the easiest approach is to set up bouncy seats or infant carriers in the bathroom or near the sink where you will bathe the babies. (It's easiest to bathe young infants in a sink or basin rather than a bathtub. You only need to use a couple of inches of water, and it will be easier to maintain a firm grip on their slippery skin within the confines of a smaller space.) Have all supplies ready and within arm's reach: soap, shampoo, washcloths, towels (plenty of them!), and diapers. Put the babies in their seats as you ready the water.

ALERT

Always fill the tub and test the temperature before you place a baby in the water. Never leave an infant in a tub while the water is running. The flowing water could change temperature and scald the baby's tender skin.

As you bathe the first baby, the other multiple(s) can remain in their seats. They are safely within your sight and will be comforted by the sound of your voice. If you have older children, they can be extremely helpful during this time by passing supplies and entertaining the waiting babies. They will enjoy participating in the babies' care, and you'll appreciate the extra set of hands, even if they are small! After you bathe and dry the first baby, he can be returned (with luck, content and soothed after the bath!) to his seat while you attend to his brothers or sisters.

Once your babies are a little bit older, you can bathe them in the bathtub using specially secured baby bath seats. One of the great joys of having multiple infants is watching the fun as they interact in the tub, splashing and enjoying the water. Of course, you should never leave babies unattended in the tub, even for a moment.

Changing Challenges

You'll do lots of changing in the first few months with multiples . . . changing diapers, changing clothes, and changing diapers again! As you get acquainted with your babies' individual habits, you'll figure out a system that works best for your family. Most families with multiples find that it saves time to change everyone together. If one is dirty, it's likely the other(s) will be too, and if not, they will be soon enough!

Diaper time is an excellent time to attend to your newborns' special needs. If your male multiples have been circumcised, you may be advised to change the dressing on their penis. Use small gauze strips and antibacterial ointment to cover the affected area until it heals, according to your doctor's instructions.

ESSENTIAL

The American Academy of Pediatrics neither recommends nor discourages the practice of circumcision, acknowledging that it is a completely personal decision that parents should decide based on the best interests of their child. Many premature infants are not able to undergo circumcision at birth, but must delay the procedure until they are ready to be released from the hospital.

For boys and girls, the umbilical cord stump should be checked daily. The remains of the cord that connected the baby's belly button to the placenta will dry up and fall off within about two weeks after birth. You should not try to remove it. At your doctor's suggestion, you can clean it gently by wiping around the base with a cotton swab dipped in alcohol. However, you may be instructed to leave the area alone, under the premise that it will heal faster on its own. Keep the area dry and protected from irritation from diapers or constricted clothing.

Crying Is Communicating

Newborn babies are a feast for the senses: the sight of ten perfect little toes, the smell of their tender skin, the silky softness of their downy hair. One of the great joys of having multiples is being able to revel in these glorious sensations. However, the sound of multiple newborns is not always quite so pleasant for parents. Researchers estimate that babies spend one to two hours a day crying. Multiply that by two for twins or three for triplets, and that's an awful lot of bawling!

Interpreting the Cries

Imagine if your babies were born with the ability to say, "Hi, Mom and Dad! We love our new home, but isn't it about time for dinner?" Unfortunately, language is an acquired skill, and until it develops, babies have to rely on other forms of communication.

Their primary mode is crying. If you think about crying as communication rather than an annoying emission of useless sound, you'll be a much more effective—and much less frustrated—parent. It's your job to translate the cries and craft an appropriate response.

ESSENTIAL

With multiples, you'll face the additional challenge of distinguishing the individual cries of each baby. Even as newborns, your multiples are unique individuals. Each has his own needs and his own style of expressing them. It's important to respond to them as individuals, rather than always as a group.

Babies cry for many reasons. They may be hungry and need to be fed. They may have a dirty diaper and need to be changed. They may be too warm or too cold. In addition to physical needs, they may also cry as a reaction to emotional needs, such as when they are overstimulated, startled, or seeking the comforting touch of a loving parent.

As you get to know your newborns, you'll learn to interpret their cries more effectively. Simply spending time with each baby will help you understand his or her language of crying. Through trial and error you'll learn how to satisfy their needs. External cues may also be helpful in interpreting their cries. A baby who is crying because she is tired may yawn, while a hungry baby may gnaw on her fist. An unusually loud or high-pitched cry may indicate illness or pain.

Coping with Crying

Crying is a part of life when you're caring for babies. Unfortunately, it can often become a source of frustration. As a parent, you want so badly to be able to soothe and comfort your children, and inconsolable crying may feel like a failure of that goal.

When the crying becomes overwhelming, it's vital that you take steps to avoid losing control. There will be times when all the babies are crying at the same time, and you simply aren't able to stop it. When that happens, try one of these coping strategies.

- **Walk away.** Put the babies in a safe, secure place, such as a crib or playpen, and walk into another room for a minute. Take deep breaths to calm down. Count to twenty and then return to the babies.
- **Use a calm, soothing voice to talk to the babies.** It doesn't matter what you say. The sound of your voice may offer some temporary consolation, or at the very least, reassure them that you are aware of their needs.
- **If their crying escalates over your calm voice, try singing!** It may not stop the crying, but it will distract you from the chaos at hand and help you endure the maelstrom.

Above all, keep a sense of humor. In a few years, this will be a funny memory of life with multiples.

Keeping Things Straight

With more than one baby in the house, it can be tough to keep track of all the details. Who ate what and when and how much? Was it Twin A who had a dirty diaper this morning or Twin B? Did you give all three babies their medicines or did someone get a double dose? Staying organized and having a system for record-keeping are important skills for new parents of multiples.

With your brain befuddled by lack of sleep, your first task is to remember which baby is which. If your multiples are identical, that can be tricky. Even dizygotic multiples can have remarkably similar appearances as newborns. Many parents of monozygotic—or identical—twins worry that they won't be able to tell their twosome apart. Veteran parents, however, acknowledge that it's not as difficult as you would think. Even though identical twins have similar physical appearances, those who know them intimately will have no trouble distinguishing them. Parents soon realize that there is more to recognizing their child than just appearance. There are exceptions, of course. Everyone gets mixed up occasionally when they are bleary-eyed from lack of sleep.

The first step in keeping things straight is to make each baby easily identifiable at first glance. Some parents find it helpful to dress each multiple in a designated color. (Twin A=green and Twin B=yellow.) If color-coordinating their wardrobe seems too complicated, consider other apparel clues: distinguishing hats, booties, or pacifier clips. There's one downside to color-coding: Eventually your babies will get undressed! If you rely too steadily on clothing cues, you'll likely become very confused when they're naked, for example, at bath time. Just in case, you can paint one tiny toe with a small dab of nail polish as a hint.

Once you can easily identify each baby, you'll need an organized system of tracking their vital information. Many parents rely on a chart similar to that found in Appendix B. During the first few weeks at home, it's vital to track crucial information about the babies' intake and output. If you are establishing breastfeeding, you'll want to keep track of how long each baby feeds and which breast they fed from. If you are combining breast milk and formula, a chart is very handy for keeping track of the alternating feedings.

FACT

Too modern for pen and paper? Tech-savvy parents can utilize programs for their smartphones or electronic devices to keep track of their babies. The programs have several handy features that give parents the ability to synch information between mom and dad and babysitters, as well as share milestones through social networking.

As gross as it sounds, monitoring the babies' diaper debris can help you ensure that they are getting proper nutrition and that their brand-new digestive systems are functioning properly. This is another instance where a chart or written record comes in very handy. Find a process that works for your family. You want a system that allows you to record important information without becoming cumbersome or an inconvenient burden.

Bonding with Everyone

When you're a parent of multiples, you become very interested in ensuring that each child receives his or her "fair share." You expend a lot of energy trying to keep things equal. Many expectant parents of multiples express concern that they won't be able to bond equally with each child. Will they have enough love to go around? Fortunately, the reality of having multiples is that a parent's capacity to love only increases exponentially in proportion to the number of children. Multiples only multiply the amount of love in a family; they don't divide it.

What Is Bonding?

Modern parents put a lot of emphasis on the process of bonding with their babies. The term describes the intense attachment that forms between parent and child. In a nutshell, it's like falling in love with your babies. In the short term it provides the motivation for parents to fulfill their child's needs, even at the sacrifice of their own. Over the long term, effective parent-child bonding is credited with numerous influences in a child's development. It provides the model for the child's future intimate relationships. It fosters a sense of security for the child and is said to enhance self-esteem.

FACT

The process of bonding with babies was first defined in the 1970s by two professors of pediatrics, Dr. Marshall Klaus and Dr. John Kennell. Their research changed the way that hospitals handle babies immediately following birth, encouraging them to give mothers and babies time to bond.

Sometimes bonding occurs instantaneously after birth, but for other families, it develops over time with routine caregiving. Sometimes the process is interrupted—for example, in situations where parents and child are separated shortly after birth, perhaps by a medical event. Such is frequently the case with multiples, many of whom are born prematurely or with other medical concerns. However, these impediments should not diminish bonding if parents are determined to overcome them.

Bonding with More Than One

There are many ways that parents of multiples can enhance their bond with their children. The strengthening of the emotional connection between parent and infant is accomplished by touch and smell. As much as circumstances permit, spend time holding and cuddling each baby individually. Face-to-face interaction is also important; look into your babies' eyes at every opportunity. Any of the following activities may be helpful in enhancing bonding. Take turns with each baby.

- Infant massage or other loving touch
- Singing
- Reading (It's never too early to start!)
- Skin-to-skin contact
- Rocking
- Talking and playing

It's not uncommon for parents to occasionally feel more attached to one baby. There's nothing wrong with that, as long as the feelings of attachment do not cause you to neglect the other multiple(s). Most parents find that feelings of partiality alternate among the children over time. If you are feeling an enduring preference for one multiple, you can overcome it by consciously spending more time with the other baby or babies.

Getting Out and About

Once you've mastered the routines at home, it's time to venture out into the world. You can't stay in the house forever! Getting out and about with infant multiples can be quite a challenge, requiring the planning skills of an army general, the packing power of a mule, and the arms of an octopus. There's no need to become a hermit, however. Some simple strategies will make on-the-go maneuvering more manageable.

The first requirement for heading out is a good stroller. You'll find that your investment in a quality double, triple, or quadruple stroller pays off the first time you leave the house. With newborns, you may need to adapt the stroller to accommodate their "floppy" bodies. If your model adjusts, fold down the seats to form an open carriage and lay the babies in the space. Or prop up the babies in their seats using rolled-up blankets or head rests to support their necks.

If you're traveling by car, it's imperative that your vehicle is equipped with approved infant car seats—one for each baby. In most states, the law requires that infants under twenty pounds be seated in the backseat in a rear-facing seat and some guidelines suggest that they should remain rear-facing until age two. Be sure that your car seats are properly installed. The make and model of your vehicle will determine the best arrangement of the seats within the car. Some cars are not wide enough to accommodate three seats across, so if you have triplets, or twins and an older child, you may have to consider other options and invest in a new vehicle.

The Diaper Bag

A diaper bag is a standard accompaniment for any family on the go with a baby, but what if you have multiples? You'll want to stock your bag with plenty of supplies, but you don't necessarily need to double or triple up. You will need a larger bag, however. Alternative bag styles might be a better option when you have twins or more. Consider a backpack or large tote.

ESSENTIAL

Always keep your diaper bag packed and ready to go. Restock items that you've depleted as soon as you return home so that you don't have to rush around the next time you're trying to get out the door.

In addition to diaper supplies, carry an extra outfit for each baby and feeding supplies (if you'll be out during mealtime). If your babies are partial to pacifiers, make sure that you stash extras and that you have enough to go around. A portable pad or blanket is a handy addition as well, providing a sanitary spot for changes when facilities aren't available on the go. Bibs, burp rags, plastic bags, and antibacterial hand sanitizers will be very helpful for cleanups. You don't want your bag to become burdensome to carry, but other handy items you might include are bottled water, toys (rattles, teething rings, or small books), medications, and an extra shirt for mom, just in case.

Here's a checklist to describe the contents of a well-stocked diaper bag for multiples.

- ❏ Diapers (one per baby for every two hours that you'll be out)
- ❏ Cleansing wipes
- ❏ Extra clothes (one outfit per baby, and perhaps an extra top for mom as well)
- ❏ Blankets or changing pad
- ❏ Bibs (one per baby)
- ❏ Burp cloths or spit-up rags
- ❏ Plastic bags (for disposing of dirty diapers or containing wet/dirty clothes)
- ❏ Accessories for temperature changes (extra socks, hats, jackets for babies)
- ❏ Food (formula for infants, baby food and snacks for older babies)
- ❏ Toys (small items, books, teethers for emergency entertainment)
- ❏ Hand sanitizer
- ❏ Emergency kit (first-aid items, sunscreen, teething ointment, cell phone, extra cash)

You may find it easier to have help the first few times you venture out. Often the first outing is to the pediatrician for a checkup, which can be a stressful experience in itself. You'll appreciate having an extra pair of hands available until you're comfortable juggling all the babies and their supplies on your own.

Surviving the First Few Months

- **One of the biggest challenges in the early months is getting enough rest.** The overnight hours will be punctuated with repeated feedings, burpings, and changings when you are responsible for multiple infants. Dealing with the fatigue and sleeplessness is one of the most daunting adjustments to having twins or more. But, with a little bit of creativity, you can establish a system to meet the babies' midnight needs, and make sure mom and dad get some shut-eye as well.

- **Establishing a schedule will make things easier for everyone.** Most families with multiples overwhelmingly agree that life is more manageable when both—or all of—the babies follow the same schedule. It may take a few weeks or months to establish a schedule for feeding and sleeping, and the babies may need some encouragement to stick together, unless they are monozygotic with similar metabolisms. Implement a system to keep track of the babies so that you can tell them apart and ensure that no one gets neglected.

- **Find ways to free up your hands so that you can focus on one baby at a time.** Slings, swings, bouncy seats, and even your car seat carriers are valuable resting spots when you need a place for one baby to wait while you attend to the others. Make use of this strategy when you're bathing, dressing, changing, or soothing your multiples.

- **Babies communicate through crying.** Get ready for some noise. Multiple babies can create quite a cacophony with their cries. Don't give in to the din. Keep in mind that they are simply trying to express their needs. Don't let the stress of crying babies overwhelm you.

- **The logistics of getting out and about with multiples may take some organization and practice.** Equip your vehicle with the appropriate restraint seats, and invest in a sufficient diaper bag to tote all of the babies' necessary supplies.

- **Enjoy this special time of bonding.** The precious early months with infants pass all too quickly, especially amidst the chaos of adjusting to multiples. Take a few minutes each day to slow down, savor the moments, and bond with each baby as an individual. You'll appreciate the tender memories of these infants as they grow up, all too quickly.

CHAPTER 19

Special Situations

Every set of multiples joins a unique family, with its own special routines, challenges, and relationship dynamics. Sometimes special family circumstances present extra factors to consider as you prepare for the arrival of multiples. No matter how your family is set up, adding multiples will mean a great deal of additional joy and love.

First-Time Parents

Here you are, new to parenting, and right off the bat you've been handed a double (or triple) whammy! Take heart. In some ways, having multiples first makes it easier to parent. With no previous parenting experience, you have no idea what to expect from one baby, much less two, three, or more. That's the good news; it's one situation where ignorance is definitely bliss! The bad news is that you have no previous experience. You haven't had the chance to develop confidence in your parenting instincts or the opportunity to create timesaving routines and shortcuts. You don't yet know your strengths and weaknesses as a parent, and your relationship with your partner has not been tested by the trials of sharing responsibilities. You won't have the luxury of adapting gradually to your expanded family, but will have to jump right in with both hands and both feet.

Getting Ready

With no children at home you have no excuses not to take it easy during your pregnancy. Use that time to read about and research parenting and pregnancy; with no prior pregnancy as a basis for comparison, you're less likely to know when something's out of the ordinary.

You have a lot more work to do in preparing your home to accommodate babies and children. With no hand-me-downs recycled from older siblings, you're starting from scratch. You'll have to spend some time—and money— to acquire all the necessary supplies and equipment.

ALERT

Don't feel that you have to buy out the baby supply store right away. Consult other parents for a realistic determination of what's essential immediately after the babies are born and what can wait until later on.

Adjusting to Parenthood

Upon being diagnosed with multiples, you may feel that the intensity of your pregnancy has been ratcheted up a notch. You may not feel "normal." As you reset your expectations for the future, you may even mourn the loss of normalcy. Now that you are having twins or more, your experience may be vastly different from your friends' pregnancies and you may feel that they can't relate to you.

As a first-time parent, it's even more important that you seek out the support and advice of other parents of multiples. A local multiples group is an invaluable resource for new parents, providing mentorship and companionship. It's also crucial that you line up a helpful support system. If you don't have an established network of babysitters and health care providers, start rounding them up well in advance of the babies' arrival. You're going to need the help!

It's easy for first-time parents to underestimate the need for assistance. You may think that you can go it alone or that you can handle it. Maybe you feel that you don't want to impose on the friends and relatives who offer to help you. Don't turn them down just yet! Ask the parents who've lived it before you; most all will agree that they wish they had accepted more offers of help.

FACT

Having multiples can put a strain on your marriage. However, while 39 percent of single parents of multiples reported that the emotional stress of having multiples contributed to the breakup of their marriage, a study by MOST (Mothers of Supertwins) found surprising results. Among nearly 3,000 survey respondents, 82 percent reported a positive level of marital satisfaction.

As new partners in parenthood, be gentle with your spouse through this experience. It's new for both of you, and you'll both have to adjust to new roles. The lines of responsibility are not yet clearly delineated; open communication about your expectations and feelings will help you establish routines and a comfortable pattern of family life. All aspects of your life and your relationship will undergo a change with the arrival of these babies. Be flexible and accommodating. Support and nurture each other through the experience.

Take Heart

Above all, don't be discouraged. One of the biggest things you lack as a first-time parent is perspective. You can't see the light at the end of the tunnel. You don't know from experience that eventually the upheaval will settle into a routine. Soon enough the babies will sleep through the night, feed themselves, and leave you for part of the day to attend school. There will be a time when you'll be able once again to sleep soundly, sit down for an entire meal, and enjoy sex.

Probably the biggest surprise in store for you is the amazing wonderment of becoming a parent. You won't believe how lucky you feel to have received the gift of multiples. Just one child is a wonderful blessing. You've been gifted with the miracle of multiples. For you, the joys of parenting are coming fast and furious, but they will fill your life with meaning and your heart with love.

Multiples After Infertility

Perhaps you've come to this point after a long battle with infertility. It's not surprising; the recent rise in multiple birth is directly attributable to advances in reproductive technology. Finding yourself pregnant with two, three, or more babies after an arduous struggle just to conceive one can leave you with some conflicted feelings.

You're not alone. It's estimated that 35 percent of pregnancies conceived with ART (assisted reproductive technologies) result in multiples. At that rate, you are quite likely to encounter other families who share your experience.

As you proceed through your pregnancy, you will likely find it very reassuring to connect with other parents in the same circumstances. During your battle with infertility, you may have felt that your fertile friends simply didn't understand your situation. Now that you're pregnant, you may feel similarly isolated and distanced from your infertility support community. But at the same time, you don't quite feel a common bond with parents who conceived spontaneously.

That's why it's important to establish a new support system, which includes other formerly infertile parents of multiples. Having an instant family after struggling to conceive will create some interesting issues for parents, and you will find that talking about your feelings with folks who have faced the same challenges can be quite reassuring. Your local parents of multiples group is a good place to start. Or your fertility specialist may be able to put you in contact with other families.

Facing Your Feelings

A common aftereffect of infertility, especially after failed attempts to conceive, is a sensation of fear—fear that this success is fleeting, fear that you'll lose these babies that you've wanted so desperately, fear that your "dream come true" will disappear. Don't let a fear of disappointment or loss keep you from bonding with your babies. Embrace your pregnancy with a positive, optimistic attitude so that you can give your babies the best possible start in life.

ESSENTIAL

While singletons conceived by assisted reproductive technology (ART) are three times more likely to be born prematurely, that trend does not hold true for multiples. The risks and complications associated with delivery were only slightly higher for ART twins than for those conceived naturally. A 2004 study showed that the risk of stillbirth or newborn death was actually lower for babies conceived with assisted reproduction.

Formerly infertile mothers often feel isolated from their peer parents when the talk turns to complaining about the negative aspects of motherhood. As someone who had to work very hard to have children, you may now feel that you don't deserve to complain about the aches and pains of pregnancy, the discomfort of labor and recovery, or the trials and tribulations of raising multiples. You asked for this, and you got it—the good, and the bad. After years of desperate wishing, you can't understand how other mothers feel resentful or frustrated by their children. You're sure you will never feel that way!

Don't judge other parents for their complaints. Deep down, they love and want their children, and they don't mean to be insensitive or ungrateful. And don't be a martyr. Pregnancy and parenthood aren't pretty sometimes. As much as you yearned for it, you don't have to like every minute of it.

Give yourself permission to join in the moaning of woeful parents, and enjoy being part of it.

Some parents feel that after working so hard to have their multiples, they can't possibly turn over their care to outsiders. Avoid that kind of "do-it-yourself" attitude. Just as you sought out assistance to conceive, don't be shy about seeking help once the babies are born.

Other Issues

Another factor for couples who come to a multiple pregnancy via infertility is the financial impact. Pursuing fertility assistance can be an expensive process. When successful, it is an investment that pays off in parenthood. However, the experience can leave parents deeply in debt, a problem only compounded by the expenses of raising multiples. If you find yourself in this situation, take action to address it before it becomes uncontrollable.

Throughout your pregnancy and as you raise your multiples, you may find yourself facing some uncomfortable inquiries. Well-meaning acquaintances and even perfect strangers will feel compelled to bluntly ask you, "Are they natural?" among other probings prompted by curiosity about multiples. They don't realize the insensitivity of their inquiry, and you're put in the awkward position of having to discuss the conception of your children. Be prepared with a response to these intrusive questions. You can be honest, polite, instructive, or simply let them know it's none of their business.

As time passes and your family becomes established, you will stop feeling "different." You'll exchange the rounds of fertility drugs and injections for baby Tylenol and vaccinations. When your children are old enough, be sure to share the story of their origin with them. Tell them how special they are because you wanted them so badly and worked so hard to become a family. Having multiples is a blessing unto itself, but having them after infertility is truly an amazing miracle.

Single Parents of Multiples

If you are facing multiple pregnancy and parenthood without a partner, you are likely all too aware of the additional challenges that lie ahead. You will be outnumbered, with more babies than adults in the household. You're going to need extra help, during pregnancy and beyond. It's never too early to start making arrangements for assistance. As your pregnancy progresses, a loss of mobility and a lack of energy may keep you from being productive.

ALERT

The National Organization of Mothers of Twins Clubs has a single parent support coordinator that serves as a source of advice and encouragement. Contact the NOMOTC (*nomotc.org*) for assistance in determining contact information for local resources, coordinating pen pals, and an informative brochure.

However, the period of time when you will most require help is during your babies' infancy. With only two hands, it will be quite a challenge to manage the care of multiple newborns. You may want to consider live-in help for a few weeks or months. If you can afford it, hire a nanny or night nurse to provide assistance. As the months pass and you become adept at single-handedly caring for your multiples, you will likely find that your need for help decreases.

Finding time for yourself is a vital issue for single parents of twins. Whether you are a single parent by choice, or through circumstances of divorce or death, you bear the primary responsibility for raising your multiples. To be an effective parent, you have to focus some attention on your own well-being. Think of it as preventive maintenance. Give yourself the opportunity to rest and relax, invest in your health, and develop your hobbies and interests.

In parenting, a partner provides emotional as well as physical support. Joining a support group where you can share advice and companionship with other single parents can fill that role for you. A list of resources for single parents is included in Appendix A.

Adopting Multiples

There are many routes by which a family adopts multiples. It could be an international adoption, where you open your home to encompass needy children from another part of the world. Or maybe you became the legal parents of additional children due to circumstances that left their biological parents unable to care for them.

No matter how it came to pass, this unique and special way of forging a family has its own set of challenges and obstacles to overcome. For parents in this situation, the need for support is great. It's important to seek out resources that address the special concerns of adoptive parents, as well as those aimed at parents of multiples.

Sometimes adoptive parents perceive a lack of acceptance from fellow parents of multiples and identify more closely with other adoptive families. Fortunately, both types of support are accessible in most locales. Your local parents of multiples organization may include members who have adopted multiples. In addition, organizations for adoptive parents provide support throughout the adoption process. There are hundreds of adoption-related support groups in North America. These groups give parents the opportunity to share their experiences and emotions, as well as information. Networking with these other parents who have similar experiences can be very valuable.

International Adoptions

In some cultures, the birth of twins or multiples is not a welcomed or cherished event. In societies plagued by famine or poverty, multiples may simply be too many mouths to feed. A desperate mother may abandon one or more of the babies in an attempt to provide for the other members of her family. In countries where male offspring are accorded precedence over females, there can be an abundance of abandoned daughters, including sets of female twins or the female of a set of boy/girl twins. Many loving families welcome the opportunity to adopt and raise these children.

Not Quite Twins

On occasion, adoption may produce a situation where two siblings are the same age, but biologically unrelated. Although not technically defined as multiples, they may be raised as such and will come to share many of the characteristics of twins, triplets, or the like. For example, if a couple in the process of adopting an infant becomes pregnant, their biological child and their adopted child could be extremely close in age, only weeks or months apart. Or a blended family might include children and stepchildren of the same age. In situations like this, it's perfectly acceptable to treat the children as twins or multiples assuming that they are comfortable with that role.

Multiple Multiples

A very few families are lucky enough to be blessed with multiple multiples: more than one set of twins, triplets, or more. It's hard to believe that some families could hit the jackpot more than once, but it does happen. With the increase in multiple birth mostly attributed to assisted reproduction, the trend in multiple multiples hasn't experienced the same dramatic uprising. Often couples who have multiples after a complicated process of conception assistance don't go through the process more than once.

ALERT

Experts claim that a previous twin pregnancy quadruples a woman's risk of having them again. That is, a woman who has already had twins is four times as likely to have them again as a woman who has only given birth to singletons or has never had children at all.

However, those identified factors only apply to dizygotic (fraternal) twinning. If your existing multiples are monozygotic (identical), then your chances should be the same as anyone else's that your next pregnancy will be multiples, right?

Except that there are two aspects of having multiples to consider: conceiving multiples and sustaining a multiple pregnancy. The first of these refers to the process of multiple sperm meeting multiple eggs, or a fertilized egg splitting. The second concerns the ability of the fertilized egg(s) to travel to the uterus, implant, and begin to develop.

Some theories hold that having a previous twin or multiple pregnancy increases the odds of having a subsequent one based on the second factor, the mother's ability to sustain the pregnancy. The reasoning is based on the high number of twin conceptions that never result in the live birth of two babies. Early ultrasound has allowed the detection of multiple embryos within a few days after conception. However, it is estimated that only 20 percent of those early pregnancies produce two or more live babies nine months later.

Because the body may consider a multiple pregnancy to be an abnormality, it may reject the pregnancy, resulting in miscarriage (a total loss of the pregnancy) or vanishing twin syndrome (reabsorption of one or more of the embryos, leaving one healthy, surviving fetus). However, if the multiple pregnancy does persevere, the body accepts it as a normal state, and subsequent twin pregnancies are more likely to thrive.

Whether that theory holds true or not, there have been cases where families produced an incredible assortment of multiples. A Russian woman in the eighteenth century reportedly gave birth to an astonishing amount: four sets of quadruplets, seven sets of triplets, and sixteen sets of twins. Several families in the state of Pennsylvania have had twins followed by higher order multiples. Perhaps best known is the Gosselin family, whose twin girls were three years old when their set of sextuplet siblings—three boys and three girls—were born in 2004. In 2002 a set of quintuplets were born to a Pennsylvania family with five-year-old twin boys. The Hayes family had two sets of twins when their sextuplets arrived. Most common, however, are double sets of twins within a family. About 1 in 3,000 women give birth to two sets of twins. Meanwhile, 1 in 500,000 will have three sets.

For families having multiples again, the news can be a mixed blessing. On the one hand, you are all too aware of the hardships, and with the other children to care for, you may not look forward to the added chaos of infant multiples. Yet you've been through the experience before—you know what to expect and many of your worries and concerns can be set aside. As an experienced parent, you've mastered the basics of baby care, and have developed efficient routines and shortcuts. You're an old pro and can look forward to the additional joy that more multiples will bring to your unique family.

Loss of a Multiple

Unfortunately, the complications that besiege multiple pregnancies sometimes result in the loss of one or more babies. Miscarriage, stillbirth, intrauterine fetal death, prematurity, and SIDS are all more common in multiples than in singletons. In addition, monozygotic multiples face potentially fatal complications such as twin-to-twin transfusion syndrome and conjoined twinning. No matter when the loss occurs, whether in the first trimester or after birth, it presents a complex situation for parents and any surviving multiples.

Losing a multiple is a unique kind of bereavement. The parents may not deal with the loss in the same way as parents mourning for a singleton. In addition to losing a precious child, they may also grieve the loss of the multiples' identity as "the twins" or "the triplets." For example, when one of a set of triplets dies, the remaining two children may be classified as twins by society, but their parents will always consider them incomplete triplets.

QUESTION

What are the chances that not all of a group of multiples will survive? Statistics on multiple mortality are hard to come by, but one study showed that one in twenty mothers of twins will lose one or both of the babies in the last half of her pregnancy.

Parents dealing with the loss of one or more multiples may follow an atypical pace and pattern of grief. When there are surviving multiples, they are told to focus on their living children and to consider themselves lucky that there are survivors. They'll experience a wide range of emotion, including anger toward other families with multiples or guilt about their inability to prevent their child's death. They may be extremely overprotective of their surviving child(ren) or, conversely, emotionally disconnected because the remaining multiple(s) are a constant reminder of the loss. They may try to deny the loss by focusing intently on the survivor(s). Or they may feel intensely determined to keep alive the memory of their lost babies, to the exclusion of other children.

CLIMB, the Center for Loss in Multiple Birth, recommends some strategies for parents of multiples trying to cope with the loss of one or all of their babies. First, they urge parents to take the opportunity to hold and spend time with each baby, even while dying or after death. Often in the crisis of a medical situation, parents of multiples are denied a peaceful opportunity to say goodbye to their child. This special time may take place at the hospital or later, at the funeral home. They also encourage parents to record the events of their lost child's life, no matter how brief, by taking pictures or videos, and by collecting mementos, such as a footprint, lock of hair, hospital bracelet, or blanket.

As part of the grieving process, many parents find it helpful to obtain a medical conclusion as to what went wrong. An autopsy or pregnancy loss evaluation can provide answers that alleviate the parents' sense of guilt or blame, as well as assist them in making decisions regarding future pregnancy care.

ESSENTIAL

Many parents who experience a loss find it comforting to send out a special announcement that explains the birth and death of their multiple(s). Samples of this type of correspondence can be found at CLIMB's website, *www.climb-support.org*.

Grief counseling is highly recommended for parents who experience the loss of a multiple. Your hospital may be able to suggest a local resource, or CLIMB can put you in touch with counselors or support groups in your area. Often, delayed feelings of grief or depression surface on significant dates, such as birthdays or anniversaries, and parents continue to need support for years after the loss.

If there are surviving multiples, you will likely be very concerned with helping these children cope with the loss of their co-twin or co-multiple. It can be a difficult parenting challenge. It's important to be honest with children about their origin in life. Even if young children don't seem to recall the presence of a twin or co-multiple, some research indicates that a subconscious awareness does exist. These children may grow up with a sense of something missing in their lives. They may experience survivor guilt, wondering why they survived when their sibling did not. The Twinless Twins Support Group International, established by a man who lost his twin brother in an accident, can provide support to children in this situation as well as to their parents.

Special Considerations

- **If you are a first-time parent.** There are advantages and disadvantages to being a first-time parent of multiples. Without the perspective of previous experience with parenting, having multiples won't seem like extra effort. Yet you haven't yet developed confidence as a parent and haven't learned the tricks of the trade that keep parents on track. You're starting from scratch and will need to wisely utilize the months of pregnancy to prepare your home and adapt your lifestyle. It's most important for you to seek out sources of support and know where to turn if you need help.

- **If you're having multiples after infertility.** For many families, twins or more are the result of a hard-fought battle against infertility, conceived after exhaustive—and expensive—medical intervention. This situation can produce some unusual emotions as the wishing and waiting transitions to the day-to-day reality of pregnancy and parenthood. It's not uncommon to feel a heightened sense of fear and anxiety, or to feel isolated and lonely once you lose your connection to your infertility community.

- **If you're a single parent of multiples.** Single parents of twins or multiples are instantly outnumbered! Without a full-time partner, the need for consistent help and routines cannot be underestimated. Be sure to line up assistance to help manage your infant multiples, and don't forget to make time for yourself.

- **If you've suffered the loss of a multiple.** Unfortunately, some families encounter tragedy and loss. The loss of one or all multiples is a unique type of bereavement that requires specialized support and grief counseling.

CHAPTER 20

Raising Multiples

Families with multiples face many unique challenges, but also enjoy special blessings. As you parent your twins, triplets, or more through infancy, toddlerhood, teens, and beyond, you will encounter some interesting situations that your friends with singleton children can only imagine. Your children are multiples, but they are individuals as well. Their extraordinary birth circumstances put them in a unique category, and as their parent, you are called on to nurture their individuality within the context of their status as multiples.

Joining a Support Group

One of the first things you should do upon discovering that you are having twins, triplets, or more is to develop a support group of families in similar circumstances. Talking to parents who have been through the experience will not only prove reassuring, but will help you prepare to face the challenges ahead. Luckily for parents of multiples, a vast network of fellow families exists throughout the world. You'll find multiples clubs and parenting organizations in nearly every region of the United States, and in most countries of the world.

These groups evolved in recognition of the tremendous benefit of sharing support and advice among fellow families of twins and other multiples. Parents of multiples face unique challenges that parents of singletons don't understand. They have much to gain from the experience of others.

The National Organization of Mothers of Twins Clubs (NOMOTC) is a nonprofit organization founded in 1960 to promote the special aspects of child development that relate specifically to multiple-birth children. To find a club in your area, visit the NOMTC website at *www.nomotc.org*.

The Benefits of Belonging

In the United States, the NOMOTC is a network of hundreds of clubs, representing over 25,000 individual families. Most NOMOTC-affiliated clubs offer monthly meetings, programs about parenting multiples, resource libraries, and clothing/equipment sales. Some groups are large and busy, while others are small and casual. Other opportunities that the club might offer include:

- Playgroups organized by community or multiples' ages
- Meal delivery for families with newborns
- Outings for moms or couples
- Babysitting co-op
- Monthly newsletter
- Family activities such as picnics or visits to theme parks

- Mentor or buddy programs for expectant moms
- Community discount programs
- Service opportunities benefiting the community or needy families
- Regional and national conferences with speakers, discussion forms, and classes about parenting multiples

Membership in a local organization gives you the additional benefit of national membership. In addition to NOMOTC affiliates, there are numerous independent clubs. If you are having difficulty locating a club in your area, inquire through your physician or hospital; they can usually put you in touch with someone.

Usually, families that are expecting multiples or have newborns are invited to visit a monthly meeting without obligation. If you decide to join, there is usually a membership fee to become a member and take advantage of the club's benefits. Part of the fee is designated for the national and regional club, while the remainder is used to fund the local club's activities.

QUESTION

I'm not really a "joiner." Will I still find a club useful?
Even if you don't like to commit to committees, it's worth investigating the multiples organization in your area. You can usually visit a meeting or talk by phone with a club representative before making a commitment. These organizations exist to serve parents, not obligate them, so don't worry that you'll be expected to participate in anything you're uncomfortable with.

Seeking Support Online

The Internet has opened up a whole new world for parents of multiples. Up-to-date information is readily available from the comfort of your living room at any time of the day or night. In addition, you can enjoy immediate access to fellow parents from around the world.

Although books like this one are invaluable collections of resources and facts, the Internet has the added benefit of providing up-to-the-minute updates about multiple birth issues, including crucial medical advances. If you encounter a specific problem in your pregnancy, such as twin-to-twin transfusion syndrome, or are fighting the battle against preterm labor, you can research in-depth explanations about possible treatments and options.

ALERT

Be sure to discuss any medical information you find on the Internet with your doctor. Just because something is published online doesn't ensure that it is accurate, or appropriate, for your individual circumstances.

In addition to factual information, the Internet is a tremendous human resource. You've already learned that fellow parents are your best source of advice, and the Internet puts that font of wisdom literally at your fingertips. You can connect with other parents via chats, discussion forums, message boards, e-mail, and instant messaging. Social networking applications like Twitter and Facebook are another way to connect. You can communicate as part of a group or one-on-one with individuals.

So how do you find fellow parents online? Start at websites focused on the topic of parenting multiples; many have community features that connect users via blogs or discussion boards. Parenting sites may also have resources devoted specifically to multiple birth families. Several online resources are included in Appendix A.

Choosing a Pediatrician

In addition to maternal medical care during your pregnancy, you'll need to choose a caregiver for your multiples after they're born. If you have older children, you may already have a pediatrician or family practitioner. That individual can probably serve your needs for your new arrivals as well. However, you may want to consider some of the unique needs of multiples. It is helpful to have a doctor for your infants who has previous experience with twins or multiples, although it's not as crucial as during pregnancy.

Once your babies have arrived, they should be treated as individuals, and you'll want doctors who are qualified to handle their individual issues. If your babies are born prematurely or have special needs after birth, they will be treated in the hospital by a neonatologist, a specialist who treats infants with serious illnesses, injuries, or birth defects. However, most newborns only require a pediatrician, a doctor who specializes in treating babies and children. Ask your fellow parents of twins or multiples for recommendations. They'll give a glowing endorsement of doctors who are good candidates, and you'll know to steer clear of any who generate complaints.

There are some further criteria to consider when choosing a doctor for your multiples. These are mostly issues of convenience, not qualifications, but they may weigh in your decision.

Convenience

Choose a doctor who practices in a location and setting that is easily accessible. You'll be paying plenty of visits to his office in the next few years; minimize the hassles as much as you can. When you visit the office, check out the facilities. Is it easy to park and enter the building? Can you easily negotiate the entry, doorways, and stairways or elevator with a stroller or with your hands full? Is the office staff friendly and helpful?

In addition, find out the practice's policies. What happens after hours? Do they offer telephone support, such as an Ask-A-Nurse service? What if your doctor is unavailable? Are there partners or nurses whom you can see as an alternative?

Some pediatricians will offer a discount on well-baby care for multiples, perhaps a percentage off the charge for the second, third, or fourth baby. It doesn't hurt to ask!

Philosophy

When you interview potential doctors, find out their stance on parenting issues that are important to you such as breastfeeding, family bed, immunizations, and circumcision. Only a face-to-face interview will reveal whether you are compatible with a doctor. It's important that you feel comfortable with her personality, and that you trust her ability to care for your children. You should not feel intimidated or rushed when you ask questions. Finally, you should get a sense that the doctor respects your intuition as a parent.

Help from Family and Friends

Many families with multiples are fortunate to find themselves the beneficiaries of numerous offers of assistance from friends and relatives. Some even have the support of an entire neighborhood or church community. However, just because help is available doesn't mean that it is helpful. You'll want to be sure that you accept help in ways that make life with multiples easier, not more complicated.

Help During Pregnancy

There are many instances throughout a multiple pregnancy when you can use a bit of assistance. Because mothers of multiples experience more complications, they may find themselves restricted to bed or hospitalized at some point during their pregnancy. To a lesser extreme, they may simply find that their physical symptoms are intensified to the point where normal activities become uncomfortable and everyday chores and responsibilities may become a burden. During those times, it's very helpful to have some assistance lined up, such as meal preparation, errand running, or child care for older siblings.

It can also be a very emotional time, with lots of anxiety about what lies ahead. Pregnancy is a good time to call upon friends for reassurance and encouragement. See a funny movie or laugh about old times together. A mother's emotional state has a great deal of influence over her physical condition; friends can play an important role in keeping her spirits uplifted.

Help after the Babies Come Home

Once your babies arrive and your family's focus shifts to round-the-clock newborn nurturing, opportunities abound for outside assistance. Don't be afraid to accept help, and don't hesitate to ask for it, either. People genuinely want to help, and you genuinely need it. Take everyone up on their offers, but utilize the help in such a way that it serves your needs.

First, be specific about what you need. Nearly everyone wants to "help" by holding or rocking a baby. Sometimes that's nice if it offers you a break to accomplish something else, but be realistic about how helpful it really is. Do you need help finishing chores? Or caring for other children? Some families with higher order multiples may require help around the clock just to get all the babies fed and changed!

ALERT

No matter what kind of help you have, don't underestimate the need to protect babies from harmful germs. Tiny newborns, especially if they were preterm, are particularly susceptible to dangerous infections due to underdeveloped immunity. Explain proper hand-washing techniques to you and your helpers, and enforce a policy that requires them to wash up before touching the babies.

Some other forms of assistance you might want to consider are:

- Extra hands at feeding time
- Telephone answering and filtering calls
- Photography (taking, developing, and/or uploading pictures to the web)
- Meals for the family
- Laundry
- Yard work
- Errand running (grocery shopping, post office, dry cleaners)
- Transportation (to doctor visits for you, or to school and activities for older children)
- Bath-time assistance
- Care for other siblings (homework help, playtime)

Once you have established your needs, organize your helpers. Preferably have someone else organize the help. The less you have to worry about anything other than the babies, the better. An efficient organizer is the best helper you can have. Have her create a list of your needs, then match helpers according to their abilities and availabilities.

Professional Services

Sometimes volunteer help simply isn't enough. There are times when you'll need to call in a professional. If you can afford to pay for help, you may find it well worth the cost. Decide how your money will be best spent by considering what services you can turn over to another party while you concentrate on the activities that mean the most to you.

Help Around the House

When multiples join a household, things change forever. If you've been accustomed to cleaning and maintaining your home, you may find that your time to devote to it is severely diminished once your babies arrive. While housework still needs to be done, it is one of the responsibilities that most people don't mind giving up. Paying for a cleaning service to maintain your home removes the burden and lets you focus your attention on your new babies. Even if you don't need ongoing service, a one-time thorough cleaning would help you put your home in order and get your expanded family off to a good start.

In addition to housekeeping there are several other home responsibilities that can be turned over to professionals in order to free up expectant or new parents' time. For example, meal preparation services are becoming very popular options for busy families. Professional landscapers can take over yard work duties. Professional organizers can help you streamline your routines and reduce clutter in your home to make your lifestyle more efficient.

FACT

Ongoing or occasional cleaning assistance makes a great gift for new parents. If you're making up a wish list, go ahead and include it! Because of the cost, a group of giftgivers may wish to combine their resources and present the gift together.

Help with the Babies

Professional advice and assistance with caring for your newborn multiples can literally be a lifesaver. First-time parents, parents of premature multiples, or parents of infants with special medical needs will greatly benefit from the personal attention of a hired nurse or caregiver, such as a doula.

Doulas provide a comforting, supportive presence to mothers—and fathers—during childbirth, but are also available for postpartum care. As an objective and neutral party, they act as an advocate for the family and an intermediary between the parents and the medical staff. Postpartum doulas assist the mother with breastfeeding, recuperation from delivery, and newborn care. Most postpartum doulas charge by the hour, so you have the option of procuring as little or as much service as you require. Even a one-hour visit with a postpartum doula can boost new parents' confidence and provide valuable information about caring for their newborns. A short-term investment in professional help may assist you in becoming better parents in the long run.

With sleep deprivation an issue for so many new parents of multiples, the promise of a good night's sleep may be worth the cost of hiring a night nurse—a professional nurse who will come to your home to care for the babies throughout the nighttime hours so you and your partner can sleep. Costs vary, but even one night of uninterrupted sleep can improve parents' perspective and equip them to cope with their babies going forward.

Meeting Milestones

Throughout their childhood, your multiples will meet many milestones. From incapacitated infants, they will rapidly progress to toddlers who can walk, talk, explore, and interact with their world. You will be amazed at how quickly time passes. One day they are crawling; soon enough they are running (usually in different directions)! From riding a bike, to learning to drive, there are so many skills and achievements that they will master. The exciting aspect for parents of multiples is that they get to watch their children rise to their challenges within the same time span.

Adjusted Age

For multiples who were born early, it is important to consider their adjusted age versus their actual age. To determine a baby's adjusted age, subtract the number of weeks he or she was born early from his or her current age. For multiples who were born at thirty-five weeks—born five weeks early—their adjusted age at three months old is actually seven weeks.

As a consequence of prematurity, your multiples may not meet early milestones on the same timetable as babies born nearer to their due date.

Walking, talking, and other developmental skills may be delayed. For example, twins who were born eight weeks early may lag two months behind their full-term peers. Whereas most nine-month-old babies are starting to crawl or explore mobility and can vocalize or comprehend simple words, these twins' abilities may more closely resemble that of a six- or seven-month-old baby.

ALERT

Don't be discouraged by developmental delays early in life. Except in cases of permanent disabilities, most preemies "catch up" to their peers by the age of two. Your pediatrician can provide more specific information about your babies' developmental progress and how it correlates with expected milestones.

Where parents of singletons can compare their offspring through a lens of memory, parents of multiples have an instant, side-by-side comparison. In this situation, it can be tempting to play the "match" game, measuring up each multiple against the other. However, your multiples will encounter enough comparison from the rest of the world; at home, they need to be nurtured as individuals on their own merits, not evaluated in relation to each other.

That is why it is vital to keep perspective as your children reach milestones, such as sitting upright, sleeping through the night, toilet mastery, and learning to read. Remember, they are multiples—not clones. While many multiples, especially those that are monozygotic (identical), will indeed reach milestones at about the same time, many others have a different pace and arrive at such achievements days, weeks, or even months apart. Boys and girls have different timetables as well, so parents of dizygotic boy/girl twins should be especially flexible in their expectations.

Walking and Talking

Two big milestones for multiples that will have a great impact on your family's life are walking and talking. While handling two stationary newborns is difficult enough, things get really interesting when your multiples gain the ability to move about on their own. From wriggling and rolling, they quickly move on to crawling and scooting. Within a matter of months, they are walking and then running.

The time of transition while your multiples are exercising their newfound mobility presents some tricky challenges for parents. Chasing after a single toddler can be a full-time job; it's a sure bet that multiples will keep their parents on their toes. It's a time to be extra vigilant. Utilize physical boundaries to keep your children safely contained; playpens and safety gates will become a necessity.

While their bodies are busy mastering their movement, your multiples' brains are engaged at a supersonic rate of learning. From early coos and shrieks emerge the formation of words and then simple sentences. Their comprehension of spoken language will soon be followed by their ability to respond with their own words.

The development of their ability to communicate—with you, and with each other—is one of the most exciting and amazing aspects of parenting young multiples. But many multiples encounter speech delays—up to half of multiples by some estimates. In some instances, the delay can be attributed to prematurity, low birth weight, or complications from other medical issues encountered at birth. But even full-term, healthy twins may lag behind their singleton peers when it comes to language. Some theories blame it on parents; babies learn to speak by mimicking the sounds and facial gestures of those around them. With two or more babies to attend to, parents of multiples spend less time in direct communication with each child.

FACT

Idioglossia is a fancy word to describe the phenomenon of "twin talk": twins or multiples who share a secret language that only they can understand. While it's fascinating to imagine that twins share such a deep connection, it's more likely that young twins are simply practicing their vocalization skills by mimicking each other's baby talk.

By being aware of the potential for language delays, you can proactively address the problem by taking every opportunity to talk and read to your multiples. Even if you feel foolish carrying on a conversation with infants who can't possibly respond to your chitchat, your running commentary of sounds and sentences will benefit your babies by stimulating their brains and boosting their language skills.

Celebrating Birthdays

Multiples are forced to share—a lot. They start off sharing a womb and may share a room. They share clothes, toys, and their parents' affection. And most multiples also share a significant milestone—a birthday.

Celebrating birthdays with multiples provides an opportunity for plenty of family fun. Every family celebrates in a unique way, but there are some things to consider when planning a birthday celebration for multiples.

While younger twins won't mind sharing a celebration, future birthdays deserve some individual commemoration. By emphasizing each child as an individual as well as celebrating them as a group, your birthday traditions will be more meaningful. Some families elect to provide two cakes for twins, sing "Happy Birthday" to each child individually, and discourage group gifts. Older multiples may even desire their own parties with their own friends, but many recognize that a combined "the-more-the-merrier" event tends to be more fun. Budget and family traditions will certainly dictate the details, but be sure to consider your multiples' individual wishes when planning birthday celebrations.

ESSENTIAL

Not all multiples have the same birthday. The interval between births sometimes extends over a day or date change, and if their birth date falls over New Year's Eve, they might even be born in different years!

Promoting Individuality

Perhaps one of the biggest hot-button issues for parents of multiples is instilling individuality—assisting your twins, triplets, or more to establish their own sense of identity. Parents are cautioned against behaviors that might impede their multiples' individuality: Don't give them matching names. Don't dress them alike. Don't call them "the twins."

For the most part, multiples will develop their own identities as they grow up; it's not something parents can control. Rather than minimizing their status as twins or multiples, parents can instead encourage and nurture their unique interests and personalities. Appreciating each of your children's special qualities and loving them unconditionally is the true goal.

Preparing for Comparisons

Despite the many benefits, one of the unfortunate downsides to growing up as a multiple is that they are subject to constant comparison. The entire world will pit one against the other, trying to determine who is smarter, taller, prettier, stronger, more outgoing, or more of a troublemaker. From every checkup with the pediatrician to every test taken in school, a set of twins will be measured against each other. It is a difficult dynamic for children. Instead of being valued on their own merits, society wants only to designate them in relation to their co-multiple(s).

In this arena, parents can contribute to their twins' sense of self-identification by making an effort to suppress contrast and comparison when possible. While you can't control how society views your multiples, you can seek to minimize comparisons within the family. Don't try to define your twins with labels—"the quiet one" and "the loud one" or "the leader" and "the follower." In many cases, you'll find that they will defy your categorizations by switching roles back and forth!

Initiate discussions with relatives, teachers, friends, and coaches and encourage them to avoid using comparisons. Cultivating individuality entails a conscious choice to view multiples as individuals; it may require several reminders to establish that viewpoint. But if you are consistent about it within the home, friends and families will follow your lead. Try these tips to enhance individuality:

- **Celebrate individual achievements.** Use plenty of praise, and don't worry about keeping things "equal."
- **Keep separate memory books or scrapbooks.** If possible, take individual pictures and produce a baby book or scrapbook for each child.
- **Discipline separately.** Don't unanimously punish everyone—at least at the same time.

- **Encourage individual activities.** Enable each of your multiples to engage in hobbies and activities, as well as relationships that are unique to them.
- **Carve out opportunities for one-on-one time.** Don't be afraid to split up your twins or multiples so that they have one-on-one time with parents, siblings, and loved ones. It's a prime time for getting to know them better and letting them know you appreciate them for who they are.

Dressing Multiples Alike

The issue of coordinated dressing is a hot topic among parents. Some find it a cute and fun aspect of having multiples. Others believe that it detracts from their children's individuality. No research exists to confirm that the practice is damaging to multiples' sense of self, but you should be sensitive to your children's feelings about the issue once they're old enough to express a preference. In the meantime, your babies won't care as long as their clothes are comfortable and cozy, so take advantage of their infancy to dress them up to your heart's content.

Duplicate outfits can be a curse or a convenience; it's certainly easier to tell twins apart when they're dressed differently. However, when you're overwhelmed with the day-to-day details of caring for twins, it's much simpler to shop for and choose two sets of the same outfit.

If you're conflicted about the issue, consider a compromise. Save the matching outfits for photo opportunities or special occasions. Use coordinated or similar outfits, rather than exact matches, to experience the fun without creating a cookie-cutter effect. Or assign each multiple a color, and then choose clothing (and toys, sippy cups, and everything else!) to match. Not only does it help identify the individual child, but it makes it much easier to settle ownership disputes in the event of squabbles.

Friends and Foes

The relationship between twins and multiples is complicated. They're blessed with companionship but also cursed by comparison and competition. Just as in any relationship, there will be tender, loving moments, and times of dissension and disagreement. These interactions are a source of tremendous joy and also great frustration for parents of multiples.

All siblings have squabbles. But the fighting between multiples can be particularly intense. The lack of a birth order dynamic dissolves some of the natural boundaries that are established within singleton sibling relationships. Multiples tend to spend more time exclusively together; they're more likely to share a room, have the same friends, and are usually in the same grade. They may even be in the same classroom at school. For the most part, they enjoy being together, but there will also be times of tension. For many families, it begins with toddlers, who lack the communication skills to express their feelings and desires, and instead lash out physically. They may bite or pull the hair of their co-multiple. As multiples grow, their relationship will evolve and transform with maturity.

ESSENTIAL

Utilize neutral systems for establishing rules and guidelines within your family. Chore charts identify and track each child's responsibilities. Color-coding or labeling identifies ownership of possessions to reduce squabbles. Take turns by days of the week to designate privileges or conduct schedules. For example, Twin A goes first on even days and Twin B goes first on odd days.

There are numerous strategies for managing conflict between multiples. What is effective for one family is less useful for another. But there are some basic guidelines that you can adapt and modify based on your multiples' ages and circumstances.

- Acknowledge and validate feelings; condemn bad behavior, not the person. Communicate with your multiples to determine the feelings behind the behavior. Help them to work out an alternative behavior to accomplish their goals. "Were you jealous of your sister because she had a toy you wanted? It's understandable to be jealous, but it is not okay to take the toy away from her. Instead, can you ask her if she will share it with you when she's done?"
- Set expectations of respect among family members; offer praise when it is exhibited, and discipline with appropriate consequences when it is violated.

- Establish boundaries to provide opportunities for individual privacy and possessions.
- Model healthy formats for disagreement by listening to both parties and responding.
- Utilize time-outs, both for kids and the objects of their disagreement.
- Intervene minimally. Act as a mediator when necessary, but allow your multiples to resolve conflicts between themselves.

Finally, release your parental quest to keep everything between your multiples fair and equal. It's an impossible goal, but one that is very easy to fall into when parenting multiples. From the outset, you set a pattern of "do for one, do for the other." While that may be reasonable when caring for newborns, it quickly becomes burdensome and unfairly presents your multiples with an expectation of entitlement. While you love them all equally, life will not treat them equally. Children need to understand that there will be situations where one receives advantages over the other, but that the tables will turn in time.

School Daze

The early years of parenting multiples pass very quickly, and soon enough it is time for them to start school. Whether they attend a preschool, kindergarten, private school, or public neighborhood school, or are homeschooled, their education is important to their future success, and you will have to make some big decisions about how to approach it.

Classroom placement is one of the biggest decisions that parents will make for their multiples. There is no right or wrong answer to the question, "Should your multiples be in the same or separate classes at school?" The best answer is different for every set of twins or multiples, and may change from year to year or school to school. As parents, you will have to evaluate the situation on a yearly basis, considering input from school professionals as well as your own children, and choose the path that makes sense for your family.

In the past, some schools had predetermined policies about placement of twins, generally mandating an assignment to separate classes. However, legislative activity in the last ten years has provided reinforcement for parents in the form of twins laws. Numerous states throughout the United States have legislation in place or in progress requiring school systems to consider the input of parents of multiples in determining classroom placement. Unfortunately, many states still lack support for legislation, and parents of multiples continue to campaign for their rights.

FACT

Minnesota passed the first Twins Bill in 2005, allowing parents of multiples to have a primary voice in the placement of their children within the classroom. The bill was sponsored by Senator Dennis Frederickson, himself a father of twins.

There are advantages and disadvantages to both keeping twins together in the same classroom and placing them in different classrooms. Your decision will be determined by your school setting, your multiples' individual needs, and the relationship between them. Ask yourself these questions in evaluating your options.

- **What does our school offer?** If your multiples will attend a small school, it may not be possible to arrange them in separate classes; for example, if there is only a single morning kindergarten class.
- **What is the best learning environment?** Your multiples may be a distraction to each other—or other students in the classroom—if they are together in class. Or the absence of their co-multiples may prove equally distracting, if children prefer to be together. Some studies have found that being forcibly separated at school is actually detrimental to multiples, especially in their initial school experience.
- **What makes the most sense for our family?** Don't discount the importance of logistics. With two or more same-age children, sometimes it simply makes sense to keep them on the same path, with similar homework and activity schedules.

What You *Need* to Know about Parenting Multiples

- **Support groups for parents of multiples can be an invaluable source of advice, fellowship, and bargains on baby equipment.** Local chapters of clubs exist throughout the United States and around the world. Check out the organization in your area to see if you'd benefit from belonging.

- **If you prefer, support can be found online.** The Internet and social networking offer many opportunities to connect and network with other parents of multiples, as well as access to parenting resources and medical advice.

- **Put some thought into choosing a pediatrician for your multiples.** Your multiples' medical care provider will play an important role in their childhood, and you'll want to establish a relationship with him or her. You'll likely pay many visits to this medical professional and will rely on him or her to provide important information about immunizations, developmental issues, and general health.

- **Multiples are individuals, not clones, and not a set.** One of your basic goals as a parent is to nurture their individuality within the context of their unique relationship. Try to avoid comparisons, and be aware of the labels and stereotypes that the world will apply to them. Work diligently to help them discover and appreciate their own unique identities.

- **Multiples who are born early may follow a timetable more suited to their adjusted age than their actual age.** Expect that multiples may lag a few weeks or months behind the standard when meeting milestones such as rolling over, sitting up, walking, or talking. Your pediatrician will advise you if the delays warrant treatment or therapy.

- **Your multiples' education can be helped or hindered by their placement in the classroom.** Once your twins or multiples start school, you'll have to make a decision about their classroom placement, and whether they should be together in the same class or separated into their own class with different teachers. Hopefully your decision will be determined by which situation provides the best learning environment, and not dictated by school policy. The right decision regarding classroom placement of multiples varies depending on the circumstances—and the solution may change from year to year.

Recommended Resources

Additional Reading

Arce, Eve-Marie. *Twins and Supertwins: A Handbook for Early Childhood Professionals* (Redleaf Press, 2010)

Boyle, Christina and Stahl, Cathleen. *Twin Set: Moms of Multiples Share Survive & Thrive Secrets* (Three Rivers Press, 2008)

Fierro, Pamela. *Mommy Rescue Guide: Twins, Triplets and More* (Adams Media, 2008)

Flais, Shelly Vaziri. *Raising Twins: From Pregnancy to Preschool* (American Academy of Pediatrics, 2009)

Ford-Martin, Paula. *The Everything® Pregnancy Book, 3rd Edition* (Adams Media, 2012)

Franklin, Rachel. *Expecting Twins, Triplets, and More: A Doctor's Guide to a Healthy and Happy Multiple Pregnancy* (St. Martin's Griffin, 2005)

Friedman, Joan A. *Emotionally Healthy Twins: A New Philosophy for Parenting Two Unique Children* (Da Capo Press, 2008)

Gromada, Karen Kerkhoff. *Mothering Multiples: Breastfeeding and Caring for Twins or More* (La Leche League International, 1999)

Heim, Susan M. *It's Twins! Parent-to-Parent Advice from Infancy Through Adolescence* (Hampton Roads Publishing Company, 2007)

Kohl, Susan. *Twin Stories: Their Mysterious and Unique Bond* (Wildcat Canyon Press, 2001)

Lage, Cheryl. *Twinspiration: Real-Life Advice from Pregnancy Through the First Year* (Taylor Trade Publishing, 2006)

Le-Bucklin, Khanh-Van. *Twins 101: 50 Must-Have Tips for Pregnancy Through Early Childhood from Doctor M.O.M.* (Jossey-Bass, 2009)

Luke, Barbara and Eberlein, Tamara. *When You're Expecting Twins, Triplets or More* (Perennial, 2004)

Lyons, Elizabeth. *Ready or Not, Here We Come! The Real Experts' Cannot-Live-Without Guide to the First Year with Twins* (Finn-Phyllis Press, 2003)

Lyons, Elizabeth. *Ready or Not, There We Go! The Real Experts' Guide to the Toddler Years with Twins* (Finn-Phyllis Press, 2006)

Moskwinski, Rebecca E. (Ed.) *Twins to Quints: The Complete Manual for Parents of Multiple Birth Children* (Harpeth House Publishing, 2002)

Noble, Elizabeth. *Having Twins and More* (Houghton Mifflin, 2003)

Regan-Loomis, Meghan. *Juggling Twins: The Best Tips, Tricks, and Strategies from Pregnancy to the Toddler Years* (Sourcebooks, 2008)

Scalise, Dagmara. *Twin Sense: A Sanity-Saving Guide to Raising Twins from Pregnancy Through the First Year* (Amacom, 2009)

Segal, Nancy A. *Entwined Lives* (Plume, 2000)

Tinglof, Christina Baglivi. *Double Duty: The Parents' Guide to Raising Twins from Pregnancy Through the School Years, 2nd edition* (McGraw-Hill, 2009)

Tinglof, Christina Baglivi. *Parenting School-Age Twins and Multiples* (McGraw-Hill, 2007)

TWINS™ Magazine
www.twinsmagazine.com
Print magazine published six times a year; available by subscription.

Online Resources

Bed Rest

Sidelines Pregnancy Support
P.O. Box 1808
Laguna Beach, CA 92652
(888) 447-4754 or (949) 497-5598
www.sidelines.org
A nonprofit organization providing international support for women and their families experiencing complicated pregnancies and premature births.

Breastfeeding Support

International Lactation Consultant Association
2501 Aerial Center Parkway, Suite 103
Morrisville, NC 27560
(919) 861-5577
www.ilca.org
Find a lactation consultant to provide breastfeeding support.

La Leche League International
957 N. Plum Grove Road
Schaumburg, IL 60173
(847) 519-7730 or (800) LALECHE
www.lalecheleague.org
Provides breastfeeding help to mothers worldwide and promotes a better understanding of breastfeeding.

Childbirth Education and Support

Babies in Belly
www.babiesinbelly.com
Online prenatal classes for parents of multiples.

Doulas of North America (DONA)
1582 S. Parker Rd., Ste. 201
Denver, CO 80231
(888) 788-DONA
www.dona.org
International, nonprofit organization of doulas.

Marvelous Multiples
www.marvelousmultiples.com
Childbirth education classes specific to multiple birth.

Multiple Birth Familes
(613) 267-6754
www.multiplebirthsfamilies.com
Prenatal education by DVD.

Clubs for Parents of Multiples

National Organization of Mothers of Twins Clubs (NOMOTC)
2000 Mallory Lane, Suite 130-600
Franklin, TN 37067-8231
(248) 231-4480
www.nomotc.org
A network of more than 400 local clubs in the United States, dedicated to supporting families with multiple birth children.

Multiple Births Canada
P.O. Box 432
Wasaga Beach, Ontario
Canada L9Z 1A4
(613) 834-8946
www.multiplebirthscanada.org
National support organization for multiple birth families and individuals in Canada.

General Information on Multiples

Guide to Twins and Multiples at About.com
multiples.about.com
Comprehensive reference site about twins and multiple birth, with parenting resources.

Higher Order Multiples

Mothers of Supertwins (MOST)
P.O. Box 306
East Islip, NY 11730
(631) 859-1110
www.mostonline.org
A community of families, volunteers, and professionals providing support, education, and research on higher order multiple births.

Triplet Connection
P.O. Box 429
Spring City, UT 84662
(435) 851-1105
www.tripletconnection.org
An international network for multiple birth families.

Loss of a Multiple

Center for Loss in Multiple Birth (CLIMB)
P.O. Box 91377
Anchorage AK 99509
(907) 222-5321
www.climb-support.org
Nonprofit organization providing parent-to-parent support for all who have experienced the death of one or more twins or higher multiple birth children.

Twinless Twins International Support Group
P.O. Box 980481
Ypsilanti, MI 48198-0481
(888) 205-8962
www.twinlesstwins.org
Community for twins and other multiples who have lost their twin due to death or estrangement at any age.

Monoamniotic Twins

Monoamniotic.org
monoamniotic.org
Information site supported by parents diagnosed with a monoamniotic pregnancy.

Prematurity

March of Dimes
1275 Mamaroneck Ave.
White Plains, NY 10605
(914) 997-4488
www.marchofdimes.com
Organization dedicated to healthy babies, particularly the prevention of premature birth.

About.com Guide to Preemies
preemies.about.com
Comprehensive resource site about premature birth written by a neonatal nurse.

Products for Twins and Multiples

By-My-Side Safety Harness for Twins by TommiGuard
P.O. Box 784
Chardon, OH 44024
www.tommiguard.com
Harness products for toddler safety.

Double Blessings
2739 Via Orange Way, Suite 117
Spring Valley, CA 91978
(800) 584-8946 or (619) 441-1873
www.doubleblessings.com
Nursing products, birth announcements, and other twin-themed products.

Double Decker Stroller
(423) 261-2248
www.doubledeckerstroller.com
Source for double/triple stroller frame to accommodate infant seats.

Great Baby Products
(800) 450-0855
www.greatbabyproducts.com/Twins-Baby-Products-s/1067.htm
Offers discounts for multiples and hands-free feeding products.

For Multiples Maternity

(404) 590-0102

formultiples.com

Maternity clothing designed for pregnant moms of multiples.

Just for Twins

www.just4twins.com

Clothing for twins from infants to adults.

Just Multiples

www.justmultiples.com

Twin-themed clothing, gifts, and novelty items.

RunAbout Strollers

18770 SW Rigert Rd.

Aloha, OR 97007

(503) 649-7922

bergdesign.net/runabout.htm

High-quality stroller products for twins or more.

Research and Support Organizations

Center for Study of Multiple Birth

333 E. Superior St., Suite 464

Chicago, IL 60611

(312) 695-1677

www.multiplebirth.com

Organization seeking to stimulate medical and social research in the area of multiple birth.

International Twins Association

10913 Turkey Run Dr.

Edmond, OK 73025

(405) 225-8829

www.intltwins.org

Nonprofit organization to promote the spiritual, intellectual, and social welfare of multiples throughout the world.

Twinsight

1137 Second St., Suite 109

Santa Monica, CA 90403

(310) 458-1373

www.twinsight.com

Counseling and support services for families with multiples.

Single Parents

Single Parenting Guide at About.com

singleparents.about.com

Comprehensive resource site for single parents

Twin-to-Twin Transfusion Syndrome

The Twin-to-Twin Transfusion Syndrome Foundation

411 Longbeach Parkway

Bay Village, OH 44140

(800) 815-9211 or (440) 899-8887

www.tttsfoundation.org

Provides immediate and lifesaving educational, emotional, and financial support to families and medical caregivers during a diagnosis of twin-to-twin transfusion syndrome.

Zygosity Testing

Affiliated Genetics

(800) 362-5559 or (801) 582-4200

www.affiliatedgenetics.com

DNA testing service that performs zygosity testing.

Proactive Genetics

2935 Walton Way

Augusta, GA 30909

(866) TWIN-DNA (894-6362)

www.proactivegenetics.com

Genetic testing service for multiples.

Charting Your Newborns' Progress

Use this chart to help you keep track of your babies' feedings, diaper activity, and administration of any medications. In each column, note the babies' names. This form will accommodate up to four babies; print out two sets if you have quintuplets or higher.

Note the time in the left hand column. Under each baby's name, fill in the four squares:

- **Feed:** Indicate the amount of formula in ounces, or the amount of time spent breastfeeding in minutes. If breastfeeding, you may also wish to indicate which breast the baby nursed from, with an "R" to designate the right side and an "L" for the left side.
- **WD:** Use this space to record the number of wet diapers since the last feeding. It's important that each baby is urinating enough to soak a diaper. A lack of wet diapers could indicate dehydration.
- **BM:** This section also represents your baby's diaper achievements. Use it to record bowel movements. You can use a tally system or just check the box after you've changed a soiled diaper.
- **Med:** If any of your babies require medications, you can use this space to keep track of the dosages. Check the box when you have administered medication to make sure that each baby is getting the right dose at the right time.

Today's Date _____

Time	BABY A:		BABY B:		BABY C:		BABY D:	
Time	Feed:	Med:	Feed:	Med:	Feed:	Med:	Feed:	Med:
	WD:	BM:	WD:	BM:	WD:	BM:	WD:	BM:
Time	Feed:	Med:	Feed:	Med:	Feed:	Med:	Feed:	Med:
	WD:	BM:	WD:	BM:	WD:	BM:	WD:	BM:
Time	Feed:	Med:	Feed:	Med:	Feed:	Med:	Feed:	Med:
	WD:	BM:	WD:	BM:	WD:	BM:	WD:	BM:
Time	Feed:	Med:	Feed:	Med:	Feed:	Med:	Feed:	Med:
	WD:	BM:	WD:	BM:	WD:	BM:	WD:	BM:
Time	Feed:	Med:	Feed:	Med:	Feed:	Med:	Feed:	Med:
	WD:	BM:	WD:	BM:	WD:	BM:	WD:	BM:
Time	Feed:	Med:	Feed:	Med:	Feed:	Med:	Feed:	Med:
	WD:	BM:	WD:	BM:	WD:	BM:	WD:	BM:
Time	Feed:	Med:	Feed:	Med:	Feed:	Med:	Feed:	Med:
	WD:	BM:	WD:	BM:	WD:	BM:	WD:	BM:
Time	Feed:	Med:	Feed:	Med:	Feed:	Med:	Feed:	Med:
	WD:	BM:	WD:	BM:	WD:	BM:	WD:	BM:
Time	Feed:	Med:	Feed:	Med:	Feed:	Med:	Feed:	Med:
	WD:	BM:	WD:	BM:	WD:	BM:	WD:	BM:
Time	Feed:	Med:	Feed:	Med:	Feed:	Med:	Feed:	Med:
	WD:	BM:	WD:	BM:	WD:	BM:	WD:	BM:
Time	Feed:	Med:	Feed:	Med:	Feed:	Med:	Feed:	Med:
	WD:	BM:	WD:	BM:	WD:	BM:	WD:	BM:
Time	Feed:	Med:	Feed:	Med:	Feed:	Med:	Feed:	Med:
	WD:	BM:	WD:	BM:	WD:	BM:	WD:	BM:
Time	Feed:	Med:	Feed:	Med:	Feed:	Med:	Feed:	Med:
	WD:	BM:	WD:	BM:	WD:	BM:	WD:	BM:
Time	Feed:	Med:	Feed:	Med:	Feed:	Med:	Feed:	Med:
	WD:	BM:	WD:	BM:	WD:	BM:	WD:	BM:
Time	Feed:	Med:	Feed:	Med:	Feed:	Med:	Feed:	Med:
	WD:	BM:	WD:	BM:	WD:	BM:	WD:	BM:

APPENDIX C

Recipes

Eating right is pivotal for all moms-to-be, but especially so for moms of multiples. As discussed in this book, protein is a key nutrient for women who are pregnant with multiples. Each of the first 15 recipes presented here has 13 or more grams of protein per serving and also happens to be delicious!

Additionally, pregnant moms of multiples need to make sure they are getting enough fiber. Fiber helps aid digestion, maintains good blood sugar levels, and prevents constipation (a common plague of pregnant women). Each of the next 17 recipes has 5 or more grams of fiber per serving, so you can fill up on your fiber with these healthy, delicious dishes.

And finally, the remaining 18 recipes are quick and easy and only take 30 minutes to prepare because when you're pregnant with multiples, standing at the stove for long stretches of time can be more than uncomfortable. With these recipes, you can have delicious meals, snacks, and desserts in less than 30 minutes. These meals are also perfect for after your babies come and time to cook is limited!

Country-Style Omelet

If zucchini is not a favorite, you could also try broccoli or spinach or some of your other favorite veggies.

INGREDIENTS | SERVES 2

2 teaspoons olive oil
1 cup zucchini, diced
¼ cup red pepper, diced
1 cup plum tomatoes, skinned and cubed
⅛ teaspoon pepper
4 eggs
1 tablespoon Parmesan cheese
1 teaspoon fresh basil, minced

1. Heat oil in a nonstick skillet. Add zucchini and red pepper; sauté for 5 minutes.

2. Add tomatoes and pepper; cook uncovered for another 10 minutes, allowing fluid from tomatoes to cook down.

3. In a small bowl, whisk together eggs, Parmesan cheese, and fresh basil; pour over vegetables in skillet.

4. Cook over low heat until browned, approximately 10 minutes on each side.

PER SERVING Calories: 253 | Protein: 17g | Fiber: 2g

Tofu Smoothie

For something different, you can substitute blueberries, raspberries, or blackberries for the strawberries in this recipe or try a combination!

INGREDIENTS | SERVES 1

1⅓ cups frozen unsweetened strawberries
½ banana
½ cup (4 ounces) silken tofu

In a food processor or blender, process all ingredients until smooth. Add a little chilled water for thinner smoothies if desired.

PER SERVING Calories: 289 | Protein: 20g | Fiber: 8g

Southwest Black Bean Burgers

If you do not have fresh herbs such as parsley or cilantro available, 1 teaspoon dried can be used in place of 1 tablespoon fresh.

INGREDIENTS | SERVES 5

1 cup black beans, cooked
¼ cup onion, chopped
1 teaspoon chili powder
1 teaspoon ground cumin
1 tablespoon fresh parsley, minced
1 tablespoon fresh cilantro, minced
½ teaspoon salt (optional)
¾ pound lean ground beef

1. Place beans, onion, chili powder, cumin, parsley, cilantro, and salt in a food processor. Combine ingredients using pulse setting until beans are partially puréed and all ingredients are mixed.

2. In a separate bowl, combine ground beef and bean mixture. Shape into 5 patties.

3. Meat mixture is quite soft after mixing and should be chilled or partially frozen prior to cooking. Grill or broil on oiled surface.

PER SERVING Calories: 230 | Protein: 20g | Fiber: 4g

Egg White Pancakes

Experiment with toast and pancake toppings. Try a tablespoon of raisins, almonds, apples, bananas, berries, nut butters, pears, walnuts, or wheat germ.

INGREDIENTS | SERVES 2

4 egg whites
½ cup oatmeal
4 teaspoons reduced-calorie or low-sugar strawberry jam
1 teaspoon powdered sugar

1. Put all ingredients in a blender; process until smooth.

2. Preheat a nonstick pan treated with cooking spray over medium heat. Pour half of mixture into pan; cook for 4–5 minutes.

3. Flip pancake and cook until inside is cooked. Repeat using remaining batter for second pancake. Dust each pancake with powdered sugar, if using.

PER SERVING Calories: 197 | Protein: 13g | Fiber: 4g

Chicken Corn Chowder

To trim down the fat in this recipe, use a reduced-fat cheese, such as Cabot's 50 Percent Light Cheddar.

INGREDIENTS | SERVES 10

1 pound boneless, skinless chicken breast, cut into chunks

1 medium onion, chopped

1 red bell pepper, diced

1 large potato, diced

2 (16-ounce) cans low-fat, reduced-sodium chicken broth

1 (8¾-ounce) can unsalted cream-style corn

½ cup all-purpose flour

2 cups skim milk

4 ounces Cheddar cheese, diced

½ teaspoon sea salt

Freshly ground pepper, to taste

½ cup processed bacon bits

1. Spray a large soup pot with nonstick cooking spray; heat on medium setting until hot. Add chicken, onion, and bell pepper; sauté over medium heat until chicken is browned and vegetables are tender. Stir in potatoes and broth; bring to a boil. Reduce heat and simmer, covered, for 20 minutes. Stir in corn.

2. Blend flour and milk in a bowl; gradually stir into pot. Increase heat to medium; cook until mixture comes to a boil, then reduce heat and simmer until soup is thickened, stirring constantly. Add cheese; stir until melted and blended in. Add salt and pepper to taste and sprinkle with bacon bits before serving.

PER SERVING Calories: 193 | Protein: 17g | Fiber: 2g

Stovetop Grilled Beef Loin

The olive oil in this recipe is used to help the "rub" adhere to the meat and to aid in the caramelization process.

INGREDIENTS | **YIELDS 1 (5-OUNCE) LOIN; SERVING SIZE: 2½ OUNCES**

1 lean beef tenderloin fillet, no more than 1" thick

½ teaspoon paprika

1½ teaspoons garlic powder

⅛ teaspoon cracked black pepper

¼ teaspoon onion powder

Pinch to ⅛ teaspoon cayenne pepper (according to taste)

⅛ teaspoon dried oregano

⅛ teaspoon dried thyme

½ teaspoon brown sugar

½ teaspoon olive oil

1. Remove loin from refrigerator 30 minutes before preparing it to allow it to come to room temperature. Pat meat dry with paper towels.

2. Mix together all dry ingredients. Rub ¼ teaspoon of olive oil on each side of the fillet. Divide seasoning mixture; rub into each oiled side.

3. Heat a grill pan on high for 1–2 minutes, until the pan is sizzling hot. Place beef fillet in pan, reduce heat to medium-high, and cook for 3 minutes. Use tongs to turn fillet. (Be careful not to pierce meat.) Cook for another 2 minutes for medium or 3 minutes for well-done.

4. Remove from heat and let the meat rest in the pan for at least 5 minutes, allowing juices to redistribute throughout meat and complete cooking process, which makes for a juicier fillet.

PER SERVING Calories: 105 | Protein: 15g | Fiber: 0g

Pork Roast with Caramelized Onions and Apples

The alcohol in the wine will burn away with cooking leaving the wonderful Marsala flavor.

INGREDIENTS | SERVES 6

2 pounds lean pork loin roast

Fresh ground pepper

½ tablespoon olive oil

½ tablespoon butter

2 cups onion, chopped

1 tablespoon Marsala wine

⅓ cup low-sodium chicken broth

1 apple, peeled and chopped

1. Preheat oven to 375°F. Season pork loin with pepper. Heat olive oil in a large skillet; sear to brown all sides.

2. Transfer roast to a 9" × 13" glass baking dish; cook for approximately 1 hour and 15 minutes.

3. While pork is roasting, prepare onions: In a large nonstick skillet, melt butter and add onions. Sauté onions until soft; add wine, chicken broth, and apple. Continue cooking on low heat until onions are soft and brown in color, and have caramelized.

4. When the roast has reached an internal temperature of 130°F, spoon onions over top; place a loose foil tent over the roast.

5. Remove the roast from oven when an internal temperature of 145°F has been reached. (Temperature of the roast will continue to rise as meat rests.) Keep the roast loosely covered with foil and allow to stand for 10–15 minutes before slicing.

PER SERVING Calories: 373 | Protein: 31g | Fiber: 1g

Healthy "Fried" Chicken

When faced with the decision of whether to have chicken with or without the skin, consider that ½ pound of skinless chicken breast has 9g of fat; ½ pound with the skin on has 38g!

INGREDIENTS | SERVES 4

10 ounces raw boneless, skinless chicken breasts (fat trimmed off)

½ cup nonfat plain yogurt

½ cup bread crumbs

1 teaspoon garlic powder

1 teaspoon paprika

¼ teaspoon dried thyme

1. Preheat oven to 350°F. Prepare a baking pan with nonstick cooking spray. Cut chicken breast into 4 equal pieces; marinate in yogurt for several minutes.

2. Mix together bread crumbs, garlic, paprika, and thyme; dredge chicken in crumb mixture. Arrange on prepared pan; bake for 20 minutes. To give chicken a deep golden color, place pan under broiler for last 5 minutes of cooking. Watch closely to ensure chicken "crust" doesn't burn.

PER SERVING Calories: 118 | Protein: 19g | Fiber: 0g

Taco Salad

A hearty, wholesome salad that fills you up and gives you the protein you need.

INGREDIENTS | SERVES 8

1 recipe Turkey Chili (see recipe in this appendix)

8 cups tightly packed salad greens

8 ounces Cheddar cheese, shredded (to yield 2 cups)

8 ounces nonfat corn chips

Vegetables of your choice, such as chopped celery, onion, or banana or jalapeño peppers (optional)

1. Prepare Turkey Chili.

2. Divide salad greens between 8 large bowls. Top with chili, Cheddar cheese, corn chips, and vegetables or peppers, if using.

PER SERVING Calories: 426 | Protein: 23g | Fiber: 13g

Sesame Shrimp and Asparagus

This meal comes together quickly, making it a great meal for weekday nights.

INGREDIENTS | SERVES 4

2 teaspoons canola oil

2 cloves garlic, chopped

1 tablespoon fresh gingerroot, grated

1 pound medium shrimp

2 tablespoons dry white wine

½ pound asparagus, cut diagonally into 1" pieces

2 cups whole-grain pasta, cooked

½ teaspoon sesame seeds

¼ cup scallions, thinly sliced

1 teaspoon sesame oil

1. Heat oil in a wok or large nonstick skillet. Stir-fry garlic, gingerroot, and shrimp over high heat until shrimp begins to turn pink, about 2 minutes.

2. Add white wine and asparagus; stir-fry for an additional 3–5 minutes.

3. Add pasta, sesame seeds, scallions, and sesame oil; toss lightly and serve.

PER SERVING Calories: 257 | Protein: 28g | Fiber: 3g

Herbed Chicken and Brown Rice Dinner

Steamed mushrooms are a great add-in to this dish to "stretch" the meat further.

INGREDIENTS | SERVES 4

1 tablespoon canola oil

4 (4-ounce) boneless chicken breast pieces, skin removed

¾ teaspoon garlic powder

¾ teaspoon dried rosemary

1 (10.5-ounce) can low-fat, reduced-sodium chicken broth

⅓ cup water

2 cups uncooked instant brown rice

1. Heat oil in a large nonstick skillet on medium-high. Add chicken; sprinkle with ½ of garlic powder and rosemary. Cover, and cook for 4 minutes on each side, or until cooked through. Remove chicken from skillet and set aside.

2. Add broth and water to skillet; stir to deglaze pan and bring to a boil. Stir in rice and remaining garlic powder and rosemary. Top with chicken and cover; cook on low heat for 5 minutes. Remove from heat and let stand, covered, for 5 minutes.

PER SERVING Calories: 300 | Protein: 33g | Fiber: 0g

Chicken Kalamata

The health benefits of olives (and olive oil) come from the monounsaturated fats they contain. Olives are usually cured in a brine, salt, or olive oil, so if you must watch your salt intake, be careful how many you eat.

INGREDIENTS | **SERVES 4**

2 tablespoons olive oil

1 cup onion, chopped

1 teaspoon garlic, minced

1½ cups green peppers, chopped

1 pound boneless, skinless chicken breast, cut into 4 pieces

2 cups tomatoes, diced

1 teaspoon oregano

½ cup pitted kalamata olives, chopped

1. Heat olive oil over medium heat in a large skillet. Add onions, garlic, and peppers; sauté for about 5 minutes until onions are translucent.

2. Add chicken pieces; cook for about 5 minutes each side until lightly brown.

3. Add tomatoes and oregano. Reduce heat and simmer for 20 minutes.

4. Add olives; simmer for an additional 10 minutes before serving.

PER SERVING Calories: 311 | Protein: 31g | Fiber: 6g

Turkey Chili

This chili packs a protein punch. If your stomach can't handle the Tabasco, then omit it for a milder chili.

INGREDIENTS | **SERVES 6**

1 pound ground turkey

1 cup onions, chopped

½ cup green pepper, chopped

2 teaspoons garlic, finely chopped

2 (28-ounce) cans crushed canned tomatoes

1 cup canned black beans, drained

1 cup canned red kidney beans, drained

3 tablespoons chili powder

1 tablespoon ground cumin

1 teaspoon crushed red pepper

Dash Tabasco

1. Brown ground turkey in a large nonstick pot over medium-high heat.

2. Drain off any fat; add chopped onion, green pepper, and garlic. Continue cooking until onion is translucent, about 5 minutes.

3. Add remaining ingredients; bring to a slow boil.

4. Reduce heat, cover, and let simmer for at least 2–3 hours before serving.

PER SERVING Calories: 281 | Protein: 26g | Fiber: 11g

Jon's Fish Tacos

Fish tacos are quickly becoming a mainstream food, and this recipe combines all the best elements of this California cuisine.

INGREDIENTS | SERVES 4

¼ cup light mayonnaise
½ cup plain nonfat yogurt
¼ cup onion, chopped
2 tablespoons jalapeño pepper, minced
2 teaspoons cilantro, minced
2 cups cabbage, shredded
¼ cup lime juice
1 clove garlic, minced
1 tablespoon canola oil
1 pound tilapia fillets
4 whole-wheat tortillas, 6" diameter
Aluminum foil
Nonstick cooking spray
1 cup tomato, chopped

1. In a medium bowl, whisk together mayonnaise, yogurt, onion, jalapeño, and cilantro. Stir in shredded cabbage; chill.

2. In a separate bowl, combine lime juice, garlic, and canola oil to make a marinade for fish. Pour over fish; cover and refrigerate for at least 1 hour.

3. Place fish on aluminum-lined grill (spray aluminum with cooking spray); cook for 6–7 minutes on each side, until fish is tender and beginning to flake.

4. While fish is cooking, loosely wrap whole-wheat tortilla in a large piece of aluminum foil to heat.

5. To assemble tacos, cut fish into strips; divide into 4 portions. Place strips in center of each heated tortilla. Top with coleslaw mixture and chopped tomatoes. Add fresh ground pepper, if desired.

PER SERVING Calories: 383 | Protein: 29g | Fiber: 4g

Scallops and Shrimp with White Bean Sauce

When cooking with wine the alcohol will burn away, so dishes like this are safe to enjoy when pregnant.

INGREDIENTS | **SERVES 4**

½ cup finely chopped onion, steamed

2 cloves garlic, minced

2 teaspoons olive oil, divided

¼ cup dry white wine

¼ cup tightly packed fresh parsley leaves

¼ cup tightly packed fresh basil leaves

1⅓ cups canned cannellini (white) beans, drained and rinsed

¼ cup low-fat, reduced-sodium chicken broth

½ pound (8 ounces) shrimp, shelled and deveined

½ pound (8 ounces) scallops

1. In a nonstick saucepan, sauté onion and garlic in 1 teaspoon of oil over moderately low heat, for about 5 minutes until onion is soft. Add wine; simmer until wine is reduced by ½. Add parsley, basil, ⅓ cup of beans, and chicken broth; simmer, stirring constantly, 1 minute.

2. Transfer bean mixture to a blender or food processor; purée. Pour purée back into saucepan; add remaining beans; simmer for 2 minutes.

3. In a nonstick skillet, heat remaining 1 teaspoon of oil over moderately high heat until it is hot but not smoking. Sauté shrimp for 2 minutes on each side, or until cooked through. Using a slotted spoon, transfer shrimp to plate; cover to keep warm. Add scallops to skillet; sauté for 1 minute on each side, or until cooked through. To serve, divide bean sauce between 4 shallow bowls and arrange shellfish over top.

PER SERVING Calories: 231 | Protein: 27g | Fiber: 7g

Vegetable Pot Pie

This recipe can go vegetarian if you substitute vegetable broth for the chicken broth.
The vegetables give you plenty of fiber and flavor.

INGREDIENTS | **SERVES 6; SERVING SIZE 2 CUPS**

½ medium onion, diced
2 carrots, peeled and diced
2 celery stalks, diced
½ cup sliced leeks
2 tablespoons butter
¼ cup flour
3 cups chicken broth
1 potato, peeled and cubed
½ cup cut green beans
1 bay leaf
½ cup frozen peas
½ cup cream
Salt and pepper, to taste
¼ cup chopped chives
1 recipe Whole Wheat Biscuits, unbaked (see recipe in this appendix)

1. Sauté onion, carrots, celery, and leeks in butter until tender. Dust with flour, stir, and cook a few minutes. Add chicken broth, potato, and green beans. Bring to a boil, add bay leaf, and simmer for 40 minutes until vegetables are cooked and liquid is thickened.

2. Stir in peas and cream and remove from heat. Remove bay leaf, season with salt and pepper, and stir in chopped chives. Pour filling into a 9" × 13" baking dish and place on a baking sheet with sides.

3. Preheat oven to 400°F.

4. Place the unbaked biscuits on top of the filling and bake for 45 minutes or until the biscuit top is baked.

5. Scoop out individual portions and serve hot.

PER SERVING Calories: 480.55 | Protein: 14.37 g | Fiber: 8.99 g

Double Corn Waffles

Cornmeal plus corn kernels equal whole-grain fiber heaven. You can use canned or frozen corn, but this is a real treat if you can get corn in season at the end of summer.

INGREDIENTS | SERVES 6

3 eggs
4 ounces canola oil
1½ cups plain yogurt
1¾ cups yellow corn bread mix
½ cup corn kernels
Oil for waffle iron

Good Company

Honey Butter Spread is a good partner for corn bread and cornmeal muffins. Whip 2 tablespoons of honey with ½ stick softened unsalted butter with an electric mixer for a delicious butter spread to accompany double corn waffles.

1. Whisk together eggs, canola oil, and yogurt.

2. Stir egg mixture into the corn bread mix to combine. There will be lumps; be careful not to overmix.

3. Fold the corn kernels into the batter.

4. Pour or ladle about ½ cup waffle batter onto a preheated and oiled waffle iron and cook according to manufacturer's instructions.

5. Serve hot with honey butter spread.

PER SERVING Calories: 434 | Protein: 11.16 g | Fiber: 5.05 g

Granola

Serve this granola with fruit and yogurt or just eat it out of hand for an on-the-go breakfast. You can also turn this into trail mix by adding dried apples and/or raisins.

INGREDIENTS | SERVES 6

4 cups rolled oats
1 cup sliced almonds
½ teaspoon cinnamon
1 teaspoon vanilla
4 ounces orange blossom honey
2 ounces canola oil
½ cup wheat germ
¼ cup sesame seeds
¼ cup millet
¼ cup flaxseeds

1. Preheat oven to 350°F.

2. Toss oats, almonds, cinnamon, vanilla, honey, and canola oil together in a large bowl. Spread the mixture on a baking pan and bake for 10 minutes.

3. Stir and add wheat germ, sesame seeds, and millet. Bake for 15 minutes.

4. Stir and add flaxseeds. Bake for 10 minutes.

5. Remove from oven. Cool and break up large chunks.

PER SERVING Calories: 565.50 | Protein: 16.55 g | Fiber: 11.56 g

Hummus Pita Sandwich

*Use the freshest whole wheat pita bread you can find for this crunchy, juicy,
cool sandwich. Some fresh, chopped mint is an excellent addition.*

INGREDIENTS | SERVES 1

¼ cup plain yogurt

¼ teaspoon ranch dressing spice mix

1 small clove garlic, peeled

Pinch of salt

¼ cup canned garbanzo beans

1 tablespoon tahini

1 teaspoon lemon juice

1 teaspoon olive oil

Pinch of ground cumin

1 whole wheat pita bread round

¼ cup shredded carrots

¼ cup diced Roma tomatoes

5 slices cucumber

¼ cup alfalfa sprouts

1. Mix together the yogurt and ranch dressing spices. Set aside in the refrigerator.

2. To make the hummus, purée the garlic and salt in a food processor. Add the garbanzo beans and purée to a paste. Add the tahini, lemon juice, olive oil, and cumin and process until smooth, scraping down the sides of the bowl.

3. Spread the hummus on one side of the pita bread. Add carrots, tomatoes, cucumbers, and sprouts. Drizzle the yogurt sauce on and fold the pita in half like a taco.

PER SERVING Calories: 452.61 | Protein: 15.55 g | Fiber: 10.17 g

Wrap It Up!

It seems that every culture has a way of putting savory and sweet mixtures into delectable wrappings. You can put sweet and savory together, as in a fruity, curried shrimp mixture. You can make your fillings rich in fiber and stuff them into a good, multigrain pita or hero roll. Just be creative and experiment to build a diet high in whole grains and fiber.

Split Pea Soup

Legumes, like peas, are a source of high fiber and a good source of protein. To make this meal vegetarian, omit the ham bone and use vegetable stock.

INGREDIENTS | SERVES 6

8 cups water
2 cups split peas
1 ham bone
½ cup diced carrot
¼ cup diced celery
1 cup diced onion
Salt and pepper, to taste

1. Simmer water, split peas, and ham bone for 1 hour.

2. Add carrot, celery, and onion and simmer for 1 more hour.

3. Remove the ham bone, season the soup with salt and pepper, and serve hot.

PER SERVING Calories: 266.45 | Protein: 20.38 g | Fiber: 17.64 g

Peanut Butter Banana Tortilla Wrap

Bananas, which contain potassium and fiber, are a naturally sweet addition to any peanut butter sandwich.

INGREDIENTS | YIELDS 1 WRAP

1 large whole wheat tortilla
2 tablespoons peanut butter
¼ cup sunflower seeds, shelled and roasted
1 banana, peeled

1. Lay the tortilla out on a flat surface. Spread the peanut butter over most of the tortilla.

2. Sprinkle the sunflower seeds over the peanut butter. Lay the banana on the peanut butter and roll the tortilla around it like a carpet.

3. Cut the wrap in half diagonally.

PER SERVING Calories: 554.83 | Protein: 18.02 g | Fiber: 10.38 g

Alternate Wrap

Instead of whole wheat tortillas, substitute whole wheat pita or lavash (cracker bread). Toasted corn tortillas are also very tasty and a fine source of fiber. You may also use whole wheat hot dog buns to make this banana sandwich.

Baked Beans

Baked beans are an example of picnic food being a sort of "health" food and not a junk food like the fried chips, French fries, and sugary snacks they often accompany.

INGREDIENTS | **SERVES 6; SERVING SIZE 1 CUP**

4 cups cooked white beans
1 cup sliced onion
4 slices bacon, chopped
1 teaspoon dry mustard
½ cup brown sugar
½ cup maple syrup
2 tablespoons ketchup
½ teaspoon salt
1 teaspoon pepper
1½ cups water

1. Preheat oven to 350°F.

2. Drain the beans and layer them with the onions and bacon in a casserole dish.

3. Combine the dry mustard, brown sugar, maple syrup, ketchup, salt, pepper, and water and pour the mixture over the beans.

4. Cover and bake the beans for 2 hours.

5. Uncover and bake for 15 minutes more.

PER SERVING Calories: 357.49 | Protein: 13.52 g | Fiber: 12.85 g

Whole Wheat Biscuit Pizza

If you have premade Whole Wheat Biscuits (see recipe later in this appendix), you can use them to make your pizzas quickly. The whole wheat in the biscuits adds fiber and B vitamins to the dish.

INGREDIENTS | **SERVES 6**

12 unbaked Whole Wheat Biscuits
¼ cup pizza sauce
½ cup shredded mozzarella cheese
¼ cup sliced black olives
¼ cup diced green peppers

1. Preheat oven to 375°F.

2. Lay the individual biscuits out on a sheet pan and press them down to make flat rounds.

3. Spoon pizza sauce over the rounds and sprinkle them with mozzarella cheese.

4. Top the pizzas with black olives and green peppers.

5. Bake for 15–20 minutes. Serve immediately.

PER SERVING Calories: 489.65 | Protein: 16.01 g | Fiber: 10.76 g

Penne Primavera

You can also enhance your primavera with a garnish of chopped Italian flat-leaf parsley, a few tiny grape tomatoes, and toasted walnuts. The walnuts add extra crunch, fiber, and protein.

INGREDIENTS | SERVES 4; SERVING SIZE 2 CUPS

½ cup diced onion
½ cup diced carrot
¼ cup diced red bell pepper
2 tablespoons olive oil
½ cup chicken broth
1 cup asparagus tips
1 cup broccoli florets
½ cup cream
½ cup peas
½ cup grated Parmesan cheese
Salt and pepper, to taste
4 cups cooked penne pasta

1. Sauté onions, carrots, and red bell pepper in oil until tender.

2. Add chicken broth, asparagus, and broccoli and simmer for 5 minutes.

3. Add cream and peas and simmer for 5 minutes.

4. Stir in Parmesan cheese and remove from heat.

5. Season with salt and pepper and serve sauce over cooked penne pasta.

PER SERVING Calories: 401.46 | Protein: 15.65 g | Fiber: 5.82 g

Pasta Fagioli

The ham in this dish makes it high in sodium, so it's best to eat this dish in moderation.

INGREDIENTS | SERVES 8

1 (16-ounce) package ziti pasta
2 tablespoons olive oil
2 cloves garlic, minced
1½ cups sugar snap peas
1½ cups diced cooked extra-lean ham
1 cup cooked navy beans
¼ cup sun-dried tomatoes packed in oil, drained and chopped
1½ cups low-fat, reduced-sodium chicken broth
½ teaspoon kosher or sea salt
¼ teaspoon cracked black pepper
¼ cup grated Parmesan cheese

1. Cook the pasta according to package directions.

2. Meanwhile, heat a large skillet over medium heat and add the olive oil. Sauté the garlic for 2 minutes, being careful not to burn it. Add the peas and stir-fry for about 3 minutes. Stir in the ham, beans, tomatoes, broth, salt, and pepper and simmer for 5 minutes.

3. Toss the stir-fried bean mixture with the pasta and Parmesan cheese.

PER SERVING Calories: 380.19 | Protein: 20.37g | Fiber: 6.25 g

Pork Chops and Fruited Veggies Bake

These homemade pork chops are tender and juicy.
They are easy to cook, and they pack a ton of fiber and protein.

INGREDIENTS | **SERVES 4**

1 cup baby carrots, washed and peeled

1 (10-ounce) package frozen organic sliced peaches, thawed

2 teaspoons brown sugar

¼ teaspoon ground cinnamon

Pinch ground cloves

¼ teaspoon freshly ground black pepper

¼ teaspoon dried thyme

¼ teaspoon dried rosemary

⅛ teaspoon dried oregano

½ teaspoon dried lemon granules

4 (6-ounce) bone-in pork loin chops

8 cloves garlic, crushed

4 large Yukon gold potatoes, washed and sliced

1 (10-ounce) package frozen whole green beans, thawed

Extra-virgin olive spray oil

Fruit Swaps

You can substitute 4 peeled and sliced apples or pears for the peaches in the Pork Chops and Fruited Veggies Bake recipe. If you do, toss the slices with 1 tablespoon of lemon juice before mixing them with the brown sugar, cinnamon, and cloves.

1. Preheat oven to 425°F. Treat a large roasting pan or jelly roll pan with nonstick spray.

2. Place the carrots, peaches, brown sugar, cinnamon, and cloves in a medium bowl; stir to mix. Set aside.

3. Mix the pepper, thyme, rosemary, oregano, and lemon granules together and use a mortar and pestle or the back of a spoon to crush them.

4. Rub the pork chops with the garlic. Evenly spread the sliced potatoes and green beans across the prepared baking pan. Place the garlic cloves and pork chops atop the vegetables. Spray lightly with the spray oil. Sprinkle with the herb mixture.

5. Spread the carrot and peach mixture atop the pork chops and vegetables.

6. Bake for 30 minutes or until the meat is tender and the potatoes and carrots are tender.

PER SERVING Calories: 682.32 | Protein: 42.69 g | Fiber: 10.49 g

Whole Wheat Biscuits

You can make breakfast sandwiches from these hearty biscuits for a boost in fiber to start your day.

INGREDIENTS | **SERVES 8; SERVING SIZE 1**

1½ cups all-purpose flour
1½ cups whole wheat flour
4½ teaspoons baking powder
1½ teaspoons salt
1 tablespoon sugar
6 tablespoons cold butter
1¼ cups buttermilk

1. Preheat oven to 400°F.

2. Combine flours, baking powder, salt, and sugar in a mixing bowl.

3. Cut butter into small pieces and add to dry ingredients. Mix butter into dry ingredients with a pastry cutter or your fingers. Add buttermilk and mix with a wooden spoon to form the dough.

4. Roll dough on a floured board to 1" thickness. Cut circles with a 2–3" round cookie cutter or drinking glass. Place rounds on a baking sheet and bake for 12 minutes.

PER SERVING Calories: 262.42 | Protein: 7.00 g | Fiber: 3.38 g

Chicken and Green Bean Stovetop Casserole

This is a dressed-up variation of a popular Thanksgiving favorite. It's meant to have a hint of the flavor of a green bean casserole, but it can stand on its own as a meal.

INGREDIENTS | **SERVES 4**

1 can condensed cream of chicken soup
¼ cup skim milk
2 teaspoons Worcestershire sauce
1 teaspoon mayonnaise
½ teaspoon onion powder
¼ teaspoon garlic powder
¼ teaspoon ground black pepper
1 (4-ounce) can sliced water chestnuts, drained
2½ cups frozen green beans, thawed
1 cup sliced mushrooms, steamed
½ pound cooked, chopped chicken
1⅓ cups cooked brown long-grain rice

Combine the soup, milk, Worcestershire sauce, mayonnaise, onion powder, garlic powder, and pepper in a saucepan and bring to a boil. Reduce heat and add the water chestnuts, green beans, mushrooms, and chicken. Simmer until vegetables and chicken are heated through. Serve over rice.

PER SERVING Calories: 305.29 | Protein: 22.85 g | Fiber: 5.56 g

Blackberry Cobbler

This recipe can also be made from raspberries, blueberries, cherries, or a combination, which is sometimes called jumbleberry. The berry juice soaks into the biscuits, giving them enormous flavor.

INGREDIENTS | **SERVES 8; SERVING SIZE 1½ CUPS**

1 recipe Whole Wheat Biscuits (see previous recipe), unbaked
8 cups blackberries
¼ cup flour
¾ cup sugar
¼ cup cream

1. Preheat oven to 350°F. Prepare biscuit dough recipe, cut biscuit circles out, and set them aside.

2. Toss the blackberries, flour, and sugar together, then put the mixture into a 9" × 11" baking dish.

3. Bake the blackberries for 25 minutes, remove from oven, and place the unbaked biscuits on top of the hot berries.

4. Brush the biscuit tops with cream and return the cobbler to the oven to bake for another 25 minutes. Serve warm.

PER SERVING Calories: 441.3 | Protein: 8.62 g | Fiber: 11.09 g

Blueberry Pie

The addition of dried blueberries to fresh blueberries makes this pie even richer in fiber and flavor. If you can't find dried blueberries, use cut-up dried apples for the same high-fiber results.

INGREDIENTS | **SERVES 6; SERVING SIZE 1 SLICE**

2 rolled-out circles of pie dough
4 cups blueberries
½ cup dried blueberries
1 cup sugar
¼ cup lemon juice
1 tablespoon grated lemon zest
4 tablespoons cornstarch
1 ounce butter, cut in pieces

1. Preheat oven to 350°F. Line pie pan with one circle of pie dough.

2. Mix blueberries with dried blueberries, sugar, lemon juice, lemon zest, and cornstarch and put them in the pie shell. Dot blueberries with butter pieces.

3. Cover the blueberries with the other pie dough circle, crimp the edges to seal, and cut slits in the top. Sprinkle with sugar and bake for 50 minutes. Cool before slicing.

PER SERVING Calories: 633.49 | Protein: 4.12 g | Fiber: 6.63 g

Trail Mix

*Pack individual baggies of this to take in the car when running errands
so you have something to snack on when hunger strikes.*

INGREDIENTS | SERVES 8; SERVING SIZE 1 CUP

2 cups dried cherries
2 cups roasted pecans
1 cup M&M's
2 cups granola
1 cup shelled sunflower seeds
1 cup Pretzel Goldfish

1. Combine everything in a large bowl.

2. Divide into individual portions and store in resealable plastic bags or serve in individual paper cups.

PER SERVING Calories: 647.58 | Protein: 12.60 g | Fiber: 8.89 g

Sweets and Fiber

The more fiber you add to a sweet snack, the easier it is to pass it out of the body. Add nuts and seeds for high fiber and protein.

Caramel Nut Apple Wedges

*Another way to serve this is to arrange the undipped apple wedges on a platter and dip the apples
into the caramel and hazelnuts. This becomes a fondue. However, the caramel may
be superhot, so be careful. Nuts and apples give you some fiber.*

INGREDIENTS | SERVES 6

1 pound caramels
¼ cup evaporated milk
2 cups chopped hazelnuts
2 red apples
1 Golden Delicious apple
2 Granny Smith apples

1. Melt the caramels and evaporated milk over low heat.

2. Toast the hazelnuts in the oven for 12 minutes at 350°F.

3. Cut the apples into quarters, cut out the cores, and cut the quarters into slices for dipping.

4. Dip the apple wedges into the caramel, then the hazelnuts. Place the wedges on waxed paper.

5. Refrigerate for 15 minutes or until caramel is set.

PER SERVING Calories: 596.46 | Protein: 10.28 g | Fiber: 7.16 g

Beef Stir-Fry

Serve this delicious stir-fry with some hot cooked rice.

INGREDIENTS | SERVES 4

1 pound sirloin steak
2 tablespoons stir-fry sauce
2 tablespoons oil
1 onion, chopped
1½ cups sugar snap peas
1 red bell pepper, thinly sliced
½ cup stir-fry sauce

Stir-Fry Variations

Once you've learned a stir-fry recipe, you can vary it with many different cuts of meat and lots of vegetables. Try experimenting with different Asian bottled stir-fry sauces.

1. Thinly slice the steak across the grain. Place in a medium bowl and toss with 2 tablespoons stir-fry sauce. Set aside.

2. Heat oil in a large skillet or wok over medium-high heat. Add onion; stir-fry for 3–4 minutes until crisp-tender. Add peas and bell pepper; stir-fry for 2–3 minutes. Add beef; stir-fry for 3–4 minutes, until browned. Add ½ cup stir-fry sauce and bring to a simmer; simmer for 3–4 minutes, until blended. Serve over hot cooked rice.

Parmesan Chicken

This simple recipe demands the highest-quality ingredients. Serve it with some hot cooked couscous, bakery rolls, and melon wedges.

INGREDIENTS | SERVES 6

6 boneless, skinless chicken breasts
¼ cup lemon juice
1 teaspoon salt
⅛ teaspoon pepper
½ teaspoon dried thyme leaves
¼ cup unsalted butter
½ cup grated Parmesan cheese

1. Cut chicken breasts into 1" pieces. Sprinkle with lemon juice, salt, pepper, and thyme leaves. Let stand at room temperature for 10 minutes.

2. Melt butter in a heavy saucepan over medium heat. Sauté chicken until thoroughly cooked, about 5–6 minutes, stirring frequently. Sprinkle cheese over chicken, turn off heat, cover pan, and let stand for 2–3 minutes to melt cheese. Serve over hot cooked couscous.

Honey Mustard Salmon

Honey and mustard make an irresistible flavor combination with rich and savory salmon filets. You can multiply this recipe for a larger crowd; marinating and cooking times remain the same.

INGREDIENTS | SERVES 4

⅓ cup honey mustard salad dressing

2 tablespoons honey

½ teaspoon dill seed

2 tablespoons butter, melted

4 (6-ounce) salmon fillets

Menu Ideas

Fish is delicious when served with a salad made from baby spinach. Toss together spinach, sliced water chestnuts, sliced mushrooms, and red bell pepper, and drizzle with some creamy garlic salad dressing. Top it with croutons or Parmesan shavings.

1. In a shallow casserole dish, combine salad dressing, honey, dill seed, and butter and mix well. Add salmon fillets and turn to coat. Cover and let stand at room temperature for 10 minutes.

2. Prepare and preheat grill or broiler. Remove salmon from marinade and place, skin-side down, on grill or broiler pan. Cover and grill, or broil, 6 inches from heat for 8–12 minutes, until salmon is cooked and flakes when tested with a fork, brushing with remaining marinade halfway through cooking time. Discard remaining marinade. Serve immediately.

Turkey Pizza

Pizza is fun to make at home. Use your family's favorite foods and flavors to create your own specialty. This one is a variation of the classic ham and pineapple pizza.

INGREDIENTS | SERVES 4

1 (12" or 14") prepared pizza crust

1 cup pizza sauce

4 cooked turkey cutlets

1 (8-ounce) can pineapple tidbits, drained

1½ cups shredded Swiss cheese

1. Preheat oven to 400°F. Place pizza crust on a large cookie sheet and spread with pizza sauce. Cut turkey cutlets into thin strips and arrange on pizza along with well-drained pineapple tidbits. Sprinkle with cheese.

2. Bake pizza for 15–20 minutes or until pizza is hot and cheese is melted and beginning to brown. Let stand for 5 minutes, then serve.

Lemon Chicken *en Papillote*

Lemon and chicken are perfect partners. The tart lemon tenderizes the chicken and adds great flavor. Serve these "packages" at the table and let your guests open them.

INGREDIENTS | SERVES 4

4 boneless, skinless chicken breasts

½ teaspoon salt

⅛ teaspoon lemon pepper

1 lemon, cut into thin slices, seeds removed

1 yellow summer squash, thinly sliced

1 zucchini, thinly sliced

¼ cup pine nuts

1. Preheat oven to 425°F. Cut 4 12" × 18" pieces of cooking parchment paper. Fold in half, cut into a half-heart shape, then unfold. Place chicken breasts on one side of the fold and sprinkle with salt and lemon pepper. Top with lemon slices.

2. Arrange summer squash and zucchini around chicken and sprinkle pine nuts over all. Fold hearts in half and seal the edges by tightly folding them together twice. Place on cookie sheets and bake for 10–15 minutes, until chicken registers 170°F on a meat thermometer. Serve immediately.

Green Chili Chicken Burritos

Just because you're pregnant doesn't mean you can't have some spice. In fact, you may even be craving it!

INGREDIENTS | SERVES 6

2 (9-ounce) packages grilled chicken strips

1 (4-ounce) can chopped green chilies, drained

1 cup sour cream

¼ teaspoon cayenne pepper

6 flour tortillas

1½ cups shredded pepper jack cheese, divided

1. Preheat oven to 400°F. In a microwave-safe bowl, combine chicken strips and green chilies. Microwave on medium power for 2–3 minutes, stirring once during cooking time, until ingredients are hot. Stir in sour cream and cayenne pepper.

2. Divide mixture among the tortillas. Sprinkle with 1 cup of the cheese. Roll up to enclose filling. Place in a 2-quart casserole dish and top with remaining cheese. Bake for 7–11 minutes, until cheese melts and burritos are hot.

Stovetop Lasagna

Try this quick and easy version of lasagna that cooks right on the stove for all the taste with half the fuss.

INGREDIENTS | SERVES 4–6

1 pound bulk sweet Italian sausage

1 onion, chopped

1 (24-ounce) package frozen ravioli

1 (28-ounce) jar pasta sauce

1 teaspoon dried Italian seasoning

1½ cups shredded Italian-blend cheese

1. Bring a large pot of water to a boil. Meanwhile, in a heavy skillet over medium heat, cook sausage and onion, stirring to break up sausage, until meat is browned. Drain thoroughly, and wipe out skillet.

2. Add ravioli to boiling water; cook until almost tender, about 1–2 minutes. Drain well. In cleaned skillet, spread about 1 cup pasta sauce, then top with layers of sausage mixture, ravioli, and more pasta sauce. Sprinkle each layer with a bit of the dried Italian seasoning. Sprinkle with cheese. Cover and cook over medium heat, shaking pan occasionally, until sauce bubbles, cheese melts, and mixture is hot, about 5–8 minutes. Serve immediately.

Grilled Orange Pork Tenderloin

The fresh citrus taste adds wonderful flavor and pizzazz to plain old pork.

INGREDIENTS | SERVES 6–8

2 pounds pork tenderloins

1 teaspoon salt

⅛ teaspoon pepper

⅓ cup frozen orange juice concentrate, thawed

¼ cup honey

¼ cup Dijon mustard

1 tablespoon lemon juice

½ teaspoon dried oregano leaves

1. Prepare and heat grill. Cut pork tenderloins in half crosswise. Then butterfly the pork; cut the tenderloins horizontally in half, being careful not to cut through to the other side. Spread tenderloins open and place in a large casserole dish. Sprinkle both sides with salt and pepper. In a medium bowl, combine remaining ingredients and mix well. Spread on all sides of tenderloins and let stand for 10 minutes.

2. Grill tenderloins, 6 inches from medium coals, covered, turning once, for 14–17 minutes, until a meat thermometer registers 160°F. Brush with any remaining marinade after turning. Discard remaining marinade. Slice tenderloins across the grain to serve.

Mushroom Risotto

Risotto is a creamy, rich dish of short-grain rice and vegetables. Cooking constantly while stirring releases starch from the rice, which makes the mixture thick.

INGREDIENTS | **SERVES 4–6**

3 tablespoons olive oil

1½ cups assorted fresh mushrooms, sliced

½ teaspoon dried thyme leaves

1 cup arborio rice

4 cups vegetable stock

1 cup grated Parmesan cheese

2 tablespoons butter

1. Place olive oil in a large saucepan over medium heat. When hot, add the mushrooms and thyme. Cook and stir until mushrooms give up their liquid and the liquid evaporates, about 6–8 minutes. Then stir in rice; cook and stir for 3–4 minutes, until rice is opaque.

2. Meanwhile, heat vegetable stock in another saucepan; keep over low heat while making risotto. Add the stock to the rice mixture about 1 cup at a time, stirring until the liquid is absorbed.

3. When all the stock is added and rice is tender, remove from the heat, stir in cheese and butter, cover, and let stand for 5 minutes. Stir and serve immediately.

Potato Curry

This rich dish uses refrigerated prepared potatoes to save time. Serve it with a fruit salad and some whole-wheat breadsticks.

INGREDIENTS | **SERVES 6–8**

1 (15-ounce) package refrigerated hash brown potatoes

3 tablespoons olive oil

1 onion, chopped

3 cloves garlic, minced

1–2 tablespoons curry powder

1 teaspoon salt

⅛ teaspoon red pepper flakes

2 cups frozen baby peas

1 cup sour cream

1. Drain potatoes well, if necessary. Spread on paper towels to dry. Meanwhile, in a large skillet, heat olive oil over medium heat. Add onion and garlic; cook and stir for 3–4 minutes, until crisp-tender. Sprinkle curry powder, salt, and red pepper flakes into skillet; cook and stir for 1 minute longer.

2. Add potatoes to skillet; cook and stir for 8–10 minutes, until potatoes are hot and tender and browning around the edges. Stir in peas and cook for 2–3 minutes longer.

3. Remove from heat and stir in sour cream. Cover and let stand for 3 minutes, then serve immediately.

Tortellini in Wine Sauce

The alcohol in the wine will cook out of this recipe, but if you still don't feel comfortable using it, you can substitute vegetable broth.

INGREDIENTS | SERVES 4

1 (14-ounce) package frozen cheese tortellini
2 tablespoons olive oil
3 cloves garlic, minced
½ cup white wine or vegetable broth
2 cups frozen baby peas
¼ teaspoon onion salt
¼ cup chopped flat-leaf parsley

1. Bring a large pot of water to a boil and cook tortellini as directed on package. Meanwhile, in a large saucepan, heat olive oil over medium heat. Add garlic; cook and stir for 2 minutes, until garlic just begins to turn golden. Add wine, peas, and onion salt and bring to a simmer.

2. Drain tortellini and add to saucepan with wine. Cook over low heat for 4–5 minutes, until mixture is hot and slightly thickened. Add parsley, stir, and serve.

Garlicky Green Beans

You can add more garlic to this simple and flavorful side dish if you'd like. Just be sure to stir constantly while the garlic and shallots are browning so they don't burn.

INGREDIENTS | SERVES 6

1 pound green beans
4 cups water
1 tablespoon olive oil
1 tablespoon butter
6 cloves garlic, peeled and chopped
1 shallot, peeled and chopped
½ teaspoon salt

1. Trim the ends off the green beans and cut each bean in half crosswise. Place in a heavy saucepan and cover with water. Bring to a boil over high heat, then lower heat to medium and simmer for 5–8 minutes, until beans are crisp-tender.

2. Meanwhile, combine olive oil and butter in a heavy saucepan and add garlic and shallot. Cook and stir over medium heat until the garlic is fragrant and turns light brown around the edges.

3. Drain beans and add to garlic mixture in pan along with salt. Cook and stir over medium heat for 2–3 minutes, until beans are coated. Serve immediately.

Super Quick Beef Vegetable Stew

There are so many types of fully prepared meat entrees in your grocery store; browse the selection and stock up!

INGREDIENTS | SERVES 6

3 tablespoons olive oil

1 onion, chopped

3 cloves garlic, minced

1 (16-ounce) package prepared roast beef in gravy

1 (16-ounce) package frozen mixed vegetables

1 (10-ounce) can cream of mushroom soup

2 cups water

½ teaspoon dried thyme leaves

1. In a heavy large saucepan, heat olive oil over medium heat. Add onion and garlic; cook and stir until tender, 4–5 minutes. Meanwhile, cut the cooked roast beef into 1" chunks. Add to saucepan along with gravy, frozen mixed vegetables, soup, water, and thyme leaves.

2. Cook over medium-high heat until stew comes to a boil, about 7–9 minutes. Reduce heat to low and simmer for 6–7 minutes longer, until vegetables and beef are hot and tender. Serve immediately.

Savory Minestrone

Minestrone is a rich vegetable soup made with beans and pasta. It's really a meal in one bowl; serve with some toasted garlic bread and tall glasses of milk.

INGREDIENTS | SERVES 6

4 cups chicken broth

1 (16-ounce) package frozen mixed vegetables

1 (15-ounce) can cannellini beans, drained

½ teaspoon dried basil leaves

½ teaspoon dried oregano leaves

1 (14-ounce) can diced tomatoes with garlic, undrained

1½ cups elbow macaroni

In a large saucepan, combine chicken broth and vegetables; bring to a boil over medium-high heat. When broth boils, add beans, basil, oregano, and tomatoes. Bring to a simmer, lower heat, and cook for 5 minutes. Add macaroni; stir and simmer for 8–9 minutes, until pasta is tender, then serve.

No Flour Peanut Butter Cookies

Believe it or not, these cookies turn out wonderfully with absolutely no flour of any kind! Do not use the refrigerated, or natural, type of peanut butter because the cookies will spread too much when they bake.

INGREDIENTS | YIELDS 48 COOKIES

2 cups peanut butter

2 cups sugar

2 eggs

1 teaspoon vanilla

½ cup chopped peanuts

1 cup miniature semisweet chocolate chips

1. Preheat oven to 325°F. Line cookie sheets with parchment paper or Silpat silicon liners; set aside. In a large bowl, combine peanut butter, sugar, eggs, and vanilla and mix well until blended. Stir in peanuts and chocolate chips.

2. Drop by teaspoonfuls onto prepared cookie sheets. Bake for 12 to 15 minutes, until cookies are just set. Cool for 5 minutes on cookie sheets, then carefully remove to wire racks to cool.

Candied Nuts

Candied nuts are a wonderful snack to have on hand for the holiday season; they also make great gifts packaged in decorative tins or glass jars.

INGREDIENTS | YIELDS 3 CUPS

1 cup brown sugar

½ cup sugar

⅓ cup orange juice

3 tablespoons butter, melted

1 teaspoon vanilla

3 cups mixed nuts

Storing Nuts

Many nuts should be stored in the freezer before use, because the oils they contain can quickly turn rancid. Pour the nuts into a freezer container such as a heavy-duty resealable freezer bag or a hard-sided plastic container, label, and freeze up to 6 months.

1. Preheat oven to 350°F. Grease a large cookie sheet with butter and set aside. Grease 2 large sheets of foil with butter and set aside.

2. In a large bowl, combine brown sugar, sugar, orange juice, melted butter, and vanilla and mix well. Add nuts and toss to coat. Spread onto prepared cookie sheet. Bake for 10–15 minutes or until nuts are dark golden brown and sugar mixture bubbles. Stir nuts twice during cooking time. Immediately place nuts onto buttered foil, spreading thinly. Let cool, then break nuts apart before storing in an airtight container.

Easy Fudge

Use just about anything as the additions in this easy candy—candy-coated chocolate pieces, gumdrops, peanuts, chopped candy bars, macadamia nuts, or toffee bits would all be wonderful.

INGREDIENTS | SERVES 8–10

1 (12-ounce) package semisweet chocolate chips
½ cup milk chocolate chips
1 (15-ounce) can sweetened condensed milk
1 cup chopped cashews
1 cup miniature marshmallows

Sweetened Condensed Milk

Sweetened condensed milk is a combination of milk and sugar with 50 percent of the water removed. Keep a can or two on hand because it's a great ingredient for making fudge and candies.

1. Grease an 8" square pan with butter and set aside. In a medium microwave-safe bowl, combine semisweet chocolate chips, milk chocolate chips, and sweetened condensed milk. Microwave on 50 percent power for 2–4 minutes, stirring once during cooking time, until chocolate is almost melted. Remove from oven and stir until chocolate melts.

2. Stir in cashews until mixed, then stir in marshmallows. Spread into prepared pan and let stand until cool.

No Bake Apple Cookies

The pectin in the apple helps thicken the cookie mixture without baking. Store these cookies in an airtight container at room temperature.

INGREDIENTS | YIELDS 48 COOKIES

½ cup butter
1½ cups sugar
½ cup brown sugar
1 cup grated peeled Granny Smith apple
½ teaspoon cinnamon
3 cups quick-cooking oatmeal
1 cup chopped walnuts
½ cup powdered sugar

1. In a heavy saucepan, melt butter with sugars over medium heat, then stir in apple. Bring to a boil, then stir and boil for 1 minute. Remove from heat and add cinnamon, oatmeal, and walnuts; stir to combine. Let stand for 5 minutes.

2. Place powdered sugar on shallow pan. Drop apple mixture by teaspoons into powdered sugar and roll into balls. Place on waxed paper and let stand until the cookies are firm.

Index

multifetal reduction, 38–40

myths about, 10, 17–18

preparing for, 40–41

raising, 257–74

reproductive technology and, 33

risks to, 38

sets of, 252–53

uniqueness of, 14–15

Myths/misconceptions, 10, 17–18

Naming babies, 72–74

Natural birth, 179–80

Nausea, 43–44, 47–49

Neonatal Intensive Care Unit (NICU), 71, 193, 205–8, 211

"Nesting," 66–67

Neurological concerns, 202

NICU experience, 193, 205–8

Nonuplets, 32

Nursery, 106–15

  baby monitors for, 110–11

  changing tables for, 109

  cribs for, 107–9

  decorating, 110

  essentials for, 115

  layette for, 111–14

  linens/bedding for, 114–15

Nutritional supplements, 81–82

Obstetrician-gynecologist, 93–94

Octuplets, 32

Packing tips, 71–72

Parenthood, adjusting to, 245–48

Parenthood, singles, 249–50

Pediatrician, choosing, 260–61

Physical changes, 47–51, 55–56

Physical exam, 98

Physical symptoms, 43–44

Placenta analysis, 27

Placenta, delivery of, 188

Placental abruptions, 139

Placenta previa, 138, 142

Placenta problems, 138–39, 142, 145

Playpen/play yard, 128

Polar body, 24

Polychlorinated biphenyls (PCBs), 89

Post-mature pregnancy, 67–68

Postpartum bleeding, 139–40

Postpartum care, 193–94

Postpartum depression, 196, 209, 214

Postpartum recovery, 193–94

Preeclampsia, 136–37, 144

"Pregnancy glow," 49, 56

Pregnancy induced hypertension (PIH), 136

Premature multiples, 198–211

  anemia, 205

  breastfeeding, 217–18

  cardiovascular conditions, 201–2

  delicate skin concerns, 203–4

  gastrointestinal problems, 202–3

  impact of, 199–200

  jaundice, 204

  medical issues of, 200–205

  neurological problems, 202

  reflux, 205

  respiratory problems, 200–201

  retinopathy of prematurity, 205

  risks to, 38

  viability of, 199

Premature rupture of membranes (PROM), 162–64

Prenatal care, 97–105

Prenatal vitamins, 79, 81

Preterm labor, 155–68

  bed rest for, 146–47, 166

  causes of, 157–60

  concerns about, 156–57

  contractions and, 162–64

  medications for, 166–67

  reducing risk of, 160–62, 167–68

  signs of, 162–64, 168

  testing for, 102–3

  in third trimester, 67–68

  treatment for, 165–66, 168

Professional services, 263–65

Progress chart, 279–80

Quadruplets, 32, 33

Quickening, 56–57. *See also* Fetal movement

Quintuplets, 32, 33

We Have EVERYTHING® on Anything!

With more than 19 million copies sold, the Everything® series has become one of America's favorite resources for solving problems, learning new skills, and organizing lives. Our brand is not only recognizable—it's also welcomed.

The series is a hand-in-hand partner for people who are ready to tackle new subjects—like you!

For more information on the Everything® series, please visit *www.adamsmedia.com*

The Everything® list spans a wide range of subjects, with more than 500 titles covering 25 different categories:

Business	History	Reference
Careers	Home Improvement	Religion
Children's Storybooks	Everything Kids	Self-Help
Computers	Languages	Sports & Fitness
Cooking	Music	Travel
Crafts and Hobbies	New Age	Wedding
Education/Schools	Parenting	Writing
Games and Puzzles	Personal Finance	
Health	Pets	